Rethinking Old Age

D0994495

Rethinking Old Age

Theorising the Fourth Age

PAUL HIGGS

and

CHRIS GILLEARD

First published 2015 by
PALGRAVE

Palgrave in the UK is an imprint of Macmillan Publishers Limited, registered in England, company number 785998, of 4 Crinan Street, London N1 9XW.

Palgrave Macmillan in the US is a division of St Martin's Press LLC, 175 Fifth Avenue, New York, NY 10010.

Palgrave is a global academic imprint of the above companies and is represented throughout the world.

Palgrave® and Macmillan® are registered trademarks in the United States, the United Kingdom, Europe and other countries

ISBN: 978–1–137–38399–0 Hardback
ISBN: 978–1–137–38398–3 Paperback

This book is printed on paper suitable for recycling and made from fully managed and sustained forest sources. Logging, pulping and manufacturing processes are expected to conform to the environmental regulations of the country of origin.

A catalogue record for this book is available from the British Library.

A catalog record for this book is available from the Library of Congress.

Printed in China

Contents

List of Illustrations

Figures

Tables

Preface

Rethinking Old Age as the Fourth Age

One of the connecting themes that has underpinned our work since *Cultures of Ageing* was published in 2000 (and which was continued in our books *Contexts of Ageing* [2005] and *Ageing, Corporeality and Embodiment* [2013]) has been to investigate the paradox that as the desire for a long life has been realised for many living in the prosperous societies of the world, old age has begun to lose its social and cultural focus. Avoiding this by calling old age 'later life' seems merely to sidestep the issue, as such redefinitions do not resolve the problem of delineating when 'later life' begins, how it should be differentiated from earlier phases of life and what exactly it represents. Starting from the assumption that later life is no longer what it once was, we need to acknowledge the continuing influence of old age's cultural and social past upon contemporary imaginings of later life. This is a difficult task; it is also one of the reasons for writing this particular book which focuses on an 'old' old age and its new imaginary of a 'fourth age'.

Our previous books and associated projects have investigated the various aspects of the transformation of ageing that we have described under the rubric of the culture of the third age. In *Ageing, Corporeality and Embodiment*, we realised that as we explored the embodied practices of the new social movements and their encounters with ageing, there was a large dimension that we had not got the space to consider but which was intrinsically connected with the themes of the book. This was the issue of corporeality in 'deep' old age. We were aware that if the 'new' ageing is represented as active, healthy, productive or successful ageing, then 'old' old age appears as a set of antonyms to this, an arena of inactive, unhealthy, unproductive and ultimately unsuccessful ageing. The foregrounding of the first positions the second as its necessary background; an old age lying in the shadows of these newly emerging cultural fields, operating silently, insidiously, behind the scenes, but all the while waiting to take centre stage. This shadowy old age is what we mean by the fourth age, the continuing background of an old 'old' age defined in the collective imagination by its negativity and otherness. While the persisting presence of *old* 'old' age forms an important aspect of the fourth age, there are other more contemporary influences at work. The fourth age is, we argue, primarily a social imaginary of old age, a product less of nature than of the 'social mind'. While past habits and past representations of agedness and old age play a major part in providing its cultural template, this is made socially real by processes operating currently within society, contemporary collective narratives and practices that actively separate the new ageing from that old, 'real' old age which we have always feared.

Our aim in this book is therefore to throw light on this dark vision of old age. In doing so, we shall explore three major themes. The first concerns the fracturing of the social organisation of later life. This has led, as we have previously pointed out, to the emergence of the third age as a complex cultural field that has become an increasingly significant part of the landscape of later life in affluent societies across the world. As this cultural field has expanded, its incorporation within society and its commodification of later life have had the effect of pushing to the margin those aspects of later life that are most discomforting, distressing and, indeed, disgusting and that have long defined old age. From this fragmentation of later life, the fourth age emerges as a re-imagined old age where all the undesirable elements of later life cluster together to create a symbolic other on the margins of everyday life.

Our second theme concerns the nature of those contemporary processes that position the fourth age as a 'social imaginary' and their role in determining the boundaries of the fourth age. The concept of 'frailty', we suggest, acts as one such boundary, its conceptual ambiguity embodying the omnipresence of risk and intangible vulnerability that are ascribed to the 'really' old. Frailty alone however is insufficient to mark the affective response that the fourth age imaginary possesses. To the concept of frailty we must add the notion of 'abjection', the sense of disgust and distaste that separates the subjective world of agency, desire and efficacy in later life from that which is abject and from those who seem powerless to mask, manage or simply distance themselves from these undesirable aspects of agedness. The fourth age is fashioned, we argue, from these discourses of frailty and associated vulnerability and by the powerlessness of those unable to adequately maintain their connection to the desirable, civilised world of later life. The third and final theme concerns what we describe as 'the moral imperative of care' that prevents the total exclusion of the fourth age from the relations of the wider society. It is primarily through care and its various narratives and practices that the fourth age is tied to the rest of the social world. Just as its imagined attributions are confounded by social bonds so the fourth age is socially realised by them. The ambivalent relationship between care and old age represented as a needy yet undesirable fourth age presents a number of ongoing dilemmas for our ageing societies and for growing numbers of people seeking to negotiate, for themselves and for others, a more reasonable and satisfying way of living in and through later life.

These then are the book's main themes. In terms of content, the first chapter outlines in some detail what we mean by a social imaginary and why what seem the most 'aged' aspects of later life are represented through this social imaginary of an 'old' old age. Part of the social imaginary of the fourth age is its historical underpinning within the social institutions of care. So, in the second chapter, we explore the history of long-term care of the aged from its medieval base in the idea of charitable giving to the rise of care as a highly marketised service industry. We highlight the importance of 'institutions of care and control' in providing relief to the aged poor, and indirectly in also establishing the fear of ageing and dying within the workhouse (or its equivalent). The institutionalisation of care, we suggest, serves as an important precursor – or template – of the fourth age. We follow this historical chapter with a consideration of demography and epidemiology and how these modern disciplines have created what has been termed an 'apocalyptic demography'. The new focus upon the ageing of ageing societies, we suggest, has spread the social imaginary of the fourth age as modern developed societies are treated as if they are heading to exhaustion and indebtedness as a result of ever greater agedness, ever increasing ill health and ever more expensive forms of dependency.

In the fourth chapter, we turn from the contextualisation of the fourth age to its substance, beginning with an examination of the concepts of frailty, risk and vulnerability. We explore how frailty has come to represent one of the defining features of the fourth age, through its inversion of all that constitutes 'active', 'healthy' and successful ageing. Despite its appropriation as a distinct and measurable biomedical phenomenon, frailty we argue is at bottom a thoroughly social construction, inextricably bound up in the narratives and practices of health and social care. Although it might seem reasonable to develop a systematic approach to the provision of health and social care services for people with impairments, there are other aspects of the fourth age that go beyond attempts to delineate the extent of an individual's physical and mental infirmity, aspects that challenge the 'objective' rationality of care.

These form the topics of fifth chapter, collected together under the rubric of 'abjection'. Here we examine those aspects of age and infirmity that reflect the affective core of the fourth age, the anger, disgust and fear of those who are witnesses to the failings of age as well as of those who embody them. We employ Kristeva's concept of abjection to various features of late life infirmity that constitute 'acts of commission' – in the form of what is commonly referred to in the professional literature as 'challenging behaviours'. The abject is a feature not just of unsuccessfully aging persons; it extends to and affects those who provide care. The network of institutional and non-institutional long-term care serves as a kind of theatre of abjection and potential abjection where the social imagination of the fourth age is animated by reports of half-hidden abuse and mistreatment.

From the topic of abjection, we turn in the sixth chapter more directly to care and its role in realising the fourth age. Here, we address the moral identity that care confers on the fourth age and the extent to which the social imaginary of the fourth age implies a moral imperative to care. We examine how that moral imperative serves in its attempts at alleviation to further darken the fourth age, by constraining the free actions of those most completely enveloped by it. Claims and counter claims over agency, personhood and self-identity provide the focus for our seventh chapter, which examines the bridges and barriers between the third and fourth ages. In this chapter, we consider the moral standing of those corporeal citizens whose agency and entitlements of personhood seem so fragile, so vulnerable and the extent to which the rhetoric of the third age acts either as a barrier deepening the divide between adult life and old age or as a bridge offering new opportunities for contestation over the fourth age's social imaginary.

In our concluding chapter, we seek to separate the idea of the fourth age as a social imaginary from the actuality of the later lives of people facing progressive mental and physical infirmity. Care, we suggest, provides a key setting for the continuing negotiation over selfhood and personal identity that frames the 'event horizon' of the fourth age. The outcome of this negotiation is not predetermined; it depends both on the strength of obligation felt by the carer and on the degree of reciprocity that exists between those who care and those who are cared for. How best to age 'unsuccessfully', how to 'fail better' as it were, is a question that we and others must answer as individuals as much as a society. The concept of the fourth age as a social imaginary can help us to confront these issues, to map its contours and trace its full implications. By throwing light on the fourth age, we hope that a greater degree of reflexivity can be realised and with it fresh opportunities to resist some at least of its more baleful influences.

One final point needs to be made in this preface. Throughout this book we find ourselves dealing with chronological age. We do so because there is so much of it about – people over the age of fifty, people in their sixties, seventy-year olds, people in their eighties, nonagenarians, centenarians and super centenarians. There is so much age and agedness in the media, in the market and in medicine that it can seem that our societies are full of chronological agedness. What it may be asked about the societies of the third world, what about those societies where the old are still thin on the ground, where they are respected, cared for and contained by their family, by their community? Are terms such as the third age and the fourth age relevant only to well-off ageing societies, the consequence of living like dukes and dowagers off the resources of younger and poorer societies?

By and large, the material from which we develop our arguments derives from the better off half of the world – Australasia, Europe and North America. Later life is no doubt different elsewhere, in much of Africa, Central and Southern Asia, and in the poorer countries of South America where there are few signs yet of the new ageing. Growing globalisation links those better off in later life with the young and the poor in many ways, not least via the rising numbers of care workers and care assistants who come from the poorer parts of the world to work in 'eldercare' in the developed world. Though we touch on these matters in some of our chapters, this is properly the subject of another book and for now we must be content to explore the fourth age on our doorstep.

But however contingent the particular dilemmas may appear in the struggle between new and old forms of ageing, these dilemmas are not going to disappear if and when the centres of capital shift around the globe. Nor are they likely to diminish with any future reduction in global or local inequalities. Eliminating the fourth age is not like eliminating polio or poverty. We just have to imagine ageing either differently or not at all. In the meantime, by proposing this account of the fourth age as a social imaginary operating within the developed economies of the world and by illuminating some of its boundaries, we hope that we may reduce or at least mitigate the power of its hidden gravitational pull.

Acknowledgements

The authors and publishers would like to thank the copyright holders for permission to reproduce the following:

Figure 1.2 from G. Doblhammer and J. Kytir (2001). Compression or expansion of morbidity? Trends in healthy-life expectancy in the elderly Austrian population between 1978 and 1998. *Social Science & Medicine*, 52(3), 385–391. Reprinted with permission from Elsevier.

Figure 2.1 from Laing and Buisson, Care of Elderly People UK market Survey 2012/13. Reprinted with permission from LaingBuisson.

Figure 2.2 from Laing and Buisson, Domiciliary Care UK Market Report 2013. Reprinted with permission from LaingBuisson.

Table 3.1 from J. Rapoport, P. Jacobs, N. R. Bell, and S. Klarenbach (2004). Refining the measurement of the economic burden of chronic diseases in Canada. *Chronic Diseases in Canada*, 25(1), 1–14. Reprinted with permission from the Public Health Agency of Canada.

Figure 3.3 from Y. Zhang and J. M. Jordan (2010). Epidemiology of osteoarthritis. *Clinics in Geriatric Medicine*, 26(3), 355. Reprinted with permission from Elsevier.

Figure 3.4 and Table 3.2 based on data from C. de la Maisonneuve and J. O. Martins (2013). A Projection Method for Public Health and Long-Term Care Expenditures, *OECD Economics Department Working Papers, No. 1048*, OECD Publishing http://dx.doi.org/10.1787/5k44v53w5w47-en. Reprinted with permission from OECD Publishing.

Figure 4.1 from D. Yoshida and colleagues (2014) Using two different algorithms to determine the prevalence of sarcopenia. *Geriatrics & Gerontology International*, 14(S1), 46–51. Reprinted with permission from John Wiley and Sons.

Figure 5.1 from E. Samuelsson, L. Månsson, and I. Milsom (2001). Incontinence aids in Sweden: Users and costs. BJU International, 88(9), 893–898. Reprinted with permission from John Wiley and Sons.

Table 5.1 based on data from F. Colombo, A. Llena-Nozel, J. Mercier, and F. Tjadens (2011). Help Wanted? Providing and Paying for Long-Term Care, *OECD Health Policy Studies*, OECD Publishing http://dx.doi.org/10.1787/9789264097759-en. Reprinted with permission from OECD Publishing.

Chapter 1

The Idea of a Fourth Age

Ageing and old age: an introduction

At the beginning of a book on the fourth age it is probably useful to describe some of the concepts we are going to be using and how they provide the context for the development of our arguments about this topic. We start by making a distinction between ageing and old age. This might seem obvious but failing to do so can have important consequences. Generally, ageing is seen as the process or processes that emerge from a person living a long life, which is a life that extends beyond the period of reproductive fitness. Despite radically differing life expectancies across time and space, there have been people in all societies who have lived 'long' lives (in the above sense of living beyond the period of reproductive fitness) and there have always been others able to both observe the changes that accompany these long lives and formulate ideas about what ageing is and what might be its cause. These ideas about ageing form part of societies' cultural knowledge of life, its origins, development and decline. In contrast to such narratives of ageing as a process, old age has typically been represented as a status or social category conferred on individuals at a particular point in their lives. The bases of such ascriptions have varied, though usually they have emphasised some particular set of physical signs, characterological features and social markers. More recently, they have included a person's recorded chronological age. A point that needs to be acknowledged is that the processes that lead to people being designated as old are therefore distinct from the processes that embody ageing. In contrast to the process of attributing old age to a

1

person or persons, ageing has been thought of as a more diffuse process, referring more often to all that takes away or lessens 'youth' and 'fitness' than to what the ageing individual acquires.

In situating the themes in this book it is also important to distinguish between different types of change over the life course, particularly the distinction between the processes of ageing and those of development. Strehler (1962), a pioneering biologist of ageing, defined ageing in terms of four key principles. First, it must be universal affecting all members of a species even if it is subject to some variation over its timing and effect. Second, it must be intrinsic in that the causes must not depend on external factors. Third, it must be progressive in that changes due to ageing must occur progressively during the latter part of the lifespan. Finally, ageing must be deleterious to the individual's health and survival. Development, like ageing, is also considered to be universal, intrinsic and progressive but, unlike ageing, it is beneficial rather than deleterious for health and survival. It is this last principle – that of deleterious change – that has made ageing so important for individuals and for society.

It is generally accepted that at some point in the life course, there is a gradual transition from increasing to decreasing fitness, and from a declining to a growing risk of illness, disability and death. Across the human lifespan, decreases and increases in morbidity and mortality can be represented on a graph as 'U shaped'. Throughout recorded history, birth and infancy have been periods of greater risk of death and disease than have been the periods of childhood and adolescence. Similarly old age, however defined, has also been a period of greater risk than has youth and young adulthood. Understood graphically the precise shape of this U curve in the risk of morbidity and mortality has varied from place to place and time to time. For much of human history death has been a significant risk at all ages a point well summed up in the words of the Old Testament's Psalm 23 where it is stated that: '*we live in the shadow of the valley of death*'.

As long as life expectancy was limited by high infant mortality rates and high attrition rates throughout the life course, the personal experience of ageing and the acquisition of the status of 'old age' were confined to a relatively small minority of the population. There are many epidemiological reasons for this. Contaminated water and food-borne diseases such as cholera alongside vector-borne diseases such as the bubonic plague had devastating effects on mortality as did periods of crop failure and civil wars. These circumstances began to change during the course of the second half of the nineteenth century when a number of initiatives in Europe and North America were undertaken to improve public health (McKeowan, 1976). These measures included the construction of sewerage systems, the provision of clean water and legislation to ensure food safety and safety at work. The cumulative effect of these processes of 'modernisation' and the improved control over the environment they achieved was to lessen the effect of infectious diseases across the life course changing the traditional pattern of morbidity and mortality – and the shape of the U curve of survival across the life course. Known as the 'epidemiological transition' (Omran, 1971), the decline in infectious diseases during development was matched by a rise in diseases that mainly affected older members of the population. During the course of the twentieth century, morbidity gradually became patterned around the so-called 'degenerative diseases' of long life such as cancer, cardiovascular and respiratory disease and metabolic illnesses such as diabetes, liver and kidney disease. This change affected both ageing and old age leading to what has come to be called the 'rectangularisation of the survival curve' (Fries, 1980). This is the next conceptualisation that we shall introduce.

Rectangularisation of the survival curve

The idea of the 'rectangularisation' of the survival curve was articulated by Fries in a paper he published in the *New England Journal of Medicine* (1980) on the 'compression' of morbidity. Fries observed that contemporary Western populations exhibit diminishing levels of mortality from childhood until mid-adulthood and then demonstrate an acceleration of mortality, roughly from the age 50 and beyond. After this point in the life course there is a steady acceleration of morbidity and mortality resulting in the greatest mortality rate in 'old age'. There is considerable variability when different populations reach the point at which this acceleration occurs and its rate. Current trends are shifting both the age at which accelerative mortality occurs as well as its speed, leading to an ever sharper 'rectangularisation' of the curve. This trend is illustrated in Figure 1.1 that demonstrates, using modelled data from the UK, the progressive shift toward a rectangular pattern of survival over the lifespan that has taken place during the course of the second half of the twentieth century.

Assuming a theoretically fixed lifespan, and following the epidemiological transition from infectious to degenerative disease, the rectangularisation of survival becomes more evident as survival in later life increases (even in the presence of morbidity) and death is compressed

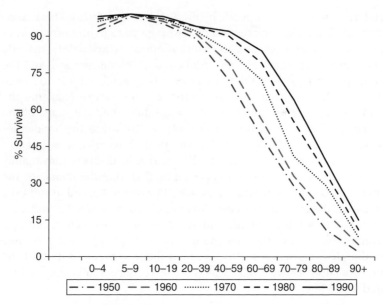

Figure 1.1   Modelled 'rectangularisation' of the survival curve
based on simulated data for England and Wales: 1950–1990

Source: Authors' modelled data.

within a narrow chronological age range. These trends – of delayed onset of morbidity, less steep decline and greater compression of mortality – have led some writers to propose a further 'epidemiological transition', the transition to 'the age of delayed degenerative diseases' (Olshansky and Ault, 1986). These relatively rapid changes in morbidity and mortality make it difficult to ascertain whether we are ageing less precipitously and at later chronological ages, or whether we are ageing at much the same rate and manner as ever but simply surviving longer in the presence of similar or even greater levels of morbidity.

This uncertainty over the rate and nature of ageing has been the subject of a number of debates both within gerontology and within the related disciplines of demography and epidemiology. One particular issue has been whether the increases in life expectancy of the last century represent a real change in the processes of ageing or whether they are simply the result of an expansion of later life morbidity (Gruenberg, 1977; Olshansky et al., 1991; Verbrugge, 1984). Gruenberg's 'failure of success' approach argues that ageing remains much the same as it ever was, a universal process whose speed and direction of travel is fixed by our biological make up. Consequently, all the apparent gains in life expectancy only mean that we are 'living longer and sicker' instead of dying 'quicker and fitter' (Schneider and Brody, 1983). Instead of the rectangularisation of the survival curve and the compression of morbidity, disease and disability are becoming ever larger features of our longer 'unhealthier' lives.

Despite such claims, Fries' prediction of a 'compression of morbidity' has challenged many of the old assumptions about the connections between ageing, illness and death. Although some analyses of subjective measures of health do seem to suggest that longer lives are resulting in an increasing burden of disease in later life, others using more objective indicators of disability suggest a different scenario (Schoeni, Freedman and Martin, 2008). For some time, US disability rates have been falling, mirroring the decline in mortality rates (Manton, Gu and Lamb, 2006). These changes look even more significant when looked at over a longer timeframe. Using US data going back to 1900, Costa has demonstrated that age associated morbidity – the diseases associated with mid-life and beyond – fell dramatically over the course of the twentieth century. She calculated that functional disability 'has fallen at an average rate of 0.6% per year among men age 50 to 74 from the early twentieth century…[with] a large proportion of the decline in disability at older ages…occur[ing] only recently' (2002: 38). This is further substantiated by data on 'healthy' and 'unhealthy' life expectancy among older people in Austria over the last two decades of the twentieth century. There has been a clear increase in the former and a clear decrease in the latter, with ill health becoming 'more and more compressed into the later years of life' (Doblhammer and Kytir, 2001: 385). These findings are illustrated in Figure 1.2 which shows the growth in Austrian women's healthy life expectancy in later life as a function of their overall life expectancy (i.e., the compression of morbidity in later life).

The accumulation of this kind of empirical data is helping shift the weight of evidence in the debate over whether ageing is an endogenously determined, universal process of bodily decline, the inevitable consequence of an unchanging and unchangeable human nature or whether it can be seen as a set of interlinked processes that are contingent on time, circumstance and the organisation of social relations. Evidence of such observed variability suggests that ageing possesses an intrinsic indeterminacy, even if that exists within some notional set of biological limits.

Some bio-gerontologists argue that age-related mortality occurs primarily because of accumulated, unrepaired damage to cells and

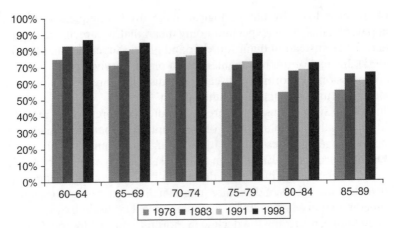

Figure 1.2   Increasing proportion of later life spent as
healthy life: 1978–1998 (Austrian women aged 60–90)

Source: Doblhammer, G., and Kytir, J. (2001).
Reprinted with permission from Elsevier.

tissues. This 'neglect', it is suggested, arises from the limited investment
that evolutionary processes have made in developing efficient, long-
term body repair mechanisms which is said to be a consequence of
somatic cells only 'needing' to last the body one generation to ensure
the survival of the genotype. This is in contrast to the resources
'needed' by those cells that provide the germ lines which can then
survive across innumerable generations (Kirkwood, 1999). These ideas
have led more speculative bio-gerontologists such as de Grey (2008)
to argue that if and when the basic biological processes of somatic
maintenance and error repair are understood, longevity can be
extended indefinitely.

Such speculations are encouraged by evidence of continuing
increases in later life expectancy. Although Fries had originally
assumed a fixed life span in his model of rectangularisation, evidence
now suggests a degree of open-ness in how long a human life might
last. As Rau and his colleagues (2006) have pointed out, while mortality rates for men aged 80–89 dropped by a mere 0.81 per cent between
1950s and 1960s, they have dropped by more than twice that rate
(1.88%) from the 1980s to the 1990s. For similarly aged women, their
rates of 'declining to decline' went further, rising from 0.91 per cent
to 2.45 per cent during this period. Schoeni, Freedman and Martin
(2008) have pointed out that greater educational attainment and
declines in poverty have affected the decline in disability levels in the

US and have opined that as long as standards of living continue to improve, ageing is likely to follow suit. Increasing lengths of life have been observed throughout much of the developed world, resulting in increasing numbers of centenarians and even super-centenarians. Evidence is mounting that the clock of life can be changed although some have questioned the idea of unending life extension (Olshansky et al., 2005; Turner, 2009).

The changing status of old age

If there are signs of contingency in the processes of ageing, contingency is even more evident – and perhaps less controversial – when it comes to the status of old age. In traditional or pre-modern societies where the experience of ageing was less common and the numbers of people surviving into old age were fewer, the status of old age was often quite high, or perhaps more accurately, the status of older men from elite groups was often high. According to 'modernization theory' the status of old age declined as societies transformed from agricultural to industrial economies (Cowgill and Holmes, 1972). The introduction of industrialisation put a premium on the selling of labour power and encouraged the migration of younger men and women to the cities where wages were often higher than in the countryside. Urbanisation favoured younger people, and old age became increasingly linked to poverty. The rise and decline of earning power over the course of a man's working life came to reflect the rise and fall in his capacity to provide for his family leading to a corresponding decline in status. Concerns about the pauperisation of old age rose markedly in the urbanised industrial society of the nineteenth century. These concerns led eventually to the introduction of the state old age pension as a means of financially securing old age. This marked the consolidation of the modern, institutionalised life course that was organised sequentially around home, school, work, retirement and death. In all of this 'chronometric' institutionalisation, women's ageing was less socially visible. It was men's old age as defined by state chosen retirement age that declined in status. In the US and UK, despite increasing numbers of men leaving work and collecting their pension at age 65, for many men retirement represented an imprisonment in a 'role-less role' within society (Burgess, 1960: 20) and a tragic loss of status within the home (Townsend, 1963).

The endless debates about when old age began that had been actively conducted in books, periodicals, reports and in the UK parliament during the latter decades of the nineteenth century were soon forgotten (Roebuck, 1979). By the time that the post-war welfare state was established in the late 1940s, old age was unquestionably placed at the chronological ages of 65 for men and 60 for women. The discrepancy in men and women's pension age that had been established as the basis for pension entitlement seemed permissible at the time, in part because women's ageing counted so much less. Her 'ageless' role within the family meant that it was her husband's retirement – or death – that represented the public onset of her old age. The internal markers of women's ageing such as the menopause and its consequences were matters that went largely unspoken, whether they were experienced personally as a loss or greeted as a relief while within the sphere of home and family, the exterior signs of ageing went equally unremarked.

Change in the social organisation of old age and its gendered nature came about after the cultural ferment of the 'long' 1960s. During this period the principal features of 'modernity' – stable occupational identities, ascribed class and ethnic identities, marriage and the nuclear family – became looser. In their place came a culture based upon consumption and lifestyle, a culture that put a premium on youth and innovation rather than age and experience. This affected the circumstances situating old age. There was a steady increase in the number of women entering, staying in, and/or returning to the workforce with a corresponding fall in the number of men staying in work into their 60s and beyond. Old age now framed as retirement was turning into a broader, less impoverishing and more heterogeneous experience, all the while becoming ever more universal. The standard of living in retirement rose, accounted for in the UK by an expansion of occupational pensions and home ownership, and in the US as a result of improvements in the coverage and adequacy of Social Security, the introduction of Medicare and rising levels of home ownership. In much of continental Europe, retirement benefited from the rise in the value of state administered pensions that were linked directly to the general rise in wages during the post-war decades of growth.

From the late 1980s, the standard of living of retired people has risen at a faster rate than that of working people (Jones et al., 2008). A new 'third age' has been fashioned from these developments, one that contrasts sharply with the narrow and gendered old age that was constructed by modernity's chronology (Gilleard and Higgs, 2005). The boundaries of what constitutes 'old age' have been challenged by these new possibilities as the circumstances of people in later life have lost much of their connection with what was once considered 'real' old age. At the same time, the last institutions housing this 'real old age', the welfare homes, the ex-workhouse infirmaries and the long stay hospitals in which the 'elderly poor and infirm' had long been confined were now seen as expensive, inhospitable and out-dated resources. De-institutionalisation and disinvestment followed in the wake of the mid-1970s' 'crisis' of the welfare state (O'Connor 1987). The rhetoric of 'community care' saw the numbers of the people aged 60 and above living 'independently' steadily increase. Despite more ageing than ever, there appeared to be less 'real' old age.

A crucial point for the analyses presented in this book is that the 1980s witnessed the demise of the category 'old age pensioner' (OAP) as the alternative archetype of old age. Rising standards of living, increased numbers of women in the work force, falling rates of employment and increased wealth and earnings redefined the economic situation of people aged 60 and above in Western societies. 'Real' old age, physically dependent, psychically impoverished and socially isolated was confined to a shrinking segment of the population while the numbers of people solely dependent on state support declined. As ageing expanded, its social identity became increasingly confusing while 'real', 'deep' or 'dependent' old age became narrower and narrower. Instead there began to emerge a new and more fearful image of old age as references to a 'rising tide' of dementia began to pervade the professional and popular media (Health Advisory Service, 1982; Arie and Jolley, 1983). Alzheimer's disease, once the little-known psychiatric name for a rare form of 'pre-senile' mental decay began to replace the term 'senility' or 'senile dementia' as the 'cause' of later life mental decline. Following the putative identification in the late 1970s of the neuro-chemical lesion associated with late life mental deterioration, and drawing parallels with the potentially treatable Parkinson's disease, the 'Alzheimerization' of ageing was underway (Adelman, 1995; Gilleard and Higgs, 2000).

By the 1990s the cultural ferment of the 1960s had settled down, its 'radical sell' more or less successfully integrated into post-war consumer society (Heath and Potter, 2005). Ageing was becoming ever more diverse as it was immersed in a mass of competing and conflicting interests. Critical gerontologists were busy identifying the accumulating economic inequalities of later life. Cultural gerontologists were equally eager to draw attention to the double standard of ageing that endorsed the status of men while consigning women to be reflections of their younger selves. In a similar fashion the increased acceptability of diversity created new cohorts of older men and women distinguished as much by their ethnicity, gender and sexuality as by their agedness.

Alongside this profound change in the nature of old age, some older people were starting to be seen as becoming distinctly 'more equal' than others. Politicians and policy think tanks began to fulminate over a growing 'generational inequity' (Kotlikoff, 1992). In this formulation older people were seen to be leaving the ranks of the poor at a faster rate than other age groups – but rather than celebrating what had been overcome, the focus was on the future 'disorder' that was threatened by this overturning of the rational economic order of the life course. In short, 'diversity' in ageing competed with 'inequality' in ageing as the dominant gerontological narrative, and generation rather than age became a focus of future division.

The new diversity of ageing became a source of commercial opportunity. Almost as soon as it had freed itself from the mantle of old age, later life became surrounded by uncertainty and confusion. Within this new anxiety over ageing – and no doubt contributing to it – anti-ageing practices and products appeared as part of a new mass market whose *raison d'être* was helping people of all ages prevent 'the signs of ageing' (Gilleard and Higgs, 2013). Following the emergence of 'cosmeceuticals' consumers across the world started to discover that 'anti-ageing' remedies could be found on the shelves of pharmacies and supermarkets. A few years later minimally invasive rejuvenative procedures such as Botox, fillers and skin smoothening agents became available and soon grew in popularity and cultural acceptability. This combination of diversity, life-style consumerism and a powerful desire to avoid the attributions of old age in later life helped shape the new culture of the third age. All the while policies and welfare constraints were busy narrowing the boundaries of 'real' or 'deep' old age.

Dividing later life into a third and a fourth age

The distinction between the third and the fourth age is of critical importance to this volume. The term 'the third age' was introduced into gerontological thinking by Laslett in his book *A Fresh Map of Life* (1989). Following a then well-established tradition of ordering the life course into distinct stages and ages, he coupled the term with the idea of a 'fourth age' and in so doing drew attention to one of the principal binary oppositions in the way later life is represented; namely the distinction between a fit, healthy and productive later life and an old age dogged by ill health, incapacity and neediness. Laslett assigned people reaching later life to one or other of these statuses, with those most aged, ill and disabled being placed in the fourth age, while those still 'young enough' to demonstrate 'tremendous reserve capacity, plasticity or latent potential' were assigned to the third age (see also Baltes, 1998: 412 for a similar argument).

But while Laslett considered the third age a distinct life stage, he was reluctant to see it 'bounded by birthday ages', insisting that 'the decision as to who is and who is not in the Third Age is (not) a straight-forward matter (1996: 443). He considered the fourth age also 'idio-syncratic' for several reasons – 'because it does not necessarily occur in every individual, it can come at any point in the life course and can be very variable in length' (444). Others like Paul and Margret Baltes made extensive use of the third age versus fourth distinction, but in contrast to Laslett, they have emphasised the importance of chrono-logical age in framing this distinction (Baltes and Smith, 2003; M. Baltes, 1998). For the Baltes, the third versus fourth age script is primarily an elaboration of the 'young-old' versus 'old-old' distinction that was introduced by Neugarten (1974) in her seminal paper on 'the rise of the young old'. They define the third age or 'young old' as 'those aged between 60 and 70 years' (M. Baltes, 1998: 411) with the 'water-shed' transition into the fourth age taking place sometime after 70 or 75. Using data from a variety of sources, Baltes and Smith claimed that during this transitional period, the resilience of later life breaks down and 'the positivity of the news about human ageing begins to crumble' (2003: 128). Although they acknowledge the contingencies of place and period in determining exactly when this 'fourth age' watershed occurs, they argue that it can be operationalised by 'the chronological age at which 50% of the birth cohort are no longer alive' (125). Under these assumptions, increasing life expectancy would lead to a concomitant increase in the age at which individuals or cohorts reach the fourth age. What we can see is that very quickly the third age and the fourth age have become concepts that can be either loosely framed as 'life stages' or tightly operationalised as 'chrono-logical age boundaries' with each framework leading to different con-clusions regarding the nature and 'inevitability' of a fourth age.

Alternative perspectives exist that critique the 'third age/fourth age' framework, arguing instead that by using it divisive categories are created among the community of old age shattering what is otherwise a common bond that exists among 'old' people flowing out of their shared experience of discrimination and social and cultural marginality (Neuberger, 2009). A slightly different criticism is postulated by those who argue that the projection of such distinctions masks a more fun-damental division between 'two nations' in retirement, the rich and the poor (Holstein, 2011; Scharf, 2009). Calasanti and King (2011) argue that multiple divisions exist within later life, but these divisions of gender, class and ethnicity act primarily as sites of inequality rather than as sources of differential adaptability and/or success. Against this position it can be argued that none of these 'divisions' are necessarily distinctive of later life. They represent divisions permeating the whole of society advantaging or disadvantaging people in every age group. Treating the issue of the divide between the third and fourth age as no more than an issue of generational solidarity or the inevitable conse-quence of the divisions between those who are better and those who are worse off does not address the difference in kind that lies between a third and a fourth age. In a similar fashion, treating the distinction in purely chronological terms assumes that it arises from some intrinsic mechanism operating within the body; thus essentialised it becomes no more meaningful than any other distinctions based purely on time. It also begs the question, why not a fourth and a fifth age? Why not talk of age in terms of decades, of age cohorts, of generations?

The fourth age: defining a social imaginary

In a number of publications we have argued that the third age can be interpreted as a cultural field that is developed most extensively – though not exclusively – during post-working life (Gilleard and Higgs, 2000; 2005; 2009; 2011a). Some people in later life participate in it more extensively than others, but it is their participation not their identity that defines this cultural field. Part of this definition of the third age is its active exclusion of 'old age' and 'agedness'. This cultural rejection of agedness helps drive the desire to consume and in so doing helps determine the contours of the fourth age. This latter phe-nomenon appears as a kind of distortion in the 'mirror' of the third age, playing a key role in forming a 'social imaginary' of 'real' old age, within the changing circumstances of ageing.

When Laslett wrote *A Fresh Map of Life*, he sought to rescue the third age from what he termed the 'ignominy' of the fourth age (1989: 3–5). For Laslett the fourth age was a period of decline and decrepitude that particularly affected those who lived beyond their mid-80s (41). While he periodised the fourth age within the lifespan of individuals, he located the third age within the history of society. The fourth age was not a matter of collective achievement but an ontological and exis-tential end that can at best be minimised by being confined to the outer edges of life. Although we share Laslett's view of the third age as a socio-historical phenomenon situated in the confluence of particular social and historical trends, we do not see the fourth age as simply a domain of exclusion from the third. The fourth age is about much more than *not* participating in this cultural field. It is more distinct and in some sense more unfathomable. It is we believe a social imaginary.

The term 'social imaginary' originated with the twentieth century French social theorist Castoriadis in his book, *The Imaginary Institution of Society* (1987). In this book, he argued that all social institutions possess a central imaginary, situated 'on the level of elementary symbols or of global meaning' that link the functions of social institutions with their symbolic forms. '[E]very society', he writes, 'posits a "view of itself" which is at the same time a "view of the world"...[which]...is part of its truth or its reflected reality...without being reducible to it' (39). As social institutions are necessarily human inventions, their particular functions are inevitably invested with symbolic meaning that make sense of their functioning within the broader structures of society. He contends that social institutions can only be understood through the organisation or network of signifiers and signified held within the social imaginary. A 'social imaginary' gives meaning to modern society's unstructured and inarticulate sense of the world.

The idea that society can be represented as a social imaginary has been explored most recently by Taylor in his book *Modern Social Imaginaries* (2004). For Taylor, the social imaginary refers to 'the ways people imagine their social existence, how they fit together with others, how things go on between them and their fellows...and the deeper normative notions and images that underlie these expectations' (23). Though linked to Castoriadis' more general formulation of society as a 'magma of magmas', Taylor's notion of 'a common understanding' among members of a society once again echoes Durkheim's notion of 'collective representations' compounded with the anthropologist Anderson's (1983) argument of how the modern nation state emerged as an 'imagined community'.

Taylor's modern social imaginary can be linked to concepts of 'social trust' or 'social capital', those shared expectations and assumptions that are deemed necessary for a society to hold together (cf. Fukuyama, 1995; Misztal, 1996). Gaonkar has summarised the various components of Taylor's social imaginary into five key ideas – (1) 'that social imaginaries are ways of understanding the social that become social entities themselves', (2) 'that modernity in its multiple forms relies on a special form of social imaginary that is based on relations among strangers', (3) 'that the national people are a paradigmatic case of the modern social imaginary', (4) 'that other social imaginaries exist alongside and compete with these national social imaginaries', and

(5) 'that the agency of social imaginaries comes into being in a number of secular temporalities rather than existing eternally in cosmos or higher time' (Gaonkar, 2002: 4–5).

We posit that the fourth age functions as such a social imaginary because it represents a collectively imagined terminal destination in life – a location stripped of the social and cultural capital of later life which allows for the articulation of choice, autonomy, self-expression and pleasure (see Gilleard and Higgs, 2010; 2011a; Higgs and Gilleard 2014). In this manner the institutional structures framing the fourth age first emerged as sites for those too poor and too ill to manage on their own. By the time of the post-war welfare state, policies addressing old age were institutionalised as either issues concerning social security and income maintenance or issues concerning sickness and infirmity. The institutional outlines of an incipient fourth age retained much of what had been most feared from the new poor law era, namely enforced indoor relief (Thane, 2000) but added to it a deeper neediness that went beyond that located within a framework of poverty and social need. These institutions helped frame the social imaginary of a fourth age as, in Laslett's terms, an 'unwanted condition of half life' whose 'onset and hence…duration should be put off for as long as possible' (1996: 154).

The post-war paternalism toward 'old folks at home' has in more recent times, been outflanked by the demands of an 'individualized' second modernity of risk management, with its emphasis on self-management of disease and the expectation of universal precautionary self-care for everyone in and approaching later life (Barlow, Turner and Wright, 2000; Higgs et al., 2009; Lorig and Holman, 2003). While in earlier times the fate of ending one's days in the workhouse cast a shadow over the working class, ending one's days in a nursing home has become a fate more universal in its potential coverage. It is a more personalised risk, and if all are at risk, then everyone must look out for themselves. Health promotion and precautionary self-care, as aspects of the 'citizen consumer', have insinuated themselves into the third age, distorting and disturbing its emancipatory messages while further darkening its borders.

Part of the social imaginary of the fourth age arises from the institutional densification of long-term care. By this we mean that reductions in the public provision of long-term care combined with the increased size of the population aged 60 and above has changed the nature of long-term institutional care toward one of greater agedness and more profound infirmity among the 'care recipients'. Ever fewer nursing home residents are able to self-manage basic activities such as bathing and dressing (Decker, 2005; Bowman, Whistler and Ellerby, 2004). The progressive concentration of infirmity that has taken place within the nursing home sector has nevertheless made long-term care an increasingly real yet alienating prospect for what may be as many as one in three of those who reach the age of 65 (Liang et al., 1996; Liu, 2000; Murtaugh et al., 1990). Predicting who will be that one in three implicates everyone aged above 65, as medicalised disabilities rather than socio-economic status form the principal determinants of nursing home admission (Agüero-Torres et al., 2001; Bharucha et al., 2004). The fourth age appears neither as a moral and final stage of life, nor as the cumulative consequence of a materially unsecured position in society. Rather it seems the result of individual misfortune.

Accompanying this interpretive change in the nature of care in old age is the abandonment of any reversibility in the status of those assigned to the communities of the old, sick and poor – the modern prototype of the fourth age. When the English medical journal *The Lancet* surveyed the state of the chronic sick in the Victorian work-houses of England, it claimed that

> If, as we assert ought to be the case, all the infirm were medically treated, there would be a very large percentage of recovery and consequently an important saving of the rates. (*The Lancet*, 1865: 9)

Similar claims of reversibility were made by other Victorian reformers who believed that

> they (workhouse inmates) are indigent in their old age after a life of toil because they have been robbed of the fruits of their labour by the class from whom our guardians and magistrates are mostly drawn. ('Nunquam', *The Clarion*, 17 September 1892[1])

Whatever the successes of the social and medical reformers of first modernity in creating 'rationalized' institutions, the result in second modernity has been the refashioning of these communities into positions characterised by the depth and the irreversibility of their infirmity – an 'event horizon' of historical contingency by which the fourth age is imagined more darkly than before.

The fourth age and its 'event horizon'

If the cultural field of the third age emerged successfully from past social contestations around 'lack' in old age, the fourth age might appear the bitter fruit of that victory. Unlike the habitus of autonomy, choice and leisure that are associated with the third age, the fourth age we would contend can neither sustain any set of cultural dispositions, nor support any subjectively construed forms of symbolic differentiation. It remains an imagined state or position that is undesired by, and distasteful to, all of those subject to its pull. The distortions in the mirror of the third age that shape it are more than the concerns of 'third agers' finding themselves at the receiving end of services labelled as 'geriatric medicine' or 'care of the elderly'; they serve as a fundamental ontological and existential challenge. The irreversibility of nursing home admission, the minimisation and often disappearance of any personal exchange in the processes of admission, and the 'de-privatisation of experience' that results from long-term care placement (Gubrium and Holstein, 1995; 1999) create an immense negative pull on both the third age that surrounds but remains imperceptive of it and the public's attitudes to what is seen as 'real' old age. In short, the fourth age acts as a metaphorical 'black hole' of ageing (Gilleard and Higgs, 2010).

This metaphor might seem too strong but our object in using it is to convey the inherent unknowability of the fourth age. In astronomy, a black hole creates a massive gravitational pull that sucks in everything that comes within range including light itself. This generates the phenomenon of the 'event horizon' which is a point where light disappears completely. Any light emitted from beyond this horizon can never reach the observer. To many people in or approaching 'later' life, the position of those in the fourth age can be likened to that of an object that has strayed too close to the event horizon and has now gone over it, beyond any chance of return. Equally, no light shines back once the event horizon is traversed. In the absence of any reflexive return it becomes impossible to separate what is projected into it and what occurs within it. The fear of the fourth age is a fear of passing beyond any possibility of agency, human intimacy or social exchange, of becoming lost in the death of the social, a hyper-reality from which there is no reality to return to. This fear is neither confined to those in the third age nor is it exclusive to contemporary society's citizen consumers. The social imaginary of the fourth age contains a universal ontological quality. As de Beauvoir remarks 'every society…dreads the worn-out sterility, the decrepitude of age' (1977: 46) and this is what makes it more than just the particular institutional organisation of frailty or the 'perspectivism' of the third age, although both play their part.

In extending this metaphor of the black hole, we are seeking to argue for an interpretive frame for old age that differs from both the classical distaste for bodily ageing and the modern stigma attached to the pauperisation of age. The fourth age represented as an imaginary black hole carries with it the notion of passing beyond the social world, beyond its connections as well as its contradictions. For observers, influenced in varying degrees by the commodification of their life world, the fourth age offers no opportunity to be able to create a status or articulate a lifestyle. In a similar fashion, nor is there reason to trust that previous choices based on personal agency will be honoured or even acted upon (Higgs and Gilleard 2006). Borrowing a phrase from the Slovenian philosopher Žižek, this is indeed 'the desert of the Real', a place where our greatest fears reside, ones that can only be addressed by allusion and metaphor (Žižek, 2002).

Attempts to measure this space within society fail to assuage its power. As relativity theory in the natural sciences has failed to resolve the dilemmas posed by quantum mechanics, so too the attempts of geriatricians and gerontologists to calibrate frailty; the efforts of policy analysts and health economists to assess the equivalencies of different forms of long-term care; and the aspirations of third sector advocates to give voice to the disempowered all cannot contain the forces that emanate from the fourth age. The inference that we are making is that as with the 'mass' of a black hole that can only be apprehended through its effects on the objects that surround it, the cultural perturbations created within the third age by the fourth age may offer the nearest approximations to what cannot itself be fully grasped.

If social reflexivity is the marker of modern social relations empowering the agency of the third age, the fourth age is marked by its opposite. There are no chosen choices in the fourth age. What may appear as choices – in terms of food, clothing or activity – are the attributions of choice created by others' actions, a 'hyper-reality' of choice. As with the event horizon where light emitted from the outside disappears, so the intentions of carers and professionals generated from outside the fourth age also get lost within it. The discourses of care and concern create their own interpretive frameworks that can never receive the confirmation of mutuality and reciprocity that characterise other everyday social relations.

The seeming mindlessness and immobility attributed to the fourth age is just that. However difficult it may be to grasp the 'real' effects that any individual has upon another, the circumstances of the fourth age are such that struggles to establish a conscious social exchange seem too intractable, beyond any possible resolution other than death and grief. All that is evident are the various 'civilized' exchanges of professionals and carers, whose discursive reality exists within the context of the agreed understandings that inevitably lie external to the fourth age itself. Although such discourses are rendered sensible by the institutional structures that generate them – the normative frameworks of professionalised care – the objects of that discourse play little active role in any part of them.

Conclusions

In this introductory chapter we have sketched out some of the key terms necessary for understanding the fourth age as a social imaginary, and outlined the elements of a model of the fourth age that we believe offers the social sciences a particularly productive way of understanding the fractured nature of old age in contemporary society. We began the chapter by outlining a distinction between ageing – as process – and old age – as status. While biological models have dominated the discourse concerning what ageing 'is', psychological and social models have focused upon what old age is – what status or social identity it possesses. It has, for this reason, been easier to accept the contingency and social construction of 'old age' than it has been to consider the processes of ageing in similar terms. Yet as we have argued the facticity of ageing and old age are equally bounded by uncertainties, subject to changing views and changing practices, their temporality provisional and forever contingent.

Most provisional of all is old age. Once rendered as a clearly chronological category, an established part of the modern institutionalised life course of childhood, work, retirement and death, much of its modern certainty has gone. The processes that institutionalised men's life course have created in their turn the conditions for its subsequent 'de-standardisation'. Later life, perhaps more than most other periods of life, has become more diverse, richer and paradoxically less distinct. Its' gendered, racialised and class-based constitution has been blurred as has its 'aged' nature. People in later life have been given the capacity to fashion new, 'third age' cultures that reject old age as both an identity and a destination. Since the generational schism that opened up in the 1960s, new voices, new narratives and new practices have begun to embody age differently – themes that we have explored extensively elsewhere (Gilleard and Higgs, 2005; 2013). While the writings of Laslett and of Margret and Paul Baltes have sought to explore the division between a third and a fourth age, their emphasis upon chronological age in the latter case and moral agency in the former renders this distinction less than helpful in understanding what is going on in later life in late modernity. We have outlined an alternative framework, one that draws upon this division between a third and a fourth age, but that posits a different conceptual approach, contrasting the cultural field of the third age with the social imaginary of the fourth.

In doing so, we recognise their inter-connectedness. While some have sought to prohibit such distinctions on the grounds that the one merely serves to oppress the other, or that the distinction masks more profound inequalities that fracture our societies – that of rich and poor – played out in later life (Grenier, 2012), we feel that this distinction reveals a very different source of tension, one that goes beyond divisions of wealth, gender, justice and rights. It concerns the problem of living well or living badly – and the problem of solidarity – of what Erikson once called 'pseudo speciation' – the cultural privileging of 'we-ness' from 'other-ness'. The third age, we have argued, contributes to the social imaginary of the fourth age, advanced as 'real' old age. By advocating diverse lifestyles, a timeless self, and an endless journey through life, the third age helps paint a darker picture of 'old age', contributes a darker narrative and exaggerates the gap between the fit and the frail; it does not mean to but, in a world of unintended consequences, it does, just as the institutional securing of later life in first modernity created the conditions for its subsequent fracturing.

In the following chapters of this book we shall explore the social imaginary that has been created of 'deep', 'real' or 'frail' old age, casting it as our model for the fourth age. In doing so, we shall investigate its origins, explore its parameters and interrogate the practices and policies that perpetuate its imaginary powers. Our purpose in providing this account is twofold. In the first place we think that such an understanding illuminates the social changes taking place in contemporary society particularly one enmeshed in reflexivity. Second and equally important, we hope this account can reduce the power and reach of this particular imaginary in framing the experiences, narratives and practices that surround illness, disability and care in later life.

Note

1. 'Nunquam' was the *'nom de plume'* of Robert Blatchford, editor and co-owner of the *Clarion*, a late nineteenth-century socialist paper published in Manchester.

Chapter 2

The Shadow of Long-Term Care

Introduction

Despite the variety of active later lifestyles evident in contemporary society, in most discourses about old age the topic of care sooner or later emerges. Even if it is not itself a normative feature of later life, long-term care has been for some time a socially imagined expectation of where later life leads. The aim of this chapter is to outline the role played by long-term care in fashioning expectations about old age and the social imaginary of the fourth age. By mapping its changing form and function, we want to draw attention to the elements of continuity in the provision of institutional care of older people as part of the 'moral identity' of old age as well as noting those transformations in institutional arrangements that have had particular significance in deepening and darkening people's fears and expectations of 'old age'. Care and especially the social organisation of care has, and continues to be an important determinant in securing the fourth age within the collective social imagination.

Much of the modern fear of the fourth age is expressed by the dread of 'ending up' as a 'non-person' in a nursing home, hospital or infirmary. Such fears have their historical origin in the evolution of the poorhouse and all its European variants. In many countries these anxieties became darker and more potent during the nineteenth-century reform of European poor law systems (Brundage, 2002; Englander, 1998; Katz, 1986; Mitchison, 2000; O'Brien, 1982; Williamson, 1984). But before the coming of the workhouse and its symbolic role as the dreaded of all 'institutions incarcérales' to use Foucault's terminology, other forms of provision had existed that constituted what may be seen as pre-cursors of or alternatives to the poorhouse or workhouse. Alongside and interwoven with the evolution of these various institutional forms were their accompanying imaginaries (ideologies) of care and control that influenced their social realisation. One central element in the transmission of these imaginaries has been the attitude of dominant groups, both religious and secular, regarding issues of charity, care, poverty and power and the effect these elite imaginaries have had on those on the receiving end of the giving and refusing of charity and relief.

To address this question of how the planning and practices of institutional care for 'impotent old age' have contributed to its evolving social imaginary, we shall briefly describe the period from the middle ages to the present through four distinct 'phases' of care. In the first, pre-modern period the focus will be on the generic practices of 'Christian' charity toward the aged that dominated the imaginary of medieval society in Europe up until the Reformation. The second period covers the 'early' modern period. It is associated with a much sharper bifurcation of the poor into a deserving and an underserving constituency and the subsequent construction of 'large' institutions to care for or contain them. This is followed by a third period, that of 'high' modernity, when the poorhouse, the workhouse and the various infirmaries associated with these 'carceral' institutions (Foucault, 1977) were replaced by non-stigmatising systems of care whose imaginary was fashioned by the welfare state. Finally, we come to a fourth period, leading to the circumstances prevailing in the present day, when the state has facilitated a commercialisation of care. During this period, long-term care of old and infirm persons has become a market sensitive modern service industry in which an individualising commercial rhetoric combines an emphasis upon 'personalised care' with that of 'consumer choice'.

Before the arrival of the poorhouse, 1100–1500

Before the creation of the poorhouse, diverse institutional practices of care for old age existed. These were mostly developed on an *ad hoc* limited scale, largely unregulated by, and of marginal concern to the crown and the state, except in so far as they provided opportunities for charitable giving by the ruler and his or her entourage. Though rural poverty was an endemic feature of life for the masses during this period, various factors mitigated against such lifelong poverty becoming an overwhelming social problem. In the first place, the regular occur-rence of local wars, pandemic diseases, crop failures, famine and out-breaks of pestilence meant that few people held any great expectations of reaching, let alone enjoying later life. Fears of old age – or at least any collective representation of such fears – were largely confined to a small section of society and were expressed most often by those whose precarious position in society rested upon patronage, but who otherwise lacked the means of the landowning classes or the collective security offered by the church to its senior clergy. In the case of the latter groups, their wealth and resources provided them with a degree of protection from some of the harshest physical, financial and per-sonal rigours of old age while in the case of the peasants the resources of their collective community would leave very few to reach old age alone and unaided. Moreover, many of the institutions of the Roman Catholic Church were specifically designed to address poverty and alleviate its more harmful effects. These included the founding of hospitals and infirmaries attached to abbeys, monasteries and churches scattered across even some of the more remote parts of the continent, where care of the poor – the *pauperi Christi* (Christ's poor) – was an expected duty of both secular and religious elites, either through the provision of accommodation, or more commonly through the distribu-tion of alms or access to the resources of chantries, hospitals and other charitable religious foundations.

Another factor mitigating against the development of large scale institutional provision for the aged were the locally negotiated forms of institutional care established by the church, the non-church aristoc-racy and some of the more successful members of the new merchant class. These included 'alms-houses', 'houses-of-God' (*Maison-Dieux*) and 'bede-houses' established during the later part of the middle ages to provide a safe haven for the genteel poor at the end of their lives. In addition to the various forms of indoor and outdoor relief noted above, the church offered other forms of 'old age security', notably that of the 'corrody' (Cullum, 1991). Corrodies could be purchased by the wealthier members of the community or granted directly by the church or the monarch. They served as a form of annuity designed to ensure the beneficiary support and care of their donors (or their rela-tives) in later life, care ensured by the monks and associated staff of the individual monasteries to which the corrody was paid (Lewin, 2003). Funds from these corrodies were intended to ensure access to financial capital to meet the particular institution's own needs (Harper, 1983). In addition to selling corrodies, the church could also offer them to its servants and fellow members in the form of regular pensions and accommodation, something that must have been of particular importance to those adults who having given up the protection of their own kin to take office in the church, could still expect support from their adopted 'family' (Harper, 1983; Cullum, 1991).

Alongside the provision of alms in kind and in cash, distributed by the lords temporal and spiritual, many churches established poor boxes and poor chests where donations from the wealthier members of the community were distributed to the *pauperes et infirmii* at appropriate times and circumstances during the liturgical year (Cullum, 1991; McIntosh, 2012). For some there were also early forms of retirement 'pension' though these were typically limited to those servants of the church who had grown too old or infirm to continue their vocation as well as those particularly favoured servants of the crown and related officials whose loyalty was ensured by the prospect of a secured pension (Lewin, 2003).

Estimates of the total level of such 'indoor' provision available to the older population – in the form of places in alms-houses, bede-houses, hospitals and related institutions – prior to the era of the poorhouse are problematic. The best data available comes from the end of this period, and especially from what later became the Netherlands where the founding of alms-houses was a late medieval and early modern phenomenon (Looijesteijn, 2012: 202). Although some alms-houses were founded as early as the twelfth century, the real 'boom' in these establishments came during the sixteenth and seventeenth centuries predating only slightly and often overlapping the arrival of the poorhouse/workhouse (Goose and Looijesteijn, 2012; McIntosh, 2012).

During the early years of the Dutch republic, Looijesteijn has estimated that 'the percentage of Leiden elderly accommodated in alms-houses rose considerably from 2.7 in 1670 to a maximum of 9.7 per cent in 1795' (2012: 204). Other estimates suggest that there were probably equal numbers of poor, frail older people in hospital beds as there were in alms-houses and approximately twice that number received some form of outdoor relief (Looijesteijn, 2012: n.24). The data from Leiden imply that up to a third of the city's elderly population were receiving some form of indoor or outdoor aid during the seventeenth and eighteenth centuries. In England, in the sixteenth century, McIntosh (2012) has estimated that the proportion of elderly people living in alms-houses, hospitals or related institutions represented just less than 2 per cent of the older population (online appendix, 7) while Goose has estimated that perhaps 1.5 per cent of the population aged 60 and above in England were housed in alms-houses at the end of the seventeenth century. Although these figures are of course not directly comparable either in time or in place, they do suggest that in the period leading to the poorhouse era, relatively benign institutional forms of long-term care were a salient feature of later life in several European countries.

These late medieval institutions were well-intentioned, especially so when contrasted with the workhouse regimes of later centuries. They were also much smaller and 'home-like'. Estimates of their size suggest that most housed no more than twenty inmates and many fewer than ten – in marked contrast to the hundreds of inmates that would 'end up' in the workhouse infirmaries during the nineteenth and early twentieth centuries. Nor were the elderly residents of alms-houses (or their equivalents) necessarily the poorest or most impotent. Often the intended residents were the frail but genteel poor, those who had fallen on hard times in later life and who were judged by the elites in their community as among the most deserving of care and support in later life.

Reflecting this view of benign charity directed toward the impoverished gentility of the 'shame-faced' poor were the codes of conduct that governed these institutions. What we might now call 'standards of care' appear to have been relatively high even in the Middle Ages. An examination of the records associated with St Leonard's Hospital, in York, for example, suggests that the care provided to the aged poor and infirm inmates was delivered largely by 'nursing sisters' and related staff, and involved 'ministering to the sick, giving them food and drink as needed, washing them, leading them about as human necessity required and if any required the viaticum or sought confession, the care staff were to tell the priests immediately' (Cullum, 1991: 15). As van Leeuwen has pointed out, unlike staying in a hospital or poorhouse 'living in an alms-house usually did not incur the stigma of shame and loss of status ... [as] ... residents were ... in respectable housing among those of similar social status and usually also with their own sex' (van Leeuwen, Meerkerk and van Voss, 2014: 8).

Of course it is impossible to know how closely the instructions governing these institutions were followed, but still the founding documents of various alms-houses and hospitals give some insight into the kinds of care that was expected to be offered to the old and infirm. As Nicholls has pointed out, what may have started out as a favourable level of provision for the residents during the initial years after an alms-house was founded may often have dwindled as a result of inflation, administrative corruption and the diminishing returns available from the original founder's bequest. Nevertheless as she points out:

> The security provided by the guaranteed nature of even a modest stipend was in marked contrast to the chronic insecurity experienced by the majority of poor people. Moreover, the physical representation of alms-house residents as the idealised, deserving poor gave them a rank and status above that of the ordinary poor, despite their economic dependence ... Status and respectability may have been their own reward, but they also brought more tangible benefits in their wake. The paucity of some of these in the more impoverished alms-houses indicates how miserable the alternative was for many of the aged poor. (Nicholls, 2012: 91)

The coming of the poorhouse

The late medieval model of charitable care, evident in the establishment of alms-houses, hospices and hospitals was overtaken by a change in the social imaginary of 'the poor'. This change is commonly judged to have taken place during the course of the sixteenth and seventeenth centuries and was associated with the Reformation and counter-Reformation that transformed Catholic Christianity (Beier, 1985; Geremek, 1997; Jütte, 1994). The rather generalised concern for the poor as representatives of Christ on earth in the medieval period was replaced by a much sharper delineation between the deserving and the undeserving poor. In effect the virtue of giving charity – and its value as credit for the individual soul after death – was questioned. A more critical approach was advocated against the generalised use of 'indulgences' and similar forms of buying one's way into heaven, and as a result attention turned toward the moral status of the recipients of alms or charity and their just deserts.

Across Europe, laws were enacted that called for the incarceration and punishment of the 'able-bodied' undeserving poor. At the same time, although the old traditions of 'caritas' were retained they were now increasingly targeted at specific groups. The targets were the 'deserving' poor – among who were ranked the aged, the sick and disabled, orphans and widows and indeed most of those persons judged unthreateningly 'impotent' (Jütte, 1994; Pullan, 1999). By the end of the sixteenth century, urban poor relief had become 'primarily a lay affair, albeit one with a strong religious motivation. The two main forms were alms-houses and hospitals caring for the sick and the aged and the poor tables' (Michielse, 1990: 3). While the able-bodied poor were treated increasingly harshly, sometimes by branding, imprisonment or whipping, punishments imposed by the new poor laws, provision for the impotent poor of whom the people aged above 60 formed a sizeable number – lacked any such punitive element retaining and even expanding the earlier forms of indoor and outdoor relief. Even where the quality of care and the care environment left much to be desired, those charged with running such establishments were nevertheless expected to act out of a moral concern for the recipients of relief.

During the latter half of the seventeenth century, matters began to change once again. New institutions appeared that were larger in size and included a more diverse collection of impotent poor people than before. In France, following an edict passed in 1662, municipal hospitals (*hôpitaux généraux*) and hostels (*hôtel-Dieux*) were built in many of the major French cities. The former were intended to serve the needs of all categories of the poor, 'the disabled, the very young, the aged, the chronically ill...as well as...those who needed to be forcibly detained' although each group was meant to be separately housed, while the *hotel-Dieux*, new and old, continued to serve the sick and infirm poor of all ages (Adams, 1990: 29). The problem with the *hôpitaux généraux* was that despite the edict, many were never built and those that were often had great difficulty in accommodating the needs of those forcibly detained. Still, the relative success of the *hôpitaux généraux* and the *hôtel-Dieux* in providing institutional care for the aged and infirm during the eighteenth century has led one author to claim that old age as a state mediated social category was born during this period (Gutton, 1988).

The medieval hospital had been primarily a place of temporary sanctuary, its wards offering shelter, a bed and food and clothing for those temporarily homeless or simply far from home. Medical care formed a small but slowly growing part of their regime. The new institutions emerging in the seventeenth and eighteenth centuries were neither hospitals in the modern or in the medieval sense but half-way houses, secular establishments charged with incorporating two diverse and divergent categories of poor, containing the one (the undeserving) while caring for the other (the deserving). In France, the strains placed on the *hopitaux généraux* by trying to cater for both groups were too great. The result was that the government established *dépôts de mendicité* in 1767. These 'new' institutions were intended to be less 'woeful' than prisons, but less containing than the general hospitals – a place where beggars could be returned to society, sent back to their families, engaged in public works, sent to serve in the military, placed in hospitals – or kept there (Bertier, cited in Adams, 1990: 71). These *dépôts de mendicité* were in effect the equivalent of workhouses, similar to institutions being set up across the British Isles, in Scandinavia, in the Netherlands and in the German States, sharing the common purpose of containing and setting to work the idle and rootless poor of all ages. These institutions were known variously as 'houses of industry', poorhouses and/or workhouses.

Regarding the problem of the aged sick, changes in their care were also afoot during this time. As noted earlier, the medieval idea of the hospital was fast disappearing. At the beginning of the eighteenth century, for example, the old Parisian *Hôtel-Dieu* was transformed from a shelter for the sick 'into an institution where the poor could seek charitable treatment from physicians and surgeons' (McHugh, 2007: 80). Hospital care lost much of its earlier religious significance as the hospital increasingly functioned as a site for the diagnosis and treatment of disease. Beginning in the seventeenth century, and accelerating in the eighteenth and nineteenth centuries, the hospital underwent a major administrative and architectural transformation. Its funding basis was changed from reliance upon charitable donations to an income derived from state taxes. It grew in size expanding the numbers of sick poor who could be housed there and extended its provision of an ever widening range of medical and surgical 'treatments' (McHugh, 2007). Within this new environment issues of 'treatability' came to the fore, and admission of elderly patients into these new clinical arenas of care grew ever rarer (Edwards, 1999; Smith, 1990). Although there were other institutions, such as the various hospices in Paris that continued to serve the needs of the aged poor, their time was limited and the new century would see most of them go or change their function entirely (Cahen, 1904).

In other Catholic countries such as Italy and Spain, while there were no equivalent edicts mandating the setting up of *hôtels- Dieux, hôpitaux généraux* or *dépôts de mendicité*, laws rendering begging illegal and enforcing work on the able bodied had been passed from the sixteenth century onwards (Jütte, 1994). Various charitable institutions such as the 'houses of misery' (*casa de misericordia*) were established from the sixteenth century onwards while licensed begging remained accepted practice for many of the 'deserving poor' (Martz, 1983; Cavallo, 1990). Alongside the continuing development of urban hospital charities and religious foundations for the needy, the counter-reformation had seen the creation of 'general hospitals' on the lines of the French model, in many Italian and Spanish cities. In addition to such developments various 'pre-modern' institutions continued to serve the needs of the poor, including the aged poor, in the 'hospitals for incurables' or the various hospices for the poor that offered shelter to the impotent poor from which they could 'go out and beg during the day' (Pullan, 1999: 28). Cavallo's research on Turin's *Ospedale di Carità* suggests that by the mid-eighteenth century, the aged poor – both men and women – formed one of the principal groups receiving the kind of indoor relief provided by these *hôpitaux généraux*, along with boys and girls aged between 6 and 12 (Cavallo, 1990: 74).

Prior to unification in the nineteenth century, Catholic Germany followed the rest of Catholic Europe, establishing general hospitals, hospices and poorhouses to provide relief for the poor and the ill. As in most other Catholic countries, this was done in a relatively 'decentralised' manner. In Polish cities, charitable hospitals for widows were established to cater for the needs of the genteel poor such that a fifth of the people receiving aid from the Brotherhood of Charity during the eighteenth century were 'impoverished noblewomen' (Kuklo, 2000: 464) but here too poorhouses were set up on a rather *ad hoc* basis, offering a combination of shelter and work whereby the inmates were expected to labour in return for their shelter. In contrast, the Protestant German states (as well as England and the Scandinavian countries) tended to organise relief through centralised municipal authorities charged with responsibility for administering the 'poor chest'. It was these states particularly that lead the way in creating municipal poorhouses/workhouses where the more able bodied poor of all ages were incarcerated and forced to work (Frohman, 2008).

Prototypical versions of the workhouse can be traced back as far as the sixteenth century, but the systematic provision of municipal workhouses across the main cities and towns of a state was a distinct feature of the eighteenth century. The driving force behind it was the ideology of instilling a new discipline of regular work among the able-bodied poor. From the earliest days of the *dépôts de mendicité*, it was clear that a substantial minority of the inmates were made up of the 'aged poor' whose productivity and health was such as warranted not work but care, not a *dépôt* but an infirmary (Adams, 1990: 72). As the number of workhouses grew, and the acceptability of providing outdoor relief, even to the aged poor, decreased, the workhouses and their equivalents ended up 'housing' ever larger numbers of aged people, much more numerous at the end of the nineteenth century than the numbers secured in the alms-houses, hospices or the 'general hospitals' in previous centuries.

As the leading industrialising power in the nineteenth century, Britain was singularly exercised by the need to control its poor. In 1832 the British parliament passed a 'new' Poor Law Act whose basic principle was the idea of 'less eligibility' – the intention that the work-house should provide less comfortable living conditions than any other obtaining for the working poor. A home 'however humble' should always seem preferable to living in the workhouse. As part of its *raison d'être* the workhouse was meant to be understood as a place lacking all comfort, devoted to the discipline of work rather than the discipline of religious service that had operated in the institutions of pre-modernity. Here even the non-able bodied aged were expected to perform some form of work, no matter how uneconomic, so long as they were not actually sick. Those who were sick would be sent to the workhouse's infirmary and from there a pauper's grave awaited. Although in the immediate aftermath of the passing of the Act, the aged poor were mostly spared the workhouse and provided with 'outdoor' relief, such attitudes changed as the workhouse became the principal source of relief for all the aged in need (Thomson, 1983).

In French speaking countries, a distinction was made between *maisons de refuge* (poorhouses) and *dépôts de mendicité* (workhouses). This distinction between the poorhouse and the workhouse was not always clear however. Similarly, the distinction between a prison and a 'house of correction/workhouse' was slow to emerge within the German states – the ambiguity associated with the latter no better exemplified than in the seventeenth-century motto engraved over the door of the Hamburg 'workhouse' – *labore nutrior, labore plector* ('through work I am nourished, through work I am punished', cited in Frohman, 2008: 37). In effect, the workhouse remained a more mar-ginal institution – as well as an institution imposing greater margin-alisation on its inmates – in Germany than it did in Britain and no equivalent to the workhouse infirmaries seem to have been built in Germany, in contrast to those in the countries making up the British Isles where so many of the aged poor ended up.

Both workhouses and poorhouses had existed in England and Wales (as well as in Ireland and Scotland) as sources of indoor relief dating back to the mid-eighteenth century when 'houses of industry' were set up in Dublin, Edinburgh, and London. In the Low Countries, similar institutions were established (in some cases dating back to the seven-teenth century), but as in Germany, these 'workhouses' tended to be sites of coerced labour that scarcely catered for the aged. Neverthe-less, during the nineteenth century, the number of institutions housing the aged increased in almost every European country where such data have been analysed. Data on the relative balance between the differ-ent institutional forms where the aged could be found, between 'alms-houses/poorhouses', 'poorhouses/workhouses' 'hospitals/hospices' and 'poorhouse/workhouse infirmaries' and the like remains to be collated, but clearly there were differences between countries in the extent and depth of the shadow cast over old age by these different institutions.

Not only were there differences in the experiences and expectations of old age in the different countries of Europe. There were also major divisions of class within nations. For those comfortably positioned not to have to live under the shadow of the workhouse, in late Victorian Britain (and one suspects elsewhere in Europe and North America) old age could be viewed as

> the close and crown of a state of existence conducted throughout in regularity and moderation [since] life orderly lived usually ends as orderly, faculties, comfort and even enjoyment continuing until as if grown weary it accepts a timely ... repose in the sleep of ages. (Editorial, *Lancet*, 6 January 1894: 41)

There were, as Benjamin Disraeli famously noted, two nations in Victorian society whose lives pursued parallel trajectories but who experienced very different life courses. For many older people in Britain during the late nineteenth century, later life was spent under the shadow of the workhouse and the prospect of dying alone in an infirmary bed. For a fortunate minority, at the same time, no such shadows darkened their later lives and old age could well seem the 'close and crown of existence'.

The next section examines the changes that took place in those various institutions, caring for and containing the aged poor and infirm – in the hospitals and infirmaries and in the poorhouses and workhouses – during the course of the twentieth century. A new imaginary was born, of universal welfare with security from the cradle to the grave. A 'welfare state' was emerging that sought to bridge those Victorian divides and in the process remove the stigma of poverty from later life.

The coming of the welfare state: a new dawn?

After two world wars, the institutional care of the aged began to change as part of a broader reform of public welfare. Across the British Isles, in Scandinavia, Belgium, France, Germany and Holland, the workhouse and all its variants were abandoned[1]. In Britain before the start of the Second World War, they had first been transformed into what were called 'institutions of public assistance' within whose infirmaries the chronic sick continued to languish. Something similar happened in France where many of the institutions of poor relief were replaced by or integrated with the new systems of indoor and outdoor 'public assistance'. In the wake of the war, across much of Europe, capitalist and communist, a policy of universal welfare was developed aimed at protecting all the vulnerable groups in society, including the aged or the 'elderly' as they were coming to be known.

In 1938, before the outbreak of warit has been estimated that just less than one-third of all the 'hospital' beds in Britain were occupied by the 'chronic sick'. They were mainly in hospitals maintained by the local authority – that is, the old workhouse infirmaries – and most of these inmates were elderly (Means and Smith, 1998: 17). As Means and Smith point out, the problem of the aged infirm was highlighted during the Second World War and various schemes were developed to house this 'vulnerable' group in hostels or in former workhouses. By the end of the war, renewed concern over the plight of this group was evident. A *Lancet* editorial noted that 'many old people are in difficulties' as 'provincial newspapers frequently report great hardship among the elderly poor whose failing powers are ill fitted to bear it' (16 February 1946: 244).

Following the establishment of geriatric medicine as a specialty in 1948 (Pickard, 2010: 1076), the problems – and status – of needy old people began to be redefined. The division between the sick and the frail that had been established by the 1948 National Assistance Act was cemented by the institutionalisation of this new medical specialty, and in 1951 the British Ministry of Health came up with definitions of the sick and the infirm, designed to improve lines of accountability within the welfare state. The aim was to ensure 'health care' for the sick and 'social care' for the infirm elderly. The sick were defined as 'patients requiring continued medical treatment [and] supervision and nursing care' including 'very old people who though not suffering any particular disease are confined to bed on account of weakness'. These were deemed 'properly the responsibility of the regional hospital board'. The infirm 'includ[ing] those who need a certain amount of help ... and those who from time to time – for example in bad weather – may need to spend a few days in bed' were to be 'the responsibility of the local authority' (*Lancet,* 10 November 1951: 880).

This new system of classification was well intentioned. The beds in the public assistance institutions (aka workhouse infirmaries) were fully integrated within a national system of health care while those old people who 'need[ed] a certain amount of help' were to be offered new accommodation under the terms of the 1948 National Assistance

Act. This was designed to remove once and for all the stigma of the workhouse as its institutions were replaced by 'attractive hostels or hotels each accommodating 25 to 30 old people who will live there as guests not inmates' with those who could paying out of their own incomes and those too poor being paid by the national assistance board' (Garland, 1948, cited in Means and Smith, 1998: 155).

By the 1970s, however there were few signs of any great changes. Writing in 1981, Townsend bemoaned the fact that 'rich societies have still to come to terms with the engineering of retirement and mass poverty among the elderly in the twentieth century' (1981: 13). Townsend pointed to the continuing dependency and demoralisation of life in the 'new' old institutions that still survived variously renamed as 'long stay' geriatric and 'long stay' psychiatric wards/hospitals and Homes for the aged. What Townsend called 'the structured dependency of the elderly' was sustained in large part by the inherited institutional regimes that were still not sufficiently changed from those of the old poor law/public assistance regime. Beginning with Townsend's classic account of residential care, *The Last Refuge*, several books appeared in the 1960s and 1970s drawing attention to the plight of old people living in the institutional long-term care setting that were supposedly 'liberated' from the old 'Victorian' regimes (e.g., Meacher, 1972; Robb, 1968; Tobin and Lieberman, 1976; Townsend, 1962).

Across Europe, in North America, Australia and New Zealand, similar stories were being told. In mid-1960s in France, according to de Beauvoir, there were 275,000 beds designated for the aged sick in 'hospices' and *hôpitaux*, of which some 178,000 were in buildings more than a hundred years old (1977: 286). She describes their setting in words that could easily be found in Townsend's book: 'dormitories [in the old hospices and hospitals] were condemned in 1958 but the majority of beds are still so arranged and in these beds the sick and the bedridden lie all day long...there is no screen between the beds, no private bed table, no private locker; the old person does not possess an inch of space he can call his own' (de Beauvoir, 1977: 286–287). As she notes, given these conditions it is understandable that 'an old person should look upon going into an institution as a tragedy' as once admitted the individual old person is soon 'reduced to the state of an object' (289).

In the US, prior to the introduction of Franklin D. Roosevelt's welfare reforms, most public provision for the care of the aged had been limited to the alms-house (equivalent to the European poor-house or workhouse). Although there was some variation from state to state and from county to county, by the end of the nineteenth century most of the poor farms or alms-houses offering 'indoor relief' to the destitute 'had become an old age home no matter what it was called ...filled with elderly people who were unable to care for themselves ...[some of which] were horrible places where the elderly met with callous cruelty and endured suffering beyond description' (Fischer, 1978: 152). Before the Social Security Act was passed, less than $200 million was spent on public welfare; a decade later the figure had jumped to $1 billion (Weaver, 1987). In 1930, approximately 3.5 per cent of the people aged above 65 were inmates of alms-houses and another 2.5 per cent inmates of prisons or mental institutions (509). Most of the residents in alms-houses were aged 60 years old or more, and more than 20 per cent were in need of regular nursing care (Munson, 1930: 1226). Within these pre-welfare state institutions, trained nurses were few and resident doctors fewer. The consequence was that 'nursing care, the feeding of bed patients and the many tasks that illness imposes are done after a fashion by other inmates – nearly always by the mentally retarded because they are the able-bodied' (cited by Munson, 1930: 1228). Unsurprisingly, these conditions contributed to a general fear and even hatred of these public assistance homes (Ogden and Adams, 2009: 142).

The passing of the 1935 Social Security Act was expected to bring about the decline of the alms-house and the rise of the nursing home. However many states failed to abolish these institutions because the infirmity of the residents was such that social insurance alone could not relieve their plight (Achenbaum, 1986: 27). It would take the passage of the Hill-Burton Hospital Survey and Construction Act in 1946, the Medical Assistance for the Aged Act in 1960 and the Medicare and Medicaid Act in 1965 to properly stimulate the development of a 'government subsidized but not government run nursing home industry' (Ogden and Adams, 2009: 142). Old Age Assistance had given many infirm elderly people the funds to purchase a place for themselves in an old age home or nursing home. Even so, the new private 'homes' set up to replace the alms-houses were 'often dilapidated and frequently unsafe; medical and nursing care was minimal [and] reports of exploitation and abuse of residents quickly circulated' (Vladeck, 1980: 38). The Act for the Medical Assistance for the Aged provided further financial resources expanding by one-third the national funding of nursing home care (Ogden and Adams, 2009: 145). Up until the passing of the Medicare and Medicaid Act, however, there was little or no regulation of standards of care. Subsequently, numerous attempts were made to improve standards, but scandals of care continued as the US government was torn between tightening standards and risking there being an insufficient stock of 'good enough' beds to meet the rising demand for places.

By the early 1980s, many felt that regulation was failing. Substandard nursing homes continued operating, where 'residents frequently received inadequate and sometimes shockingly deficient care' (Ogden and Adams, 2009: 152). The alteration between regulation and deregulation lead to a feeling that little really was changing and by the end of the 1990s, US nursing homes remained variable in their quality of care and the balance they achieved between containment and comfort. Reviewing progress, Ogden and Adams concluded, rather wearily, that 'more than two centuries of public policy have not moved us much beyond the alms-house' (2009: 154). Meantime US politics continued to focus upon the growing influence – and presumed unsustainability of – public provision of health and welfare – whether via Medicare or Medicaid. The dread shadow of the poorhouse was consequently more often blotted out by the more powerful nationally voiced threat of a mounting, unsustainable public debt.

A new century and the growth of the long-term care industry

Across a growing number of national economies it seemed that by the end of the 1980s, a kind of impasse had been reached in welfare spending. Although some aspects of the welfare state continued to expand and some countries still hurried to realise the levels of welfare provision that those at the forefront of change had long since achieved, there was a pervasive sense in the developed economies that the welfare state could not continue as it had been conceptualised after the Second World War (Pierson, 1998). Something had to change. Although concerns were being voiced over almost all aspects of welfare, throughout the 1980s and 1990s, our concern here is with the consequences of this re-thinking of policy for the future of long-term care services as the alarmist demography of the 'ageing of society' merged with the rhetoric concerning the 'fiscal crisis' of the welfare state (Gee and Gutman, 2000).

Although it is not easy to provide a comprehensive, let alone internationally adequate account of all the changes in long-term care of infirm elderly people that have been initiated since the 1990s, four features seem to stand out. In no particular order of importance, these are (1) the growth of a social market in care, (2) the increased use of assessments and 'targeting' of care, (3) the rise in less institutionalised forms of long-term care and (4) a clearer separation between the state as co-purchaser of services and the state as co-provider. Let us start with the development of a social market in care. Already in the 1980s, there was a general concern over the future affordability of long-term care, a concern that was paralleled by the equally widespread desire to deliver care in ways that were less patronising of the people who were receiving care. The solution proposed was for the state to develop a 'quasi-market' for services – for both indoor and outdoor forms of relief, or as it has come to be known, for institutional and community care. An important step in creating this market was to separate the purchasing of services from their provision and then encourage competition between different providers; in addition, there was also a desire to turn patients and home residents into clients or consumers by encouraging them to be 'co-purchasers'. All of this was done with the desire – the need in some analysts' minds – to strategically target those for whom the services should be provided and for whom differing levels of funding would be offered. The state was not particularly keen to broaden the range or quality of the services purchased, but was interested in the creation of a tightly targeted market. In effect this meant that the recipients of care services were expected to be those who were the neediest or most at risk – which was typically translated as the oldest and frailest. This led to an emphasis and an investment in assessment technologies. In addition, these targeted customers were expected to contribute to the cost of those services (whenever they could) and thus be in a stronger position to consider themselves as customers rather than recipients of services (although many had grown up and learned under the old universal welfare regime to think of the receipt of services as a social right as citizen). Alongside this change a new language emerged with a new glossary which utilised new words to describe the inmates/patients/residents as clients, customers or consumers, and new categories to sub-divide the elements of care, beyond classifying them simply as health or social care. This allowed for further sub-division allowing individuals to be assigned to various packages of financial, medical, personal, social and therapeutic care, each element or item capable of being priced and rendered locally or nationally accountable.

The new welfare also required the stimulation of a market, particularly in those states where there was little or no history of significant participation in care services by non-state actors. Whether through national legislation, international prompting or through local political decision making, the result was a requirement for purchasing authorities to formally bid for services from non-state organisations or actors either in direct competition with or alongside local or national 'state' provider-actors. This led in some cases to the emergence or the increasing growth in others of the private sector, in the form of both 'for-profit' and 'not-for-profit' nursing home providers, and community care and home nursing service agencies. These various provider bids were co-ordinated by a plethora of 'care managers' and 'service managers' and 'commissioning agents' operating at the level of a sector, locality or individual 'client'.

How successful has this 're-framing' of the welfare state been and what consequences has it had in either limiting or extending the 'shadow' of the fourth age? To address such questions, we shall of necessity draw upon findings with which we are most familiar, namely those observed in the UK. No doubt other countries have experienced somewhat different timescales, different emphases and different levels of legislative effort, but we are convinced that the overall result has been the emergence of a substantial global 'market' in long-term care of elderly infirm people with many of the same features and same consequences in shaping the social imaginary of the fourth age (Kraus et al., 2011; Mot and Willemé, 2012; Mot, Geerts and Willemé, 2012; Rodrigues, Huber and Lamura, 2012).

First, let us consider the institutional long-term care sector. Figure 2.1 illustrates the relative size of the provision of institutional care for older people in the UK segmented by public health care (NHS long-stay hospital beds), by Local Authority provision (Specialist and non-Specialist Residential Homes) and by the Independent (private and voluntary) sector from 1970 to 2010. What this graph shows is the relative rise in the number of long-stay institutional care beds up to 1990 followed by their subsequent contraction; and second, the progressive shift from state to private provision in institutional long-term care.

Turning from institutional to domiciliary long-term care, similar trends toward privatisation and individualisation can be observed, magnified in this case by an ever expanding rate of provision. Figure 2.2 illustrates both the rise in overall provision as well as the expansion of private provision of home based long-term care albeit over a somewhat shorter period from 1990 to 2010.

Such figures reflect international trends evident across Europe, North America and East Asia. Despite the ageing of the ageing population, a containment of institutional long-term care has been achieved by increased targeting (rationing) of all services together with the steady expansion of cheaper home care services. In addition, a greater 'individualisation' of care has been developed through the

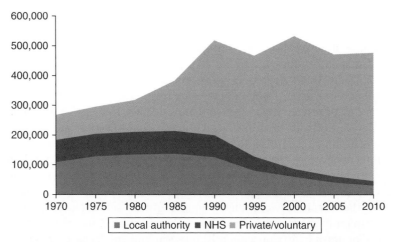

Figure 2.1   Number of residential and nursing care long-stay beds
in the UK, by sector 1970–2010

Source: Data from table 2.2, in Laing and Buisson Care of elderly people
UK market survey 2012/13. Reprinted with permission from LaingBuisson.

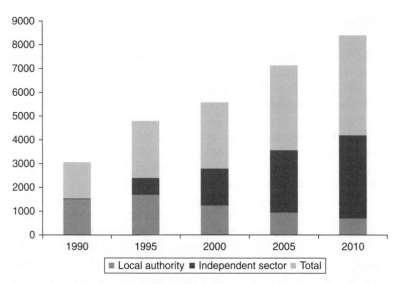

Figure 2.2   Local authority funded home care (000s contact hours/week):
England, 1990–2010

Source: Data from Laing and Buisson, Domiciliary Care UK Market Report 2013.
Reprinted with permission from LaingBuisson.

combined rhetoric of 'personalised care' and 'consumer choice'. This transformation has been achieved in the UK and US with complex systems of co-payment; in Germany and Japan, it has been realised with mandatory long-term care insurance (Rothgang, 2010); in Scandinavia, by some degree of co-payment, alongside a growing 'customer/consumer' re-framing of the care recipient as well as the greater targeting of service 'eligibility' (Blomqvist, 2004; Kemeny, 2005) while in the Netherlands there has been a steady centralisation and tightening of entrance controls into institutional care ever since the late 1980s, with a continuing decline in the proportion of people aged more than 65 in care homes since then (van Hooren and Becker, 2012). The common denominator across these countries has been the expansion of the home care service industry 'enabling' more infirm elderly people to remain in their own home while tightening the basis for eligibility for long-term care. Consequently, those in 'nursing homes' or similar institutional settings have become older, mentally and physically more infirm, with ever greater dependency on the assistance of others in activities of daily living and personal hygiene and, inadvertently, more frequent 'challenging behaviour'. In short, it has lead to the densification of age's disablement and the deepening of the fourth age's imaginary.

Going back to data collected in studies of institutional care in the 1960s and 1970s gives some illustration of the extent of this 'densification of disability' or 'compression of morbidity'. When Johnson and her colleagues set out to revisit the institutions portrayed in Townsend's book, '*The Last Refuge*', in 2005/6, they were able to trace 39 of the original 173 'homes for the aged' and completed data collection on 20 (Johnson, Rolph and Smith, 2010: 50). Where direct comparisons were possible, they found that the residents in 2005/6 were older, more dependent and mentally frail than in 1962 (Johnson, Rolph and Smith, 2012: 93). Surveys conducted over the last decade indicate that such long-term trends are continuing. In the words of one recent market report: 'care homes are moving away from being an alternative form of housing for frail older people towards a location of last resort for individuals with high support needs near the end of life' (Lievesley, Crosby and Bowman, 2011: 8). The last refuge is now a more accurate description now of long-stay institutional care for elderly people than it was when Townsend wrote his book more than half a century ago. This institutional structuring of the fourth age is in some ways a growing market opportunity, but for many older people living alone it has become a much deeper, denser and more threatening space than even the workhouse, despite the presence of kinder and more competent care.

Conclusions

The aim of this chapter has been to provide a synoptic view of the history of long-term care of older people. The main thrust of our argument is that a critical turning point first occurred during the sixteenth and seventeenth centuries when the earlier medieval model of religiously inspired care was replaced by a secular preoccupation with the 'able-bodied' 'idle' poor. States and nations alike struggled to devise effective strategies to manage this essentially 'urban' problem of able-bodied unemployed people begging, stealing and importuning the townsfolk across Europe. Almost unintentionally, the aged poor were caught up in these institutional responses – whether as inmates of the *hôpitaux généraux*, the *depots de mendicité*, the poorhouses or the workhouses. The consequence was that the aged poor became a distinct constituency within the institutional representation of the poor in what has been described as a period of *grand enfermement* (Foucault, 1975: 28). From the late eighteenth century, the size of that constituency grew both in size and arguably in infirmity as the 'clinical gaze' of the late eighteenth century hospital increasingly averted its eyes from the aged sick.

By the nineteenth century, the benevolent face of institutional care for the aged in need had largely disappeared. The era of the medieval hospital was well past; similarly that of the alms-house though some scattered groups of alms-houses and charitable retreats for the 'genteel' aged still existed. Little relief was to be found in the specialised hospitals that were being established in most of Europe's cities at this time. For the majority of the aged poor, the shadow of the workhouse loomed ever larger and the prospect of dying a pauper in the institutions' infirmaries grew ever more likely. While relatively less stigma seems to have been attached to the receipt of outdoor poor relief by elderly people, through much of this poorhouse' period, 'aversion to the 'House' is absolutely universal ... [where] ... there is widespread dread of the separation of man and wife' (Booth, cited in Thane, 2000: 176). Similar fears applied increasingly to the alms-house in America during the nineteenth and persisting into the early twentieth century. Despite these fears, estimates suggest that by the start of the twentieth century perhaps one in ten of the aged in Britain would end their days there – and similar estimates might well apply to the elderly population in many US states (Thomson, 1983: 63).

The early years of the twentieth century saw the beginnings of a new approach toward poverty, with the emergence of ideas of social citizenship and a belief that all members of society should expect a degree of protection bythe state against the exigencies of life and the market. A raft of measures were enacted, first in Germany, and subsequently across Western Europe, ensuring the provision of systems of child welfare, unemployment benefits, and insurance against injury, sickness and old age that reached their highpoint in the early 1980s before signs of 'retrenchment' began to appear (Huber and Stephens, 2001: 222).

Amid the slaughter of two world wars, the problems of caring for the aged in need had taken a back seat, but by 1946 a new world view was emerging that sought to provide welfare for all across all stages of life. The universal welfare state was born. Within this new system the elderly (a new term that replaced 'the aged' in the discourse of welfare) were to be given a better place in the national health service, a more secure home in the community, a pension upon which to live if not well then at least not badly and a welcome in the new 'residential' institutions replacing the poorhouse.

As the historian Webster has pointed out, 'on the eve of the modern welfare state the elderly counted as one of the great groups of the deprived and they bore all the scars of this deprivation'(1994: 187). Since then, he wrote, 'services for the elderly have improved in some respects, but the scale of response has been inadequate to the magnitude of the problem' (188). Change however has continued. The number of people aged 65 and above in long-stay hospital beds has fallen dramatically while the residential home for the elderly has all but slipped from memory, along with the imaginary of the workhouse and its infirmary. In Scandinavia, even the Swedish term 'nursing home' (*sjukhem*) has disappeared as the aged infirm are increasingly looked after in what are termed 'special living' apartments (*särskilt boende*).

Despite these changes, institutional care of the aged infirm continues to be an unappealing and frightening prospect facing people as they get progressively older and less able to look after themselves. The compression of morbidity (and mortality) in society at large that was observed during the last half century has been matched by a similar compression in long-term care in this century – leading to the densification of disability within long-term care. This has added to, or perhaps we should say modified the feared imaginary of old age that was previously associated with the workhouse infirmary, inserting in its place the universalised risk of ending up 'in care' in a manner even more abject and non-agentic than was the case for those old people from the past forced into a life of labour in the poorhouse. Although they could at least resist the impositions the workhouse placed upon them, the rhetoric of consumerism in the face of incapacity has rendered the positions of these 'customers' more one of pity than of protest. How far this 'demographically informed' depiction of old age contributes to the new social imaginary of the fourth age is the topic of our next chapter.

Note

1. According to Elise Feller the *dépôts de mendicité* continued to the end of the nineteenth century the majority of the inmates being elderly 'voluntary' residents who chose to end their days there because of their indigent circumstances alongside their importunate peers (2000: 10).

Chapter 3

Demographic and Epidemiological Aspects of the Fourth Age

Introduction

In this chapter we examine the enumeration of the fourth age within the discourses of demography and epidemiology. This process plays an important role in the framing of the 'negative' social imaginary of the fourth age. Unlike the threats to society attributed to groups such as asylum seekers, teenage gangs or illegal immigrants, the nature of the threat posed by 'the old' is based not upon their being a danger to the majority but rather rests on the extent of their neediness and society's potential inability to meet this need. The metaphors employed to illustrate this danger are typically those of ecological disaster, rising tides, tsunamis, an apocalyptic demography made up of an ever increasing number of frail elderly people over-whelming society and its resources (Robertson, 1997; Zeilig, 2014). A less often used metaphor is that of disease, a growing pandemic of 'agedness', a plague of age laying waste to our already weakened 'ageing societies'. These dangers are made more salient because they are also represented, albeit indirectly, as the possible fate of our future selves, of becoming 'other' to ourselves – or if not us then those whose identities are intimately linked to our own, like our parents or partners.

Although the earlier debates over the 'problem' of an ageing society focused on the post-war growth of the population aged 60 and above and the future costs of pension and social security schemes (Aarons, Bosworth and Burtless, 1987; Clark and Spengler, 1980; Johnson, Conrad and Thomson, 1989s; OECD, 1988a), these concerns have since merged with, and increasingly been overtaken by the new threat associated with the ageing of the older population itself. Within this new locus of concern, the number of people reaching retirement age – 60 or 65 – has become of less import compared with the numbers of older people who will continue to age, ending up as denizens of a 'fourth age' – people worn down by the weight of their own ageing, and no longer able to manage as 'senior citizens' without the aid and assistance of others.

When the term 'apocalyptic demography' was coined by Robertson in an article written in 1990, it quickly established itself as a common motif employed by academics and journalists alike. But instead of being applied with the critical edge that Robertson intended, the apocalyptic nature of this latest demographic transition is now regularly used to preface numerous research grant application designed to secure funding to address, or to contextualise journal articles addressing one or the other of the frightening aspects of later life. A noteworthy example of this kind of narrative is the book, '*The Coming Generational Storm*', written by US economist Kotlikoff and his journalist colleague, Burns. These authors start by drawing the reader's attention to 'the tidal wave of baby boomers that is moving inexorably from changing diapers to wearing them' (2005: xx). They go on to claim that 'we are heading toward a planet that is big, blue and wrinkled all over' (35). '[T]he developed world' they prophesy, 'is plunging into a new demography: inescapable old age' warning that 'human demography driven by simple changes in life expectancy and childbearing is about to trump the power of economic growth' (38–39).

But if Kotlikoff and Burns make their case so egregiously, many other more seemingly neutral books and journal papers adopt a milder version of the same rhetoric, irrespective of whether they are demographers, epidemiologists, clinicians or social scientists. Before we examine the social facts on which these papers base their judgements, it is important to recognise the recent history of the tropes that form much of their discourse. One of the earliest examples is to be found in a paper published in the *British Journal of Psychiatry* in 1987, commenting upon a British government White Paper on planning services for elderly mentally infirm people, titled 'The Rising Tide' (Health Advisory Service, 1982). The author, a senior research fellow dealing with 'performance and standards' in a British health authority, wrote:

> The rapid increase in the number of elderly people, especially the very
> elderly, is widely recognised and is likely to continue into the next

century ... this means almost inevitably a growth in the numbers of mentally ill old people, the so-called 'rising tide'. (Ineichen, 1987: 193)

What started as a phrase used in local policy discussions has over time become 'an international rising tide of late life dementia' (Larson, 2010: 1196). Contemporary epidemiological reviews of the ever 'rising tide' of dementia are represented through numerous ecological metaphors as well as in terms relating to 'looming epidemics' and 'growing global burden'. These move in an un-problematical fashion from the restricted concept of dementia to the generalised problem 'of the aging of the world's population' (Brookmeyer et al., 2007: 190; Kukull, 2006). Such metaphorical framing of the ageing of our ageing societies consequently reflects a shift from earlier concerns with planning services and the professional framing of that concern in terms of demands for greater resource (cf., Arie and Jolley, 1983: 326) to a much more explicit concern over the economics of disease and the threat to wider society. Reframing the idea of dementia from representing a 'rising tide' requiring additional services to a 'global burden' incurring increasing costs reflects this shift in perspective.

Since the second crisis of the welfare state in the era of austerity, there has been a return to the preoccupation with rising health care costs and the need for 'containment'. Importantly, there has been a widespread acceptance of the notion that the rise in health care costs is a direct result of the ageing of ageing societies and the 'morbidity' attributed to the oldest old (Lehnert et al., 2011). Demography and epidemiology have been combined in order to render 'apocalyptic' the ageing of ageing societies. These narratives and how they shape the social imaginary of the fourth age provide the focus of this chapter. We begin the chapter with demography, exploring data on the ageing of the population aged 60 and above over the last half century (1961–2011) in the UK, USA and other Western countries and the evidence for a second 'demographic' transition emerging in the latter decades of the twentieth century, that of the ageing of ageing societies. In the second section, we turn from demography to epidemiology and the 'epidemiological' transition that resulted from the decline of infectious diseases in early life asd the main causes of morbidity and mortality shifted to those associated with the degenerative diseases of later life (Omran, 1971). In particular, we examine the extent to which data on chronic disease, multi-morbidity and frailty in later life (defined for present purposes as that period of life after reaching 60) help support the imagery of a fourth age as one deepened by age and darkened by disease. In the third section, we address the public anxieties regarding the costliness of this imagined fourth age and the assumptions that increasing disease and disability will place an intolerable burden on national finances and the tax paying public all the while consigning ever larger numbers of people to an old age dominated by illness, infirmity and incapacity. We conclude by considering how these academic debates have percolated into the various forms of the mass media thus extending the narratives of the fourth age into the field of public opinion.

The demography of later life

For later life to age, people aged above 60 must live longer. This was not the case in the first half of the twentieth century. The substantial increases in overall life expectancy were achieved by the fall in infant and childhood mortality rather than through longer later lives. In a letter to the *Lancet*, written in April 1926, the medical director of the New York Life Extension Institute observed that

> about a dozen years have been added to the average lifetime in the past 37 years but this certainly has not been accomplished by prolonging the lives of people over 60. It has been accomplished chiefly by a reduction in the death rate under age 5. There has been little extension of life beyond the age of 50. (Fisk, 1926: 844)

How dramatically the demographic picture changed during the course of the second half of the century is shown in Figure 3.1. This figure charts the rise in life expectancy after the age of 65 for men and women from 1951 to 2011.

The effect that this 'later life extension' has had on the composition of the population aged 65 and above is shown in Figure 3.2. It shows how the proportion of the 65+ population in the UK that is made up by people aged 85+ has increased from approximately 5 per cent in 1961 to approximately 15 per cent in 2011. This growth in the 'oldest old' segment of the population is by no means confined to the UK. Commenting on the 'rapid emergence of a new population in Switzerland, the oldest old', Robine and Paccaud note that while Swiss life expectancy at birth rose from the 1870s onwards, it was only after the 1950s that a decrease in mortality in later life occurred leading to the emergence of this 'new' demographic – the oldest old (2005: 35).

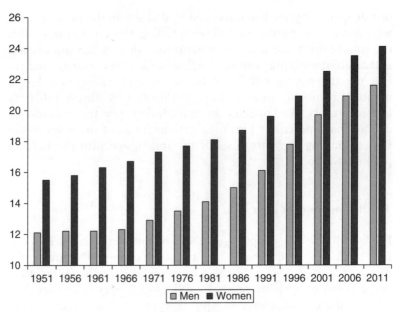

Figure 3.1   Life expectancy at age 65, men and women,
England and Wales, 1951–2011

Source: https://www.gov.uk/government/uploads/system/uploads/attachment_data/
file/223190/life_Expectancy.pdf.

Similar trends can be found in most developed countries, with an
anticipated doubling (or more) of the population aged 80 and above
in the OECD (Organisation for Economic Co-operation and Development) area, over the next 30 years (OECD, 2013c: 171). The question is not whether such trends reflect social facts – they clearly
do – but what exactly those social facts mean. What does it matter if
there are more octogenarians, nonagenarians and centenarians in the
population? Are the 'oldest old' the major category of frail and infirm
persons? Are they the most disabled and the most likely to be found
incapable? While pensions and social security are paid out to everyone over a certain age, the costs of pensions and social security are
not themselves affected by the age composition of the pensionable
population. The apocalyptic demography argument assumes that
other costs – medical, personal and social – are. Hence we turn from
considering the demographic transition represented by the ageing of
ageing societies to the epidemiology of ageing and the costs of health
and social care.

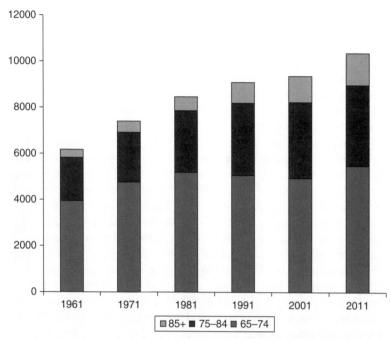

Figure 3.2   Change in the age structure of the 65+ population
in the UK, 1961–2011 (000s)

Source: Census data, England and Wales, 1961–2011.

The epidemiology of disease and disability in later life

In Omran's seminal account of the epidemiological transition, the principal causes of death in most developed economies have ceased to be the consequences of infectious diseases and become the result of degenerative illnesses such as coronary heart disease, cancer, hypertension, metabolic disorders and stroke (Omran, 1971; see also Gilleard and Higgs, 2014). The prevalence of these diseases has grown throughout the twentieth century and some 80–90 per cent of the population aged above 65 are estimated to suffer from one or more clinically ascertained degenerative conditions (ILSA Working Group, 1997). Terminology is not fully consistent across studies and countries, helping sustain the ambiguity and uncertainty that surrounds the fourth age. Co-morbidity and multi-morbidity are used interchangeably while the definition and delineation of chronic conditions varies from study to study. Some studies focus upon the prevalence of multiple conditions, while others restrict the conditions to long-term or chronic illnesses. But, whichever way the cake is cut, the rise in the prevalence of chronic degenerative disease with age and the increased frequency of multi-morbidity seem pervasive features of contemporary ageing societies (Marengoni et al., 2011; Salive, 2013). That there is a rise of chronic disease with age is indisputable, as is illustrated below with data from a Canadian national survey of chronic disease among the adult population.

The majority of people in the oldest old category (those aged 80 and above) have some degree of multi-morbidity, however defined, that is typically associated with multiple chronic illnesses (Formiga et al., 2013; Marengoni et al., 2008). But whether this is inevitable, intrinsic and universal feature of living longer or even whether it is a continuously increasing trend through each decade of adult life is less clear. One of the largest surveys of the oldest old ever conducted, in mainland China, observed that the prevalence of chronic disease actually *declined* after age 80, with fewer nonagenarians and centenarians suffering from chronic diseases compared with their octogenarian compatriots (Dupre, Liu and Gu, 2008). Studies of so-called 'super-centenarians' suggest that those who live longest show generally later onset of such diseases as cancer, cardiovascular disease, dementia and stroke as well as of cognitive and functional decline (Andersen et al., 2012). What these and other related studies suggest is that living through 'the oldest ages' may not lead to progressively greater enfeeblement and even raise the possibility of a kind of 'age barrier' beyond which the progress of debility and disease no longer applies.

Table 3.1   Prevalence (%) of one or more chronic diseases across the adult life course

Age group (years)	None	One	Two	Three	Four or more
20–39	62.0	26.5	8.0	2.4	1.1
40–59	43.6	30.1	14.4	6.8	5.1
60–79	20.1	25.2	24.0	14.5	16.2
80+	11.7	24.3	22.3	16.8	24.9

Note: Chronic diseases in this study comprised asthma, arthritis, cancer, cerebrovascular disease, Type 2 diabetes, dementia, chronic bronchitis or emphysema, sinusitis, epilepsy, ischaemic heart disease, high blood pressure, migraine, low back pain, osteoporosis and thyroid condition.

Source: National Population Health Survey, Statistics Canada (Rapoport et al., 2004). Reprinted with permission from the Public Health Agency of Canada.

Even if morbidity and multi-morbidity generally increase with age, at least until the very oldest ages, the consequences of such morbidity may be more contingent that is generally assumed by the 'growing pandemic' narratives. Disease and the outcome of disease change over time and not always – perhaps not usually – because of improved medical care and technology. Morbidity, multi-morbidity and infirmity are potentially separable phenomena, and each has distinctly different and arguably contingent associations with age and ageing. Three particular issues need to be considered about the effect of ageing of the older population on health illness and disability. First is the relationship between age of disease onset, progress and long-term outcome; second is the extent to which disease interferes with older people's activities of daily living; and third is the degree of tractability of such consequent impairments.

None of these phenomena are fixed. There is good evidence that (1) the age of onset and rates of progression of chronic diseases vary over time, (2) the disabling effects of disease are by no means constant and (3) the tractability – or intractability – of disease and disease-related impairment is also subject to change as a result of both 'treatment related' and 'treatment unrelated' factors (Costa, 2000; 2002). Let us consider the first issue – changes in the incidence and prevalence of 'degenerative' diseases. Since the 1960s, there has been a decline in the rates of coronary heart disease and associated mortality rates (Schmidt et al., 2012; Tunstall-Pedoe, 2012). These trends seem to apply to all age groups, as well as both genders and across all socio-economic status groups. The result paradoxically is that because of the 'ageing' of the population, a greater number of people aged more than 70 are now hospitalised for these conditions while fewer people aged less than 60 are leading, in effect, to the 'ageing' of coronary heart disease (Gerber et al., 2006; Floyd et al., 2009; Schmidt et al., 2012). Attempts to identify the reasons for these gains in health and life expectancy are tentative but suggest that both 'lifestyle' and 'treatment' factors have contributed (O'Flaherty, Buchan and Capewell, 2013).

Similar trends have been observed for stroke which has shown a downward decline in incidence and mortality over the last half century (Caradang et al., 2006; Rothwell et al., 2004). As with coronary heart disease, paralleling the decline in incidence has been an increase in the age of incidence – in effect the 'ageing' of stroke. This effect can be illustrated by reference to a study conducted in Oxfordshire comparing incidence mortality and severity of stroke in the 1980s with that in the early 2000s. The incidence of stroke among men and women aged 60s and 70s declined, while the incidence of stroke among those aged 85 and more than that was unchanged. Whereas stroke among men and women aged more than 85, in 1981–1984, represented only 15 per cent of all strokes in the pensionable age population, by 2002–2004 it represented almost a quarter (23%) (Rothwell et al., 2004: table 1: 1927).

Can much the same be said for other degenerative conditions? For much of the twentieth century cancer incidence rates increased, leading to yet another 'moral panic' over the state of people's health in society. These concerns were expressed most vociferously in the period between the wars (Chief Medical Officer's Annual Report, 1928) but continued in more muted form during the 1950s. There are now signs that cancer rates are declining (Jemal et al., 2010; Wingo et al., 1998). Although cancer tends to develop more often with increasing age, its incidence peaks around 85 years and seems to decline thereafter (Piantanelli, 1988; de Rijke et al., 2000). Survival rates have increased in recent decades, at all ages, and hence the prevalence of cancer among the older population – and particularly the oldest old – has increased. Fewer people die and more (continue to) grow old with cancer – presenting again the apparent ageing of yet another 'degenerative' disease (Edwards et al., 2002).

Unlike cancer, coronary heart disease and stroke, arthritis is not a terminal illness. But, similar to other degenerative illnesses, its prevalence rate rises with age. In one of the early Framingham studies, radiographic evidence of marked osteoarthritic changes rose from 11 per cent among those aged 60 to 69 to 19 per cent among those aged 80 and above; symptomatic arthritic complaints on the other hand only rose from 7 per cent to 11 per cent in the same age groups (Felson et al., 1987). Subsequent studies of the incidence of osteoarthritic changes in the hand, hip and knee also suggest that while incidence rates rise until age 80, after that age they seem to either stabilise or decline. This is illustrated in Figure 3.3 below drawn from a review of the field by Zhang and Jordan (2010).

Turning from considerations of incidence and prevalence of disease to considerations of its consequences, how much do the chronic 'degenerative' diseases of later life affect and impair the ordinary activities of daily living in later life? Not all degenerative diseases are equal. While the diagnosis of dementia increases the risk of dependency and institutionalisation many times over, this is not the case for other degenerative diseases whether they be potentially fatal conditions such as cancer, cerebrovascular disease, heart disease or Parkinson's disease (Agüero-Torres et al., 2001; Luppa et al., 2012) or

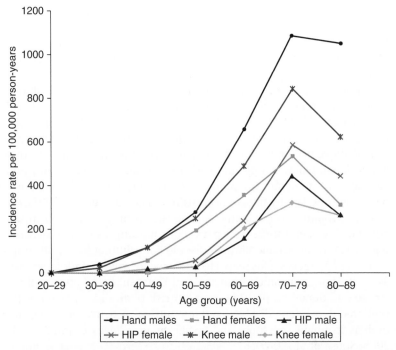

Figure 3.3   Age-associated incidence of osteoarthritic changes in
the hand, hip and knee

Source: Zhang, Y., and Jordan, J. M. (2010). Epidemiology of osteoarthritis.
Clinics in Geriatric Medicine, 26(3), 355. Reprinted with permission from Elsevier.

non-fatal, limiting conditions such as arthritis (Verbrugge, 1992). Does
the same apply to disability and dependency more generally?

Just how disabling is chronic disease in later life?

As implied in the last section, not all chronic diseases are a major
source of disability and therefore constitute a need for care. While
in-patient and out-patient hospital costs accrue from incident disease
or exacerbations of existing disease, the costs of long-term care –
whether delivered in a person's own home, in a nursing home or in
adapted housing – arise primarily from an inability of an individual
to perform the various instrumental or personal activities of daily
living, such as shopping, preparing meals and eating. Thus chronic

disease in later life can be any combination of life threatening, life shortening or life restricting conditions. Despite an extensive literature examining chronic disease, multi-morbidity and disability in later life, there are only a limited number of studies examining which diseases have which consequences.

In one of the earliest studies addressing the problem of which disorders contribute most to loss of independence, Agüero-Torres and her colleagues (1998) reported that, in a three-year follow up study, only a specific diagnosis of dementia predicted the risk of people aged 75 and above becoming dependent and only dementia predicted worsening dependency among those who survived. The significance and centrality of dementia for predicting disability and dependency has been confirmed many times since. Wolff and her colleagues (2005), for example, found that dementia showed the strongest effect on future dependency over a three-year period of follow up, as well as identifying stroke as the second chronic disease contributing to the development of dependency. This seems to hold true for low- to middle-income as well as high-income countries and suggests that between them stroke and dementia pose the greatest risk of an older person being rendered dependent, disabled and institutionalised, irrespective of his or her economic, personal and social circumstances (Nihtilä et al., 2008; Sousa et al., 2009).

We acknowledge that there is an intrinsic difficulty in identifying the extent to which any illness affects any particular person. Diseases that lead to a much shorter life – such as cancer, end stage renal disease and ischemic heart disease – may be less likely to yield prolonged periods of disablement while osteoarthritis may have little effect on life expectancy but lead to a mild but prolonged degree of disability. How can these very different conditions be easily balanced against, say, a short but serious degree of disability faced by some with end stage kidney disease. It is not clear that the disability associated with any chronic disease is fixed; clearly all chronic diseases are not equally disabling and the disabilities associated with some conditions may over time decrease, increase or remain the same. There is some evidence, for example, that the disabling effect of some chronic diseases has grown less over time as a result of earlier detection, more extensive and more effective treatment and improved rehabilitative measures (Hoeymans et al., 2012). Some researchers have suggested that while the disabling effect of fatal diseases in later life has decreased over time, the effect of non-fatal diseases has actually increased (Puts et al., 2008). In addition to any so-called 'period' effects on the relationship between disease and disability, ageing may further complicate the relationship between disease and disability. Some diseases developing in very late life may be more – and others less – disabling than they prove to be at other, earlier stages in life (cf. O'Hare et al., 2007; Reistetter et al., 2011). As the effect of disease on disability changes, as rates of institutionalisation decline and as chronic disease affects more people at later ages, the consequence may be that ill and dependent old age becomes 'compressed' and increasingly dominated by the disabling effects of some diseases even as other diseases and their effects are alleviated.

Whatever the changing patterns studies have observed between age, disease and disability, there is consistent evidence that irrespective of disease, chronological age per se leads to a growing difficulty in managing the activities of daily life. Thus even as survival with disease increases, and disability onset is deferred, the last years of people's lives may become more likely to be affected by ill health and disability. Maintaining an ethos of 'successful ageing' in these circumstances may call for a different response, one that requires greater resilience in resisting the attributions of frailty and incapacity conjured up by the spectral presence of a fourth age than is the case for people earlier in later life for whom only wrinkles and greying hair may serve as its harbinger. As reports multiply concerning the growing costs of health care arising from the diseases and disabilities of later life, people who reach older ages risk finding themselves the public embodiment of such costly diseases and, in consequence, might well experience these attributions as yet another, additional burden, that only further deepens and darkens the shadows of their days. In the next section, we consider the evidence supporting this 'burdensome' perspective.

The ageing of ageing societies and the costs of health care

In her article on apocalyptic demography, Robertson (1990) questioned the prevailing belief that an increasingly ageing population meant increasing demands on the resources of society. She argued that the rising costs reflected more the response of the health care system to changes in demography and disease distribution than to the number of older people or their increasing morbidity. In a follow up paper, she added:

> According to this scenario, people will live longer but sicker. The greater morbidity of increasing numbers of elders, so the argument goes, will drive up health care costs. In addition, public pension plans will collapse under the

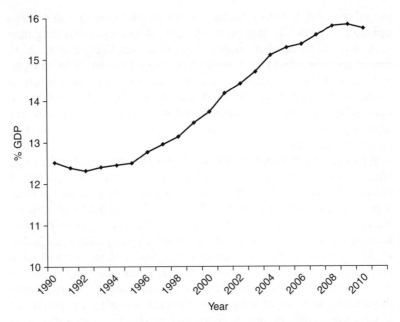

Figure 3.4   Average growth in expenditure on health care and
long-term care, as a percentage of GDP (OECD countries, 1990–2010)

Source: de la Maisonneuve and Martins, 2013. Reprinted with permission
from OECD Publishing.

sheer weight of the numbers of older people. This 'bankruptcy hypothesis of
aging' in which 'oncoming hordes of elderly' (Barer et al. 1987) deplete societal resources, constitutes apocalyptic demography. (Robertson, 1997: 426)

There is no doubt that health care expenditure is rising as a proportion
of national GDP. Across the whole of the OECD during the last two
decades (1990–2010), it has grown by 3.5 per cent (de la Maisonneuve
and Martins, 2013).

However there have been cautionary responses to this narrative. In
1999 a paper appeared in the journal *Health Economics* debunking
the idea so frequently propounded by journalists, health policy analysts and international bodies alike (cf. OECD, 1988b;World Bank,
1994) that the ageing of the population was leading to elevated health
care costs. Zweifel, Felder and Meiers argued that such views were 'a
red herring' and that there was no specific *age- associated* rise in health
care costs once proximity to death was controlled for (1999: 493).
Their findings (based on Swiss health care insurance data) only confirmed what an earlier paper had observed in relation to US Medicare

expenditures, namely that 'demographic changes in the population of Medicare enrolees should affect the program's expenditures principally through the increased number of elderly persons, not through increased longevity among the elderly' (Lubitz, Beebe and Baker, 1995: 1003).

Since then, several other studies employing different methodologies, in different countries, have confirmed that the influence of increasing age on health care costs is either negligble or very small even after considering potentially confounding effects or possible differences in the effect of age upon different elements of health care (Breyer, Costa-Font and Folder, 2010; Felder, Werblow and Zweifel, 2010; Polder, Barendregt and van Oers, 2006; Shang and Goldman, 2008; Seshamani and Gray, 2004; Werblow, Felder and Zweifel, 2007). As Polder and his colleagues concluded 'Western societies should not worry about the effects of ageing. Since other factors such as technological change and increasing service levels have much more influence on the cost development in health care, policy makers should focus on the creation of a sustainable health care system' (2006: 1730).

In 2006, the OECD published a working paper that sought to break down the rising costs of public health care expenditure from 1970 to 2002. The authors observed that across the OECD countries, changing demography – which incorporate increases in the longevity of the population aged 60 and above – 'only accounts for a small increase in [health care] expenditure' contrasted with the increasing costs associated with technological developments and rising salaries (OECD, 2006, table 2.2 p.33). A more detailed study of expenditure trends in France from 1992 to 2000 also demonstrated the same point, namely that it was changes in practices not the ageing of society that appeared to be 'the main driver in the increase in expenditures' (Dormont, Grignon and Huber, 2006: 959). In short the ageing of the pensionable age population neither constitutesthe principal, nor is it even a very important factor in the rising public health costs that have taken place over the last four decades.

Other studies have questioned certain of the generalisations of the 'red herring' hypothesis, arguing that while rising *health care costs* may not be attributable to the ageing of the older population, rising *social care costs*, and particularly those associated with long-term care, do show strong 'ageing' effects. Larsson, Kåreholt and Thorslund (2008) conducted a study of more than 500 Swedish individuals aged 75 and older who died between 1995 and 2004. As in other studies of the red herring hypothesis, they found that 'approaching death, rather than

chronological age is the major determinant of health care utilisation'
(Larsson, Kareholt and Thorslund, 2008: 355). Home care costs,
however, were influenced more by chronological age than proximity
to death while the costs of institutional care were influenced by both –
although 'time to death care had twice the effect of increasing age'
(356). A subsequent whole county study in Sweden confirmed these
findings in relation to long-term care leading the authors 'somewhat
pessimistically' to conclude that

> even though care costs of the elderly are strongly associated with local
> mortality rates…the age structure of a municipality remains a strong pre-
> dictor of overall LTC costs even after we account for mortality. Especially
> the number of the oldest old remains a relevant predictor for LTC costs.
> (Karlsson and Klohn, 2011: 17–18)

A study of the Dutch population aged above 55 reported similar
results – with the further complication that age 'and informal care
availability remain important determinants of LTCE (long term care
expenditure)' (de Meijera et al., 2011: 434). In summary, while the
ageing of ageing societies accounts for relatively little of their growing
health care costs, it does seem to play a significant role in determining
public expenditure on institutional and home based long-term care. If
one examines the relative size of these two sets of costs (health versus
long-term care) as a function of overall national expenditure, however,
long-term care costs account for approximately one eighth (12.5%) of
the combined expenditure, as illustrated in Table 3.2.

Even if the rise in the number of octogenarians, nonagenarians and
centenarians were to double or even treble the long-term care costs
across the OECD over the next two decades, the effect upon most
Western countries would be little different to what Denmark is experiencing already – that is, an apparently sustainable 25 per cent of all
health and long-term care costs being diverted to long-term care.

Despite the weakness of the data and the shoal of 'red herrings'
swimming around claims that the ageing of ageing societies is mas-
sively escalating the costs of health care, framing the demographic
phenomenon of an ageing society in terms of escalating costs further
engenders the imaginary of 'deep' old age – the fourth age – as a
demographic black hole depleting society's resources as it grows ever
larger. The tropes and discourses of apocalyptic demography and its
accompanying epidemiology have moved beyond academic debate to
become public currency via the print and broadcast media, in effect
extending the shadow of the fourth age ever wider. It is to this topic
of extending media coverage of population ageing that we next turn.

Table 3.2   Relative costs of health care and long-term care
expenditure in selected OECD countries (2006–2010)

Country	HC expenditure[2b] (as % of GDP, average 2006–2010)	LTC expenditure[1a] (as % of GDP, 2008)	LTC (as % of HC expenditure)
Australia	5.6	0.03	0.5
Canada	5.8	1.17	16.8
Demark	6.3	2.18	25.7
France	7.4	1.18	13.8
Germany	7.3	0.89	10.9
Japan	6.1	0.63	9.4
Korea	3.3	0.28	7.8
Netherlands	6.4	1.23	16.1
Poland	4.1	0.36	8.1
Spain	5.5	0.57	9.4
Sweden	6.6	0.65	9.0
USA	7.1	0.57	7.4
OECD average	**5.5**	**0.8**	**12.7**

Sources: [a] OECD (http://dx.doi.org/10.1787/888932844277) [b] C. de la Maisonneuve and J. Oliveira Martins, 2013. Reprinted with permission from OECD Publishing.

Representations of apocalyptic demography in the mass media

In the previous sections we addressed the 'social facts' concerning the changing demographics of contemporary developed economies, the ageing of their older populations and the anticipated rise in morbidity associated with this change. While there is reason to believe that such changes can reasonably be exemplified by the idea of an epidemiological 'transition' (Omran, 1971; Olshansky and Ault, 1986), the likely effect on society is by no means as great as is often implied (Gee, 2002; Mullan, 2000; Spijker and MacInnes, 2013). But since the introduction of the term 'apocalyptic demography' in 1990, the theme of a global ageing crisis has begun to fascinate the mass media. Within the print media this has resulted in what one author has described as a bifurcation between 'good' and 'bad' representations of ageing (Vickers, 2007). While individual ageing and ageing individuals tend to be represented through positive – or 'successful' – images of ageing, population ageing and ageing societies are more often treated as its 'bad' side. In one study of two Canadian national newspapers, Rozanova, Northcott and McDaniel observed how 'the apocalyptic demography / inter-generational conflict theme was manifested in the discussion of seniors in the role of clients of the health care and social security systems. The older the seniors of both genders were, the more likely they were to be portrayed as dependent on the social security system. Similarly, concern about the sustainability of an adequate health care system highlighted the "tough choices" necessary to deal with the needs of an aging population' (Rozanova, Northcott and McDaniel, 2006: 381).

In another study of relatively recent depictions of ageing and old age between 1998 and 2008 in the weekly magazine, *The Economist*, Martin, Williams and O'Neill

> found that nearly two thirds of the relevant articles portrayed them [older people] in a negative light, effectively as a burden to society. The subject matter in three quarters of the articles involved pensions, demography, health care, and politics; and the theme of apocalyptic demography was widespread. Older people were often portrayed as frail non-contributors to society. The alarmist words 'time bomb' were commonly used in relation to demography and pensions. (2009: 1436)

Examining the representation of demographic ageing in the Swedish press, Lundgren and Ljuslinder observed how it was treated as an established fact, an undefined element within an 'expert discourse' whose meaning for the reader was almost universally framed 'as a threat and a future problem in the making' (2011a: 173). These authors found that the topic was most often presented as 'news' – in contrast to reportage or comments on social or cultural life – positioning old age as an urgent phenomenon that threatened the country's welfare and future growth. Such representations were made more vivid by frequent references to an ageing population as a gathering storm or 'a bomb' ready to explode (Lundgren and Ljuslinder, 2011b:53).

In Eastern Europe similar themes were found. Research into portrayals of old age in the Polish print media found a discrepancy between 'good' and 'bad' ageing. Good ageing was represented through the themes of the family and the market, while bad ageing was portrayed in articles about the future ageing population and issues of welfare policy (Wilińska and Cedersund, 2010). Metaphors of ecological disaster also appeared in the Polish press, as elsewhere, warning of a future avalanche of old age that is 'unpredictable, perilous and unstoppable' (Wilińska and Cedersund, 2010: 339). No doubt further analyses of the media in other countries would be valuable, though we suspect that they would all yield very similar results. Despite the limited academic literature examining media representations of 'population ageing', that which has been published is consistent in supporting the thesis that, unlike more individualised aspects of ageing and old age, treatment of population ageing in the media is dominated by images of a 'bad' old age, threatening to attack, engulf or otherwise overwhelm society.

We would argue that the mass media in contemporary affluent countries actively reproduces the sort of apocalyptic demography that Robertson described decades earlier. But unlike the early concerns over pensions and social security, there now seems to be a more generalised fear that the ageing of ageing societies threatens much more than purely fiscal concerns. Apocalyptic demography is seen to pose a danger to modern, Western society as a whole, which seems poised to be submerged by a process that, like ageing itself, appears to lie beyond human hands. In this sense it echoes earlier demographic debates concerning the 'degeneration' of modern society as a result of rising numbers of another dangerous class – the mad and the mentally deficient (Soloway, 1990). During the late nineteenth and early twentieth century, predictions concerning rising levels of madness and mental deficiency were seen to threaten the 'social' or 'racial' degeneration of society, leading to a variety of proposals to exclude, incarcerate or even emasculate the degenerate 'stock' in society (Ewart, 1910; Rentoul, 1906; Tredgold, 1909). But while sharing a similar rhetoric of impending social decay, the apocalyptic demography of the twenty-first century differs from that of a century ago in one important way – that, like ageing itself, the 'ageing' of society is 'unstoppable'. And, of course, it contains an undisputed core of social 'facticity' that was lacking in the assumptions made in the early twentieth century about the incidence of mental illness and mental deficiency, that the population aged sixty and above is indeed ageing more deeply and more thoroughly than before. But the accompanying rhetoric of rising disease, spiralling costs and endless incapacity that sets the conditions for a more pervasive social imaginary of dark old age is as we have tried to show much less bounded by facts despite being trumpeted in the popular and professional press.

Conclusions

Demography and epidemiology provide twin narratives for the ageing of ageing societies. These disciplines have tended to represent this societal ageing as either an ecological disaster or a global pandemic, threatening to swamp or in other ways undermine the stability of society. The general tenor of such concerns is not new – and arguably has always accompanied the rise of demography as a field of study

and its close links with 'political arithmetic'. But these recent preoccupations do represent new ways of thinking about and understanding
ageing and old age that are serving to frame much contemporary
political rhetoric and public opinion in the contemporary world. In
terms of sheer numbers, of course, low- and middle-income countries
such as India and Nigeria contain far more people aged 60 and above
and many more people with chronic disease, but they are neither yet
seen, nor yet see themselves as being 'ageing societies'. Hence the
social imaginary of the fourth age is shaped more profoundly by the
media and the academic and professional literature of the developed
societies in the East and in the West, whose populations aged 60 and
above are becoming noticeably older.

At the centre of this imaginary is the fear of personal and societal
enfeeblement, a fear that is often linked with the idea of mental and
moral enfeeblement. Throughout history and across nations, there has
been a clear recognition of – and often quite specific words for – the
mental infirmity that old age often brings. Such terms however did not
dominate Western concerns in the eighteenth, nineteenth or early
twentieth century – any more than they dominate the media in low-
and middle-income countries today (Prince et al., 2008). It is only after
the post-war crisis of the Welfare State, in the mid-1970s, that the
demographic concerns regarding the numbers of old people in society
began to emerge across North America and Western Europe. In place
of earlier population concerns over rising numbers of the 'dangerous
classes' (beggars, paupers, idiots and the insane), the 'old' became the
new unhealthy, devitalising segment of the population (Mullan, 2000:
80). Although the worries over population ageing were initially represented as fiscal concerns, expressed as the rising proportion of
national product being directed toward pensioners or social security
beneficiaries and the likely sustainability of national pension schemes
(and in the USA, of the Social Security programme), a concomitant
concern was also beginning to be expressed over the effect of dementia and its link to the rising numbers of older people in society (Arie
and Jolley, 1983; Kramer, 1980).

The somewhat limited concerns of the 1980s have since evolved into
a broader fear – of a 'global aging crisis' that threatens to engulf the
world economy and 'even democracy itself' (Peterson, 1999: 55). Such
hysteria – in suitably modulated academic tones – has also pervaded
much of the epidemiological literature on ageing as it increasingly
focuses upon the pandemic of age-associated chronic disease and the
related costs that make ageing 'a global public health challenge' (Esser
and Ward, 2013). In such narratives, Alzheimer's disease represents

the iconic frontline, the new site of an anticipated national enfeeblement. The framework of the fourth age as social imaginary is constructed in no small measure by such developments, their metaphorical expressions a legacy of population science and its political arithmetic.

We have tried in this chapter to show that while there is evidence of an ageing of the ageing population in Western (and East Asian) societies, the degree to which this will necessarily involve rising costs, in terms of health care expenditure, rising levels of disease, in terms of a greater prevalence of so-called 'degenerative diseases' and rising levels of incapacity is difficult to predict because the various elements – disease, costs, disability are themselves not fixed derivatives of demography. Marshalling evidence from various sources in economics, epidemiology and public health, we hope to have shown – or at least to have raised the clear possibility – that there is no intrinsic, universal link between rising amounts of 'age' and increasingly burdensome and costly disease and disability. Of course there are associated risks of living longer lives; but their quantification, extent and inevitability are insufficient to justify the kind of apocalyptic assumptions that currently surround the ageing of ageing societies. Ironically, however, as a widening gap emerges between which diseases can be treated, which limited, and which can have their disabling effects mitigated, it may be these very improvements in morbidity and mortality that will deepen the divide between those who age successfully and those who fail. It is to this question of 'failing' and 'frailty' that we turn to in the next chapter.

Chapter 4

Frailty and the Fourth Age

Introduction

The concept of frailty is central to the process of 'othering' old age and therefore plays a crucial role in the articulation of the social imaginary of the fourth age. We would argue that the idea of frailty contributes, both directly and indirectly to the creation and maintenance of the boundary of the fourth age and helps separate it from the cultural field of the third age. In our view, frailty serves as the *residuum* of an imagined old age defined as much by its potential as by its actual morbidity (Gilleard and Higgs, 2011b). In this chapter we explore the clinical, historical and social construction of the idea of frailty, the objectifying practices involved in 'frailing' (i.e., assigning someone to the category 'frail' – or 'infirm') and the dilemmas of individuals who risk becoming identified as 'frailed' (i.e., being imputed or actually assessed as a potential or actual 'frail elder').

Pivotal to concepts of frailty are judgements of mental and physical incapacity which in turn focus on the extent to which this incapacity is deemed unmanageable by the individual older person within his or her currently existing physical and social environment. Frailty reflects a global judgement about individual older people but as Brunk has observed, frailty is 'an attribute created by and for others – not owned by individuals themselves' (2007: 40). The parameters of frailty are not fixed but evolve over time. In a similar way the means by which older people have been categorised as frail – of being 'frailed' – have varied over time, although we would argue that they have always invoked a degree of activation of otherness, of a generalised, third person discourse about the 'state' a particular elderly person is in. The objectification of frailty therefore confounds the possibility of agency all the while privileging the moral imperative for others to care for or manage the person, not as a personal 'I' or a 'you' but as a social 'him' or 'her' or 'it', in effect as managing a state of risk.

Cutting through the various dilemmas of becoming an object of such frailing is the limited scope frailty seems to offer the older person to assert – and insert – his or her human subjectivity into the process of his or her transition into 'real' or 'deep' old age. These limitations are framed by three elements or facets of frailty, the first is found in its ambiguous, 'epigenetic' nature, a nature that floats across biomedical, social and psychological domains; the second is represented by the processes of being or becoming frailed, whether this is viewed as the natural course that frailty framed as a 'geriatric syndrome' is observed to follow, or as a socially organised process of assessment and management that allocates care and 'caseness' to individual older people; the third facet lies in the particular dilemmas faced by older people and their relatives in accepting, negotiating or resisting their being labelled as frail as well as the consequences of living under the shadow of frailty. We first address the nature of frailty and its functional significance in demarking the 'event horizon' of the fourth age.

The nature of frailty

The biomedical perspective

Frailty is used within the world of geriatrics and gerontology to describe older patients who are in poor health (without necessarily being diagnosed as 'ill'), who are more vulnerable than others equally old to the effects of various environmental stressors and who are judged to lack the resilience to cope with disease, disability and decline (Fisher, 2005: 2229). The term has replaced more traditional words used to describe the sick and vulnerable aged, such as decrepitude, infirmity or senility; however, despite attempts at objectifying the nature of frailty through the creation of numerous scales and indices, it still remains an 'emergent' construct which 'like the weather…resists facile measurement and definition' (Bortz, 2010: 255). Although more recent research consensus has expressed the view that 'frailty has a clear conceptual framework', there is still no agreed 'operational definition of frailty that can satisfy all experts' (Rodriguez-Mañas et al., 2013: 66). Different instruments lead to differing numbers of older people being 'frailed'; one review reported that 'the prevalence of frailty ranged between 33% and 88% depending on the frailty tool used' (van Kan et al., 2010: 275), while another reported 'enormous' variations in the prevalence of frailty among people aged above 65 living at home, varying from as low as 4 per cent to as high as 59 per cent (Collard et al., 2012). Even in clinical settings, such as those of acute geriatric admission wards, where the patient population might be expected to be more homogeneous, studies have reported rates of frailty varying from 36 per cent to 88 per cent (van Iersel and Rikkert, 2006: 729). Much of this variation can be attributed to the scales and criteria being used in 'diagnosing' frailty. The more scales used the greater seems to be the variability. Comparing eight 'commonly used scales' applied to more than 27,000 non-institutionalised persons aged 50 to 100, surveyed across 11 European countries, Theou and her colleagues (2013) found rates from as low as 6 per cent to as high as 44 per cent depending on the particular scale. Another study reported that the proportion of residents in assisted living facilities designated 'not frail' by various 'frailty' scales ranged from as few as 3.5 per cent to as many as 32.3 per cent (Hogan et al., 2012: 4) leading the authors to conclude that the capacity to predict the 'adverse outcomes' said to define the frail state, 'requires further work' (8).

The persisting vagueness of the term has not prevented researchers trying to turn frailty into a more precise biomedical concept – if anything it has served as a stimulus for yet more biomedical research effort. Two lines of enquiry can be discerned in such efforts. One is to define frailty as a distinct syndrome or phenotype observed in particular old people, one that is capable of being identified by 'objective' signs (Fried et al., 2001). The other is to view frailty as a composite made up of a number of dimensions, a multi-factorial combination of particular physical, psychological and social deficits which can be observed to varying degrees within older populations. In this way, summary scores can assign older individuals to varying degrees of frailty which in turn can be seen to predict varying degrees of risk of suffering various adverse outcomes (Rockwood et al., 1999; Mitniski et al., 2002). Measures of frailty based on the former, syndrome approach, have proved capable of distinguishing frailty from related indicators such as 'agedness', 'co-morbidity' or 'disability' (Fried et al., 2001; 2004) suggesting that despite its vague nature, frailty can be represented as something other than either functional impairment or disabling ill health. We would argue that the term continues to have 'purchase' outside the existing framework of disease or disability. The question remains however what gives it such purchase? In order to pursue this problem researchers have begun to examine the various constitutive elements seen to underlie the biomedical concept of frailty to find which ones 'work' best. When examinations of individual frailty criteria are undertaken, it is clear that they are not all equally predictive of adverse outcomes. Single or limited indices seem to be at least as predictive as more cumbersome multi-dimensional measures of accumulated deficits. Studies have found that measures of motor activity such as 'slow gait speed', 'low physical activity' or even 'lower extremity function' are predictive of falls, chronic disability, institutionalisation and death among non-disabled people aged more than 70 years while self-reported measures of muscle weakness, depression, exhaustion and weight loss are either not predictive or much less predictive (Houles et al., 2010; Rothman, Leo-Summers and Gill, 2008; Vermuilen et al., 2011; van Kan et al., 2010; Woo, Leung and Morley, 2012). One set of criteria, linked with the so-called 'Fried phenotype', reflecting muscular weakness and limited physical activity overlaps considerably with another less popular 'geriatric' syndrome, that of 'sarcopenia'.

Sarcopenia is a term coined in 1989 by Rosenberg to describe age related 'decline in muscle mass and strength' (Roubenoff and Hughes, 2000). It provides a narrower concept that might serve just as well as frailty as a predictor of adverse outcomes, but lacks many of the intimations of infirmity, weakness and lack that have sedimented around the latter term. Although it might be harder to measure the loss of muscle quality that constitutes sarcopenia, it is possible to compare and contrast its utility and purchase against that associated with frailty – framing it less as a thing apart – a dividing practice – but more as a parameter of biological aging that should nevertheless not go 'unchecked' (Roubenoff and Hughes, 2000: M721). Significantly, sarcopenia seems to show a different relationship with gender to that of frailty, being more common among 80 year or older old men than it is among women in the same age category (Yoshida et al., 2014) as Figure 4.1 shows.

Cruz-Jentoft and Michel have suggested that sarcopenia, defined as 'a syndrome characterized by progressive and generalised loss of skeletal muscle mass and strength' (2013: 103) is the major determinant of physical frailty and hence should serve as the biomedical core of frailty. Others disagree with this conclusion, arguing that sarcopenia is 'a non-specific clinical sign that can be age associated phenomenon but that may also be caused by a multitude of clinical conditions that are independent from the aging process' unlike frailty which, because of its very complexity and multi-dimensionality, possesses 'specific clinical relevance for the elderly population' (Bauer and Sieber, 2008: 677).

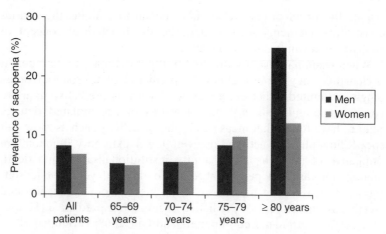

Figure 4.1   Prevalence of sarcopenia by age and gender (n=4811)

Source: Yoshida et al., 2014, figure 1, p.48. Reprinted with permission
from John Wiley & Sons.

While less dismissive of sarcopenia's relevance to ageing and old age,
the *European Working Group on Sarcopenia in Older People* has rein-
forced this distinction between the singularity of the syndrome of sarcopenia contrasted with the complexity of the concept of frailty. Thus
they defined sarcopenia as the presence of low muscle mass, combined
with low muscle strength and/or low physical performance (Cruz-Jentoft
et al., 2010: 413). Frailty, in contrast, they suggested extends its points
of reference beyond any single physical domain – indeed it extends
beyond the physical altogether. Thus they conceded that while 'frailty
and sarcopenia overlap...the general concept of frailty ... goes beyond
physical factors to encompass psychological and social dimensions as
well' (415). In short, frailty in all its ambiguity, complexity and multiplicity serves as the 'real' boundary of the fourth age; sarcopenia is too
narrow and too under-socialised a concept to be professionally effective.
So it is to frailty's 'social dimensions' that we now turn.

Frailty and the social sciences

The definitional separation of frailty from agedness, disability and
illness is important not just for geriatric medicine but also for the light
it casts on structuring a sociology of ageing and old age. From the
perspective of medical sociology, it is more than the extension of
a biopsychosocial model to ageing, however satisfactory such a

representation may be for professional engagement. Frailty represents, we would argue, a more profound re-organisation in the relationship between ill-health and later life, one that has arisen, at least in part from secular changes in the institutional organisation of, and cultural interpretations given to, ageing, health and well-being (Higgs and Jones, 2009; Jones and Higgs, 2010; Pickard, 2011). During the course of the twentieth century, agedness, chronic illness and disability have become distinct, coherent, social and cultural locations. They may bring either respect or neglect but crucially they allow scope for individual agency and subjectivity, supporting personal identities and lifestyles and providing sites of contestation within society. Crucially, they are also capable of sustaining first person narratives.

The condition of frailty denies such options. It functions neither as an identity nor as a stabilising social position – it is at best a syndrome, and at worst an accumulation of lifelong debts deficits and disease. While such formulations allow for the categorisation of older people into an ascribed community of 'the frail', this categorisation is neither individually owned nor is it capable of being subjectively defined by and within a collective of individuals. It reflects the viewpoint of others, a judgement that such people present a condition of high but poorly specified risk. It is a judgement located outside the discourses of disease 'self-management' or 'co-creating health', serving as a focus for others' actions, not as a guide, for example, to living well with chronic illness or disability. In short it represents a residual state that remains when other narratives and identities can no longer be asserted or enacted. In this sense, frailty represents ageing deprived of both narrative and 'performative' agency (Gilleard and Higgs, 2010).

The frail are neither defined by particular cultural markers, nor do they occupy particular social positions; rather they are defined by what is thought to be about to happen to them both as 'corporeal citizens' and as persons. In other words, they are defined by their ubiquitous risk and personal vulnerability. In this sense it could be argued that the contemporary term of frailty is marginally more oppressive than the traditional categories of the 'elderly chronic sick' or the 'old and infirm'. In the past these terms applied to those poor old people who were also judged infirm, sick and in need of whatever care could be afforded. There was no ambiguity, no uncertainty and no projected future concern. The reframing of this category into a 'geriatric syndrome' or 'geriatric index' has been shaped by the totalising influence of perceived risk now attached to it. This is not just the risk of physical harm, but a more pervasive, all enveloping risk, of becoming 'lost' from the ranks of citizenship and of the 'civilised' (Higgs and Gilleard, 2006).

Growing older, most people, most of the time, manage more or less successfully to distance themselves from what is perceived as the more oppressive elements of agedness, in much the same way that most people growing up with an impairment are able to distance themselves from or at least manage and modify the oppressiveness of disability. Age and impairment provide material points of reference from which these new contested positions can be wrested (Gilleard and Higgs, 2011b). Frailty lacks such ready reference points. 'Mental and physical frailty' implies not so much that one suffers from a particular social or medical condition but that a person so categorised faces some undesirable yet unspecified future that most people would rather avoid. Frail people are now seen by health and social care staff as well as by the lay public as old people who are intractably at risk.

How far are those so marked out defined by their socially structured disadvantage? Unlike 'pensioners' or 'people with disabilities' for those judged primarily as 'a complex system on the threshold of breakdown' (Nowak and Hubbard, 2009: 98), there seems to be no prospect of political resistance, no opportunities for collective affirmation, no emancipatory or transcendent narratives allowing them to escape from the 'social imaginary' of agedness because frailty is deemed a biosocial medical syndrome or state into which the rejected elements of the now positively framed discourses surrounding age and disability are deposited. While the frail seem to be defined, not just by their physical state, but by their marginality and social impotence, nevertheless there have been few attempts to frame this state as one determined by any avoidable social disadvantage. Overwhelmingly considerations of age dominate the framing of frailty. This is illustrated in Figure 4.2 which draws on more than 40,000 observations from the European SHARE survey presenting rates of frailty by age decade where frailty was operationalised as presence of at least two or more pre-designated frailty indicators (see Sirven, 2012 for details).

Not only do frailty levels increase with each age group but the risks of becoming frail also increase. People aged 80 and above are some three and one half times as likely *to become* 'frailer' than are people in their late 50s and early 60s. Does this mean that there are no socially determining influences affecting the assessment of frailty? Clearly such a conclusion need not be the case. Processes however strongly influenced by aspects of biological ageing may nevertheless vary in their realisation depending upon social factors.

Within the social sciences there has been a tendency to leave frailty alone, as if its 'social' elements were the secondary concerns of epidemiologists and public health specialists. That said, there have been

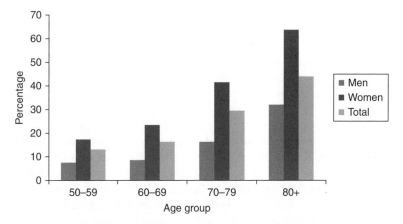

Figure 4.2   Rates of frailty by age and gender

Source: Authors' own chart based on information in *Working Paper No.52*, Institut de Recherche et Documentation en Économie de la Santé (IRDES), Paris. Table 4, p.11.

some attempts to consider the 'social construction of frailty'. One of the first was in an article with exactly that title, by the social anthropologist Kaufman (1994). Writing just before articles on frailty began to flood the academic literature in geriatrics and gerontology, Kaufman noted both the lack of precision in definitions of frailty and the restricted focus in framing frailty by 'the elderly's "need" for services or the assessment of their losses' (49). Frailty, she argued, is articulated within a discourse of 'surveillance, safety and care' (50) thereby placing the resolution of those needs over and above the potential compromising of the individual's need or wish for autonomy and independence. A decade later, Grenier and Hanley took up Kaufman's argument, noting how frailty serves as an organising theme for public health and social care discourses directed toward the older population and processes that reflect 'how older women's bodies are managed' (Grenier and Hanley, 2007: 214). Focusing especially on the gendered nature of frailty, they noted how older women commonly resist the label of frailty while noting that some nevertheless manage to employ it tactically as a means of garnering support, playing the 'little old lady card', as one of her informants said (220). Frailty was, she found, an active site of resistance for many older women, or if not resistance then at least a site of negotiation as older women sought to develop a less marginalised place for themselves, in the context of declining health and fitness. The problem with frailty, Grenier suggested in a later work, was not so much its ambiguity or even its biomedical representation, but how such representations serve to 'obscure the way frailty is structured by cumulative disadvantage' and the various social determinants of functional impairment (2007: 437).

Research into the social determinants of frailty – broadly conceived – supports her argument. Drawing upon data across 11 European countries, Theou and her colleagues (2013) reported that country-based mean scores on a frailty index reflected the relative wealth of the country. Older people surveyed in richer countries were assessed as having lower levels of frailty while the survival rates of those people classed as 'frail' were better in richer countries than in poorer ones. Drawing on the same data base and using a longitudinal 2 year follow up study design, Etman and her colleagues (2012) reported that female gender and limited education both contributed, independently, to worsening frailty among the nearly 15,000 men and women aged above 55 for whom there was adequate follow up data. Sirven (2012) also drawing on SHARE data demonstrated that women have higher levels of frailty and that more educated people have lower levels. Using reported life history data, he also observed that individuals with a history of poor health in childhood or adulthood and individuals who have experienced periods of financial hardship in both cases are assessed as having higher levels of frailty. Other studies conducted in non-European countries have also observed socio-economic correlates of frailty, observing that older people judged as frail are more often people in blue collar occupations, with less education and more often female (Alvarado et al., 2008; Casale-Martinez et al., 2012; Woo et al., 2005). Studies conducted in the US have proved less conclusive. One study found evidence of an association between Fried's index of frailty and lower socio-economic status, limited education and limited household income (Szanton et al., 2010) while another failed to find evidence of such an association (Hirsch et al., 2006). Both concurred that there appeared no relationship with race, arguably one of the key sites of socially structured disadvantage in the US.

Despite these attempts in the social sciences to construe frailty as constituted primarily by health and social care assessment practices, or by epidemiologists to frame it as the product of cumulative disadvantage associated with lifelong poverty, limited education and gender, frailty remains equally elusive to social and biomedical researchers. For both disciplinary groups 'confusion, contradiction and ambiguity reign supreme' (Ferrucci, Mahallati and Simonsick, 2006: 260). From the perspective of the social sciences, the roots of this ambiguity may lie less in social inequality and divisive assessment practices than in the progressive fragmentation that has taken place in the hegemonic representation of 'sad old age'. Once a partner in want with other groups of 'needy others', facing chronic sickness, orphanhood, widowhood, mental or physical impairment, the delineation of the group of needy aged into those whose needs are primarily financial, those whose needs are mainly social, and those whose needs cannot be met by either pensions, social security payments or increased social solidarity has radically changed this link. It is in seeking to further divide this last group and clearly delineate their needs that the steady development of 'geriatric' assessment technologies has taken place. As Grenier and others have argued, the processes of delineating what provisions individual needy older people are entitled to has contributed to giving frailty a purchase it might not otherwise have possessed (Grenier, 2007; Weicht, 2011).

To understand the nature of this particular 'purchasing power', it is helpful to consider the historical positioning of needy old age during the course of the twentieth century. As the financial position of later life was secured in the emerging welfare state, as part of the predictable and standardised life course, those who had been recipients of indoor poor relief, in the workhouse infirmaries, the hospitals for the chronic sick and the almshouses became the focus of policy makers' attention. Much of this attention was concentrated on the distinction between those needing nursing or medical attention and those whose institutional position was not considered to be the result of sickness and infirmity.

Following the fiscal crisis of the welfare state which occurred in the mid-1970s and alongside the growth of the de-institutionalisation movement, there was an increasing incentive to reduce the level of 'care' provided to older people. Consequently, long-stay hospital beds were closed; residential provision was more carefully reviewed and much effort was given to developing 'care in the community'. The fears of the workhouse, of hospitalisation and of the old infirmaries declined. During the 1980s community services expanded and the extent of the institutionalisation of older people declined. Those deemed in need of continuing hospital care were increasingly marginalised, as geriatric medicine became seen as the 'plumbers' of the health care system, unblocking the 'blocked bed' occupied by the older patient and supervising the enhanced discharge packages of the same patients who were sent either to their own homes or into nursing homes. The 'densification' of the disability of those in later life in long-term care was underway, and frailty acquired a powerful if largely unspoken role as the feared future of a deep or real old age, a fourth age vividly if somewhat unfeelingly described by Laslett as 'a condition of half-life; 'sans teeth, sans eyes, sans everything" (1989: 13).

Attempts to rationalise the term by locating it within various forms of calculability have served, we would argue, only to reify what is not so much an acquired identity but an assigned state that, however framed or intended, has become a social signifier of an unwelcome 'fourth age' that threatens to make us strangers to ourselves. What such a formulation means for an emancipatory sociology of later life is not straightforward. It is possible to critically interrogate the various analogies and metaphors through which deep old age is represented, exposing the ideological framework contained within such narratives (Zeilig, 2014 Van Gorp and Vercruysse, 2012); it is equally possible to advocate for those deemed too frail to speak for themselves – seeking to give voice to their needs through patient and carer advocacy organisations (Splaine, 2008); and finally it is possible to explore through some combination of social, medical and psychological approaches, ways to prevent the more tractable intimations of the fourth age from passing into the realm of the intractably frail (Daniels et al., 2008; Liu and Fielding, 2011). But even when the metaphors are challenged, the silence of the old and abject is broken and the arena of frailty's tractability expanded, it may be that by so narrowing its boundaries, the fourth age grows only darker, denser, more distant and more impenetrable. Perhaps to throw more light we need to turn to the processes of becoming frail – or of being frailed.

Entering the fourth age: becoming frail or being frailed?

If frailty serves as a socially negotiated biomarker of the fourth age, how best might we understand the process of becoming frail? Taking a biomedical perspective, the process can be represented as the endpoint of a number of separate but inter-related biological or biosocial processes, varying perhaps in the strength of their influence or their potential tractability. Alternatively, still keeping within a biomedical framework, the process of becoming frail can be represented as a single pathway of physical and mental decline that is fundamentally distinct from the many alternative pathways toward loss and decline in later life pursued by particular disabling, degenerative diseases. An example of this approach might be defining the specific molecular or cellular pathways that lead to the development of sarcopenia. On the other hand, should 'becoming frail' be understood differently, as the process of 'being frailed', treating frailty, not as an achieved identity or status that one acquires, but rather as an assigned state that, in certain circumstances of age, health and impairment, one is given? If frailty is an assigned state and not an identity acquired through the workings of our body, should we analyse the processes of frailing as the exercise of a Foucauldian 'disciplinary power', one that is invested in those professionals assigned to manage risk and allocate care? Is 'frailing' thus conceived only and always a matter of 'risk management'? Or is it also the exercise of the moral imperative to care? In the previous section, we described how empirical studies have been used to represent frailty as a measurable endpoint that is distinguishable from agedness, disability and ill health and the conceptual difficulties this has led to. In this section, we consider how frailty becomes such an endpoint in later life, a corporeal state that is nevertheless defined and surrounded by ubiquitous risk and the 'need' for care.

If frailty is *neither* agedness *nor* chronic disease *nor* functional impairment, how exactly might it come about? In trying to gain a better handle on its conceptual status, biomedical and public health researchers have for some time now been turning to a consideration of the antecedents of frailty, seeking to determine its putative aetiology. Like the last section, we shall begin this section by addressing biomedical approaches to understanding the development of frailty. Later we shall address the social aspects of 'frailing', on the one hand as an extension of the biosocial-epidemiological approach, aiming to reveal the 'social determinants' of frailty, and secondly by considering how individuals might come to be judged as frail, how older people are frailed by the system.

If one assumes that frailty is the net result of an accumulation of multiple adverse physical psychological and social outcomes, then clearly there can be no single pathway and neither can there be one single aetiological model. Under these circumstances, searching for such 'aetiological pathways' becomes little more than a series of investigations into the origins of any one of the numerous impairments and illnesses that arise in later life, and their equally multiple interactions with each other. This multiple deficit model espoused by researchers such as Rockwood and his colleagues does not provide any strong stimulus to research identifiable pathways in becoming frail since, as Sirven has noted, it is in essence a piece of 'black box epidemiology' that 'mak[es] use of a large set of criteria [but] without any theoretical backdrop' (2012: 7).

Hence the search for a coherent pathway or set of pathways is usually based on an adherence to frailty as a phenotype, the model of frailty that is associated with Fried and her group (2001). Even with this syndrome approach, there is a tendency to adopt tautological explanations of frailty. Although researchers are generally eager to argue that 'old age is not necessarily accompanied by frailty', explanations of frailty nevertheless treat it as caused by 'ageing of the cardiovascular system, the skeleton, metabolism, the immune system, the hormonal system and brain' (Pel-Littel et al., 2009: 391). Others have argued that while frailty is linked with age and ageing, it represents a distinct kind of 'critical point' whereby a cascade of irreparable errors occurs across some set of potentially inter-dependent organ systems precipitating the transition into frailty (or its precursor 'pre-frailty') (Walston et al., 2006: 994–995). While intriguing, such hypothetical critical moments remain undetermined and perhaps may prove indeterminable in the absence of any identifiable rate limiting event that could trigger such a cascade. They also echo what was once called the 'catastrophic error' theory of ageing! (cf. Orgel, 1963).

The search for biomarkers of frailty has revealed some positive evidence although it remains a bit of a hit-and-miss affair. Indicators of inflammation such as white blood cell count and pro-coagulant markers such as D-dimer and fibrinogen have been associated with both ageing and the onset of 'frailty' (Kanapuru and Ershler, 2009; Baylis et al., 2013), although other research has not always replicated these findings (Collerton, Martin-Ruiz, Davies et al., 2012). Others have suggested that frailty is determined not by any particular systems showing dysregulation but by the overall number of dysregulated systems (Fried et al., 2009). From this latter perspective, even though frailty is deemed to be a unitary syndrome, no single set of biomarkers are thought to cause frailty since it is assumed that there is no single biological core determining the 'trigger point' for becoming frail. It could be argued that by choosing not to place sarcopenia or some other similarly distinct physical process at the conceptual core of the frailty syndrome, any search for the aetiology of frailty is rendered every bit as complicated as the search for the mechanisms of ageing. Frailty consequently appears as the inverted image of 'ageing well'. What requires explanation therefore is not so much frailty itself but ageing without frailty – what might be considered in other circles as 'successful ageing'.

Of course, it could be argued that ageing without disease or disability is the marker of successful ageing, and frailty either ceases to be unsuccessful, if successful ageing is ageing without disease or disability, not without frailty, or it becomes a different kind of unsuccessful ageing – an unfortunate ageing defined by what is to come not what has already befallen. The search for a distinct aetiology may thus make little sense if frailty is simply the uncertain future we all face as we age. The longer one lives, the greater the odds must be that our luck will run out and frailty will inevitably follow as a consequence of successful ageing. Looked at this way, investigating the aetiology of frailty becomes an attempt to answer a question that has always been asked over the centuries – namely what is the best way of maximising one's good luck in the business of ageing? The same answer follows as that given by Galen that we should seek to minimise the degree of impairment and prevent as far as possible the onset of degenerative disease in later life by living carefully. The pathways to frailty may be described in contemporary medicine using different terms, but the framework seems pretty much unchanged, as frailty's paradigm proves nothing other than the flip side of 'successful ageing'.

Faced with such intrinsic dilemmas, one pragmatic approach has been to trial 'interventions' aimed at preventing or delaying the onset of frailty. Two broad approaches have been adopted, one aimed at preventing frailty from 'disabling' or 'damaging' those already considered frail, the other aimed at preventing frailty in the first place – what might be called in health promotion terminology, secondary and primary interventions. One recent review of the first area – secondary prevention – concluded that (1) there is no evidence that nutritional interventions for frail older persons...result in positive effects on disability-level (2) that single lower extremity strength-training has no significant effect on disability for physically frail older persons but (3) there is some indication that long-lasting high-intensive exercise programs for moderate physically frail older persons can have an effect on disability outcomes, although half of these studies failed to observe any significant effects (Daniels et al., 2008). Another review, focusing upon both the primary and secondary prevention of what the authors termed disablement, 'identified many areas of conflicting evidence, along with substantial areas of unknown effectiveness' although they did find some 'evidence to support the implementation of exercise interventions, particularly for the prevention of falls', although even here they were not sure how cost-effective they might be (Frost, Haw and Frank, 2012: 225).

Although there is growing acceptance of frailty as a geriatric fact, the continuing interest in defining, refining and redefining it overshadows these kinds of attempts to prevent delay or reverse the processes of 'frailing'. While preventive health measures are commonly adopted in trying to ensure and prolong 'active' or 'successful' ageing, these seem to exist outside the frailty domain, as if frailty must be something other than, something distinct from the mirror image of active, healthy ageing. If on the other hand, frailty is a socially constructed term realised by its use in distinguishing between people needing and people not needing social care (as distinct from constructions of health and illness, such as 'Alzheimer's' or 'Type 2 diabetic' or 'arthritic' etc.), then interventions only make sense when applied to the processes involved in allocating, managing or organising care. The question is how to stop older people from 'being frailed by the system'. One solution would then be to treat frailty as an oppressive, redundant construct of benefit only to those who categorise but never to those who are categorised. The focus of concern should then be on the prevention, remediation or amelioration of illnesses and/or impairment, so that ill and/or impaired elderly people are helped and actively treated for their illnesses and impairments as much as there is evidence of effective interventions to do so. Where there is not, help and care are still required – but care for the ill person, care for the person with impairments. The processes of becoming frailed are less easily identified than the pathways proposed in the course of becoming frail. They do not follow the impersonal systemic pathways of deteriorating muscle power, decreasing immuno-competence or declining cognitive reserve but rather reflect the complex negotiations that take place over risk and care.

Frailing: the 'othering' of old age and the consequences of being 'frailed'

The increased targeting of long-term care on the 'sickest', 'most vulnerable', 'most dependent' or 'most infirm' has been translated into a variety of assessment procedures designed to enumerate to quantify need. Given the vagaries of clinical practice, the ambiguities of terminology and the overriding need to control demand; the assessment process has become central to the negotiation of care, in effect distinguishing between the deserving and undeserving aged. However, just as with past attempts to judge the eligibility for indoor or outdoor relief of the aged poor, the process of assessment is itself part of the othering of a class, in this case of the abject aged and the truly frail. This othering is rendered unproblematic by the instrumental objectification of need, the totting up of what an elderly person can or cannot do, in the way of 'managing their daily round' (Daatland, 1985). No personal judgement is required – or implied. There is a standardised impersonal procedure to be followed – based upon information gathered about the to-be frailed person – that seems objective (unbiased) but is objectifying (impersonal): the thing to be met is need not want.

When what is gained is also a loss, the process of assessment operates ambiguously. On the one hand it seems to seek to help those in need of help but on the other in offering help, it leads in the end to constraint, which devalues, in the eyes of both helper and helped, the status of the successfully 'frailed'. The frailed individual is caught in a system of care that is doled out, rationed and increasingly driven by a rhetoric of choice within a social reality made up of constraint and dependency.

Conclusions

Frailty, we have argued, forms a central component of the fourth age's social imaginary. Despite attempts to define and distinguish it from agedness, disability and morbidity, its resonance lies less in its particular biomedical delineation than in its moral and metaphorical significance. As Grenier has pointed out, the etymology of the word implies both physical and moral weakness connected with powerlessness impairment 'and with an implication of blame' (2007: 430). When Shakespeare has Hamlet cry out: '*Frailty, thy name is woman*', he expresses the long-held belief in the character flaws in female nature; the gendered link is retained in contemporary accounts as illustrated in Figure 4.1. Why it might be asked does frailty still cling more easily to women? Should we assume biogenetic causality, or rather posit that there is something inherently gendered in current thinking about 'unsuccessful' ageing such that men succeed or die, while women linger on in their ever deepening fragility?

Not only is gender implicated in frailty's conceptual network: there is equally consistent evidence of links between frailty and socio-economic status. The poor and uneducated aged are more often designated frail and seem to become frailer faster (Etman et al., 2012; Sirven, 2012; Szanton et al., 2010). It is as if the socially disadvantaged are also the potentially frail, those least likely to age successfully, those most likely to be frailed. Whatever the basis for such links, the point is that they serve to confirm the centrality of failure and its connections with disadvantage along with a persisting suspicion that there is some inherent moral weakness that underpins the frailing of old age – a 'self othering' of old age. The notion that frailty is not just imposed as an objectifying discourse but somehow engendered by social and moral weakness leads us to consider in the next chapter the links between the infirmity of age and the condition of abjection.

Chapter 5

Abjection and the Fourth Age

Introduction

If frailty represents the externalisation (or reification) of the various degenerative processes deemed to be at work inside the ageing body, the theme of this chapter, abjection, can be located in the reactions of self and others toward those various physical and mental failings that are objectified as frailty. It is as much through abjection as through frailty and dependency that the fourth age is culturally imagined and socially realised. Although frailty represents weakness and vulnerability, the abjection of the fourth age treats agedness as a source of contamination, disgust and otherness, a 'dirty' old age threatening all who come close to it. If frailty is framed by an imperative of care, then abjection places constraints around the desire to help, rendering care both problematic and a site of conflict.

As we demonstrated in the last chapter, frailty is made a social reality or reified through the practices of assessment, evaluation and observation of the older person with impairments. Abjection is a term that is neither so easily conceptualised, nor so readily externalised that it can become either an acceptable way of describing people in later life or a topic for serious academic inquiry. It is the less acceptable side of the fourth age, one that renders its social imaginary, darker and more distant. Our aim in this chapter is to explore the term abjection and the various ways it has been interpreted since it was first introduced into cultural studies by Kristeva. Following this discussion of terminology, we consider those aspects of the fourth age that are most rooted in abjection before in the final section examining how abjection operates within the matrix of care undertaken in the shadow of the fourth age.

Abjection

The term abjection was introduced into the sociological literature by the French author and philosopher Bataille. Bataille is perhaps best known as a writer of controversial fiction, an early advocate of the literature of transgression who was equally fascinated by Marx and Nietzsche, de Sade and Freud. He was the author of numerous essays on art, economics, literature, philosophy and sociology. In a series of essays written in the 1930s but not published until after his death and only translated into English at the end of the twentieth century, Bataille (1999) wrote on the topic of 'abjection and miserable forms'. Although he thought it 'impossible to give a positive definition' of abjection, Bataille linked the idea to the direct consequences of having contact with abject things (11). These he defined as that which is excluded or excreted from the body and from mainstream society. Those whose life and work kept them tied to the gutter, unable to escape regular contact with and contamination by such abject things constituted what he called the 'abject class', those most oppressed by their poverty and lack of resources and who were the prime targets of the emerging Nazi regime.

Much later and in different circumstances, the French Feminist writer Kristeva took these ideas and developed them further in her book, *Powers of Horror*, which she sub-titled '*An Essay on Abjection*' (1982). This work was influential in transforming the idea of abjection from its pre-war origins. In particular, Kristeva re-oriented the concept of abjection away from Bataille's socio-structural emphasis upon an 'abject class' and instead aligned it more closely with psychoanalytic ideas of purity, dirt and contamination, the mother-child relationship and the development of women's gendered consciousness. Consequently, while Bataille's work has not been particularly influential, Kristeva's analytic writing has led to abjection becoming something of a key term in cultural studies, literary criticism and the sociology of gender and sexual relationships (Covino, 2000; Menninghaus, 2003). Menninghaus has somewhat wryly noted that 'the academic career of the abjection paradigm could easily fill a whole book' (2003: 393). While Kristeva's theory of abjection 'has had an extraordinary influence on feminist theory', most subsequent work has limited itself to either 'theoretical and philosophical exegesis' of her work or its application 'to specific areas of cultural production' such as film and fiction (Tyler, 2009: 82). In Tyler's view, Kristeva's thinking on abjection has had much less application to considerations of 'unbearable life on the margins of social invisibility' – remaining a psychic phenomenon rather than a material, social thing (94).

The relationship between abjection and disgust has been explored by Menninghaus who describes abjection as 'the newest mutation in the theory of disgust' (2003: 365). Disgust, whose intellectual history she traces up to Kristeva's utilisation of the term, is obviously closely aligned to the idea of abjection. There are, however, points of distinction that justify keeping it as a separate concept. First, disgust is almost unavoidably seen as an emotional reaction – 'a strong sensation' as Menninghaus' translator called it – giving it both an affective particularity and a more bounded quality. Although the power of objects to elicit disgust may be stable, the state they induce is not, unlike abjection whose power and influence persists. Furthermore, disgust tends to define the person experiencing the emotion, as set apart from that which has elicited disgust (though of course one can experience self-disgust); abjection applies both to a person's situation, through their state of being abject and to their association with abject things – in other words, it operates through social relationships. Third, disgust implies a state of disapproval, a state of being disgusted with something or someone. The powerful are more prone to be disgusted and disgusting, and shocking them with disgusting work can seem a radical, transgressive act. Abjection, on the other hand, is a state defining those without power, without civility. Unlike disgust, it implies a personal incapacity to free oneself from abject things and as a result it limits any possibility of the abject casting that which is abject back at those who have power. Thus while abjection may seem to be another mutation of disgust, its range of meaning is considerably wider and can be said to possess greater resonance than that of a merely strong sensation or emotion. The analysis of abjection is therefore neither primarily an analysis of what makes those appalled, appalled, nor can a study of it be undertaken through the readings of aesthetic philosophy (Menninghaus, 2003) or the anatomy of the psychopathology of emotions (Miller, 1997). Although these factors are useful points of reference, the analysis of abjection requires consideration of not only what is disgusting but also what material social processes render a person or persons abject, by what kinds of abject things and what principles of social organisation govern its associations and attributions.

In Kristeva's account of abjection, she defines the nature of the abject as those body products which are meant to be contained inside or otherwise kept from public view – what the anthropologist of purity Douglas refers to as 'matter out of place' (1988: 41). Abject corporeal matter may include menstrual blood, faeces and urine, vomit, mucus and saliva – but not necessarily blood, sweat and tears (Kristeva, 1982). While the former constitute dangerous, potentially contamin-able materials, blood, sweat and tears possess other qualities, signify-ing not waste but effort, not shame but pride. As we have noted, the concept of the abject cannot be separated from that of disgust – objects or matter that evoke disgust form a major category of abject things, but it is not enough to list as abject body products such as urine and faeces without considering their relationship to the embodied person who has excreted them.

Let us begin with urine and faeces, vomit and mucus. It is generally seen as good to evacuate one's bladder and bowels, to purge one's stomach and to clear one's lower and upper respiratory tract. Such actions seem to purge oneself of excess or waste. What renders urine and faeces abject is the failure to be rid of them, to be still attached to that which is meant to be excreted and then excluded. If the signs of dirt or wetness, vomit or mucus remain 'on the body', it is their remains that render the person abject. Not that abjection is simply a matter of neglect. While it may be shameful to find one has wet one's pants or soiled the bed, more abject yet is the shameless voiding of urine or faeces in public, wetness in the corner of the bedroom, faeces placed in the bedside drawer or encrusted in one's finger nails. What most crystallises abjection is the imputation about what it is that attaches the person or persons to these abject things – the matter of agency. In the next section, we shall explore in more detail the abject and its particular role in relation to agency and self-management, within the social imagining of the fourth age.

Abjection and agedness

In later life, it is not only Kristeva's concern with bodily fluids that constitutes matter out of place. Food spilled down the front of one's clothes or in one's lap, toenails thickened, stained and curled deep into the flesh, hair matted and greasy, skin covered in sores, hairs sprouting from the nose, the ears or the chin, growths on the face, swollen and sagging flesh round the ankles, the abject objects of old age extend beyond the products of the body, serving as signs of weakness, the failings not just of the body but of the will. Many of these abject things are not only 'aged' but like frailty they are also 'gendered'. When

Menninghaus discusses the aesthetic preoccupations of the Enlightenment, she notes how 'all of the defects addressed and rejected by the
discourse on disgust are repeatedly compressed into one single phan-
tasm: that of the ugly old woman' (2003: 84). Aged femininity, she says,
was the 'maximum disgusting evil', echoing the topos of the *vetula*, the
despised image of the aged naked female so often described by the
classical writers of Greece and Rome (Falkner and Luce, 1989).

The *vetula* embodied disgust in her corporeal entirety, or at least
did so when viewed through the eyes of male sexual desire. To understand the centrality of this image, it is necessary to move beyond these
obviously gendered aesthetic judgements and consider the conscious
and unconscious aspects of bodily imagination (Menninghaus, 2003:
101). Drawing upon ideas from Bataille, Freud and Kristeva, Menninghaus proposed that there were close links between disgust and
sexual desire, on the one hand, and the process of 'individuation'
whereby the child 'sheds' her ties with the all-embracing mother,
rejecting that which is 'not I' as abject or disgusting in favour of the
true 'I', the clean and new boundaries of the pure self. The *vetula*
becomes the emblematic 'mother' from whose diffuse enveloping corporeality, the child seeks to separate itself – and abjection the imagined collapse back into the primal mess of birth.

However one is attracted to, or distanced from such psychoanalytic
notions, the abjection of old age is in part a gendered imaginary. It
includes but goes beyond the close attachment to abject excreted
things and is present in the evident deformities that age has wrought
on the flesh. But without another's gaze, without another's imagined
presence, such things might matter little at all. Most women manage
their leakages of blood and urine with pads and pant-liners, plenty
pluck out their facial hairs, dye their hair or have prominent skin
growths removed – they strive in short to distance themselves from
the ur-mother, the *vetula* imago. How does this relate to men and their
aged abjections? Is the dirty old man rendered abject by his dirt or
by his desire – or by both?

Although most Greek sculptures in the classical age shaped the
faces of gods as old, they rarely did so for their bodies and most
Roman statuary that sought to represent old men confined themselves
to a bust of their head. Similarly while the desires of the aged man
were held to ridicule in Greek and Roman comedies, the assumptions
of senior power and authority were rarely traduced by reference to
an old man's dirtiness, ugliness or misshapenness. Was the patriarchal
system of the pre-modern era so powerful that it prohibited men and
women writing of, or depicting, male old age as in any way abject?

While old men's sexual impotence, youthful pretensions or insightless self-regard might be the subject of much comedy concerning them as persons, no one treated old male bodies as simply abject objects, or as pure abjection. Even in Shakespeare's gendered depiction of the penultimate stage of life – 'the slippered pantaloon' – he pays no attention to signifiers of dirt, smell or decay and his last stage is simply one of losses before death.

Are the soiled pants of an old man, his matted grey hair, dirty fingernails or his sagging flesh not equally abject signifiers of the fourth age? Does his male gender allow a distance of such signifiers from the ur-mother, the maximum evil of the *vetula?* It could be argued that there may be other reasons that make such signifiers less characteristic of old men compared to old women. There are after all, fewer very old men than there are very old women in contemporary ageing societies. Faecal and urinary incontinence are less common in men than in women, but this difference is more marked before the age of 65 than it is after that age. Age associated skin deformities such as actinic elastosis, benign growths such as actinic keratosis, seborrheic warts and skin tags, malignancies such as basal cell carcinomas and melanomas, and skin discolorations such as purpura and rosacea are equally common among men and women (El Safoury and Ibrahim, 2011; Jafferany et al., 2012). Though there is some evidence in the psychology of ageing literature that gender influences *perceptions* of facial agedness with old women perceived as older and more negatively than old men (Hummert, Garstka and Shaner, 1997), gender differences in the extent and severity of skin wrinkles and greying of the hair in later life seem at most, minimal (Boas and Michelson, 1932; Morton et al., 2007; Schnohr et al., 1995). On the other hand, the growth of male-patterned facial hair in women indicates marked age effects, with more than one-third of women aged above 75 showing significant hair growth on their upper lip and chin (Thomas and Ferriman, 1957; Lunde, 1984). While women's self-care regimes can easily and effectively remove these signs of bodily matter 'out of place', the abandonment or neglect of these practices only intensifies their signification as gendered abject things.

The relation between abjection and abject things is complex. The disgust elicited by abject things can be separated from their capacity to embody abjection. The relationship between abject things, abject persons and the ' imaginary' of abjection is mediated – by attributions of agency and desire, by the potential physical (and maybe social) separation that the embodied person can realise from abject things and by the aged and gendered identity of the person. The cultural imaginary of the *vetula* in particular serves to align abjection and the abject with femininity making dirty old women more central to the social imaginary of the fourth age than is the case with dirty old men. To explore the imaginary of abjection within the social materiality of later life, we now turn to the topic of incontinence, and its iconic place in the link between abject things and abject doings.

Incontinence and abjection

As we have seen, both Bataille (1999) and Kristeva (1982) focused upon abject things – matter out of place, bodily impurities, excreta – bodily products that are rejected as the 'not I'. Soiling and staining one's clothes, one's bed or the cushions of one's chair seem especially to symbolise the dirt, pollution and neglect associated with deep old age. When associated with a person, these become signifiers that the individual has gone beyond vulnerability to a position of either shameless neglect – by self or by others who serve as proxies for the self – or shameful behaviour. Although it is possible to find incontinence as markers of abject old age in pre-modern literature, such examples are remarkably rare. Before the modern era, aged naked flesh was enough to signify a disgusting old age. During the 'classical' modernity of the early and mid-twentieth century, the corporeality of the body ceased to be the main focus of old age as chronological age, poverty and disease dominated the imaginary (Gilleard and Higgs, 2013). Even when gerontology and geriatrics began to study the 'problem' of the aged chronic sick, attention was paid largely to counting and placing these people (Lowe and McKeown, 1949; McEwan and Laverty, 1949; Thompson, 1949; Warren, 1946). Their infirmity and vulnerability was addressed and enumerated, but not their abjection. In a provocative piece written in the *British Medical Journal*, Newman drew back the curtain when he described the processes of institutional denial in relation to urinary incontinence among elderly patients:

> Before the visiting physician does his round there is a period of intense activity in which the staff see that all is shipshape. If he turns the bedclothes down and finds a wet patch he pretends he has not noticed; the sister hastily covers it up again, and when he has gone she may have something to say to the junior nurse. How different if it had been blood; then they would have been all eyes and interest....One is respectable and the other is not. (1962: 1824)

Soon after this paper was published, studies began to appear quantifying the 'symptom' of incontinence. Though deprecating the term

'senile incontinence', geriatricians Isaacs and Walkey (1964) nevertheless sought to demonstrate the link between incontinence and other
aspects of 'senility' – such as low mental test scores, inability to dress,
feed and walk independently and so on. A decade later, Isaacs (1972)
now included incontinence as one of the four 'geriatric giants' – the
impairment of intellect (cerebral dysfunction), incontinence, immobility and instability (falls) – that constituted the central 'symptoms', the
four 'I's' to which geriatric medicine should apply itself. Ironically
these symptoms were both 'I's' and 'not I's', in the sense that they
represented the reified otherness of 'the elderly' – as problems to be
counted if not always countered – and the 'not I' otherness that
Kristeva made central to the abject (1982: 1–2).

The placement of these chronic infirm and sick patients was a continuing problem throughout the 1950s, 1960s and 1970s. The effective
institutional separation of poor old people from sick old people was
a site of continuing struggle, where the enumeration of impairments
played an increasing role in determining each old person's fate.
Incontinence became reified and its enumeration a mechanism of
assessment and placement. As a future professor of geriatric medicine
noted,

> Incontinence of urine and faeces provides one of the great problems in
> geriatric medicine. It is a problem to which physicians on the whole have
> given little thought. Yet urinary incontinence in particular keeps large
> numbers of elderly people in hospital who could otherwise leave, and
> involves a disproportionate amount of nursing time. It is important, there-
> fore, that physicians should have some knowledge of aging as it affects the
> bladder and the bowel and that they should develop a rational approach
> to the problems of incontinence. (Brocklehurst, 1967: 527)

The wet bed was the blocked bed and the incontinent were costly bed
blockers. Preventing and controlling these symptoms would clean up
dirty old age, rendering the bed blocker free to re-enter the community – or at least leave the hospital bed. In marked contradiction,
however, the abject leaked out into the community. By the 1970s,
epidemiological surveys of urinary and faecal incontinence 'in the
community' were being undertaken. They started on a rather small
scale (e.g., Yarnell and St. Leger, 1979) but soon expanded their
ambition, and incontinence within 'whole communities' became the
object of study (e.g., Diokno et al., 1986; Resnick, Yalla and Laurino,
1989; Thomas et al., 1980; Vetter, Jones and Victor, 1981). By the start
of the twenty-first century, the mapping of incontinence was truly
globalised, as worldwide indicators of the extent and costliness of

incontinence were reported (Minassian, Drutz and Al-Badr, 2003; Irwin et al., 2011). Although most of these studies continued to focus upon women, the age range studied expanded and more reports appeared detailing the epidemiology of incontinence for men and women across adulthood. In one review collating data from some 35 studies, worldwide, the prevalence of any episodes of incontinence of urine showed a consistent increase with age and at least 10 per cent of women reported some episodes whatever their age, however, few felt it had a major effect on their quality of life and most did not seek help for it (Minassian, Drutz and Al-Badr, 2003).

Such epidemiological reports indicate that most women do not seek help, whatever their age (Hagglund et al., 2003). Episodes of urinary incontinence are usually contained – whether by preventative regimes of going to the toilet more often and more regularly, maintaining close contact with public toilets or by wearing pant-liners or pads (Siddiqui et al., 2013). Even so, there remains for many women a degree of distaste for their incontinence, either because of the disgust engendered or the guilt of doing something 'naughty'. At the same time, some women report a sense of it being a 'normal consequence' of sex (pregnancy, childbirth) or age. For men, a similar pattern is evident, with most men prioritising regular preventative toileting – day and night, reducing or avoiding fluid intake at certain times and places, maintaining close contact with public toilets and wearing protective pads or devices to absorb any leaking (McKenzie, St John Wallis and Griffiths, 2013). Both men and women seem to adopt the strategy of 'making managing leaking a normal part of daily life' (47). This is the normal competency of everyday life; the awareness of incontinence's potential abjection and its prevention by both narrative and behavioural agency (e.g., treating it as a normal consequence of ageing and using protective pads).

What makes the abjection of incontinence a social reality? Studies of people reporting incontinence suggest that within unselected samples of men and women 'in the community' only a small percentage are seriously affected by their incontinence – perhaps as many as 10 per cent or as few as 5 per cent (Fulz and Herzog, 2001). Mitteness and Barker (1995) have noted how incontinence is viewed very differently by health care workers and the general public, with the former framing it as a major health problem that is nevertheless treatable and reversible, while the latter deem it an inevitable irreversible part of growing old. What makes the difference, these authors suggest, is the extent to which the incontinence is linked to incompetence – with a continuum of competence associated with maintaining the total invisibility of incontinence versus failing ever to do so. Failure is associated with lack of resources – financial, physical and psychological – and the 'risk' of institutionalisation. Studies in non-Western countries reinforce these findings. Yuan, Williams and Liu (2011), for example, reported that while more community nurses than elderly people felt urinary incontinence could be effectively treated managed and/or prevented, more elderly people perceived it as shameful, frustrating and their own fault. The use of continence aids increases with the severity of incontinence and arguably serves as a proxy of potential abjection. Figure 5.1 below indicates the strength of this association between age and gender drawing upon data on the use of incontinence aids in Sweden, extrapolated from a whole county enumeration.

Incontinence becomes an increasing presence in people's lives as they age; this is the case for both urinary and faecal incontinence, which arguably is even more of a proxy sign of abjection in that it is relatively uncommon at all ages (Al-Ameel, Andrew and MacKnight, 2010; Goode et al., 2010; Pretlove et al., 2006). While people are observed to become faecally incontinent with greater age, the pattern of 'age association' is less marked than that observed with urinary incontinence. Drawing upon four national community surveys from

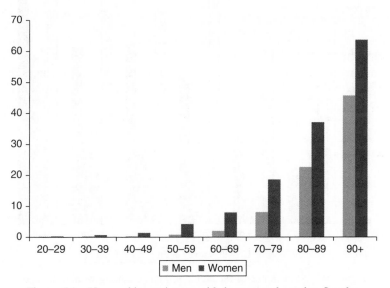

Figure 5.1   Users of incontinence aids by age and gender, Sweden

Source: Samuelsson, Månsson and Milsom, 2001, table 1, p.896. Reprinted with permission from John Wiley & Sons.

England, Finland, Norway and the US, Figure 5.2 illustrates age trends in faecal incontinence.

Although faecal incontinence is less powerfully associated with agedness, it is nevertheless a major risk factor leading older people to move (or be moved) into a nursing home along with other factors such as cognitive impairment and reduced mobility (Al-Ameel, Andrew and MacKnight, 2010; Chassagne et al., 1999). The management of faecal incontinence is carried out in nursing homes without the privacy observed when people are living in their own homes, usually because the residents are considered less aware of their bowel movements and less able to clean themselves afterwards compared with 'normal' persons (Akpan, Gosney and Barrett, 2006). Residents thus face the double abjection of soiling themselves without being able to hide such leakages from the gaze of others.

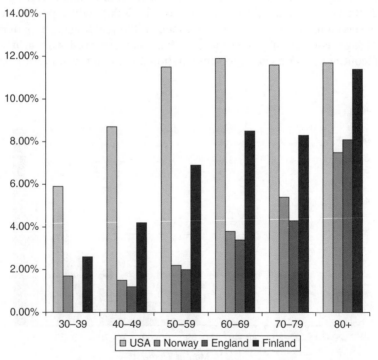

Figure 5.2   Prevalence of faecal incontinence among women by age:
international comparisons

Source: Authors' own calculations drawn from Aitola et al., 2010 (Finland); Bharucha et al., 2005 (US); Perry et al., 2002 (England); and Rømmen et al., 2012 (Norway).

Faecal and urinary incontinence are not simply sources of abjection because of their association with the negligence (and by implication incompetence) of the embodied person; a further assumption enters into the social reality of the abject – the problematic assumptions concerning agency. Those who care and therefore serve as proxies to the person who cannot keep his or her body clean and dry may not always feel compassion or even pity toward the abjection of those they care for. Disgust or anger may be expressed after witnessing the action of someone wetting or soiling 'him' or 'her' self again and again. Instead of the shameful abjection associated with an inability to remove oneself from the 'not I' excreted material, attributions of shamelessness and of seeming deliberateness may be made. 'Why have you done that?' This capacity to 'upset' or 'anger' those with power over the resident or home care client is not agonistic, rarely defiant, and seldom does it constitute the kind of 'anti-ageist' radical transgression that is associated with wearing purple, letting your hair grow grey or leaving hair on your lips which is sometimes advocated by anti-ageism campaigners. Abject doings constitute a problematic kind of agency, not so much a shameless as a mindless agency that is left in the main to the interpretations of others.

Agency, abjection and 'othering'

If incontinence draws attention to the embodiment of abjection in old age through unavoidable contact with abject things – the shame of failing to maintain a clean and civilised appearance, the abjection of owning a dirty body – it can also be seen, alongside confusion, falls and agitation as representing a less material source of abjection. It is abject not only, or perhaps not even because of its material dirtiness, but because of the implication of failed agency present in soiling or wetting. Being seen to fall over, to be evidently lost or refusing to be helped can also be understood as forms of abjection, an abjection that is based not on disgust but on the implicit failure of agency, self-management and necessary self-care. Such lapses go beyond simple acts of omission that need managing by others. These and similar actions can elicit other interpretations if they are understood not in terms of incompetence and self-neglect, but as signifiers of a malign transgression, a harm or hurt directed toward those who care.

The clinical literature on dementia has become preoccupied of late with phenomena that go under various terms – ranging from the pseudo-clinical 'neuropsychiatric' or 'non-cognitive' symptoms, the pseudo-descriptive 'behavioural and psychological symptoms', to the more judgmental 'aberrant', 'difficult', 'recalcitrant' or 'troublesome behaviours' through to the more euphemistic term – 'challenging behaviours'. What this plethora of terms refers to is a range of actions that distress, disgust or annoy the caring other. This includes agitation and aggression (Cohen-Mansfield, Marx and Rosenthal, 1989), inappropriate sexual behaviour (Black, Muralee and Tampi, 2005), screaming, shrieking and muttering (Nagaratnam, Patel and Whelan, 2003), stripping or disrobing (Victoroff, Mack and Nielson, 1997), wandering and faecal smearing (Ata et al., 2010). Such behaviours seem more common in institutional settings – though the role of cause and effect is not easy to untangle – and become more frequent as the person with dementia becomes progressively more mentally frail (Sloane et al., 2004; Selbaek et al., 2007). In the past, medication and physical restraints were widely used to control these behaviours, but restraint in their use has been called for either through the development of 'good practice' or through legislation (Aiken et al., 2010; Castle, 1998; Ronald, Fought and Ray, 1994). Still there exists large variation between nursing homes and across nursing homes between countries in the frequency of behavioural disturbances, the extent of physical restraint and the use of psychotropic medication, and it seems likely that factors other than agedness or the neurobiological processes of dementia are at work (Feng et al., 2009; Ljunggren, Phillips and Sgadari, 1997; Pekkarinen et al., 2006; Phillips et al., 1996; Zuidema et al., 2010). But whatever may account for this variation in care and the burdens of care, one finding is consistent, the rise in the age and degree of mental and physical frailty of residents in institutions for the care of older people (Boyd et al., 2011; Broad et al., 2011; Lövheim et al., 2008).

This transformation began in the 1980s (Berringer et al., 2003; Bishop, 1999; Wimo et al., 1999). Since the widespread adoption of policies supporting 'ageing in place' it has accelerated, resulting in a steady 'compression of morbidity' within the institutions of old age care (Boyd et al., 2012; Johnson, Rolph and Smith, 2010). Accompanying the compression of morbidity is the parallel densification in the abjection of the fourth age, as ever more dirty bodies and ever more dirty deeds contribute an ever heavier load of 'dirty work' for those paid others who provide the care (Wimo et al., 1999). This risks rendering ever more abject the workforce whose experience of old age is increasingly shaped by the demands of keeping mentally and physically frail aged bodies and the places they live in, clean, civilised and restrained, struggling in an unending battle against the threat of unmanageable abjection. In the final section, we turn to the carers whose dirty work serves to manage the boundary between the abject aspects of deep old age and the clean and civilised world outside.

Abjection's dirty work

'The unclean side of nursing is rarely (if ever) accounted for in academic literature: it is silenced' (Holmes, Perron and O'Byrne, 2006: 305). In writing about nurses' dirty work, these authors sought to acknowledge and reflect upon the feelings evoked in those whose job exposes them to the necessary contact with the abject. Of course it is not only nurses whose work involves close contact with the abject, and not only health care workers based in institutions. Long-term home based care for chronically ill, frail and often aged persons is expanding and an ever wider variety of people are employed as a 'recommodified' workforce in this sector of the economy (Doyle and Timonen, 2007: 118–119). Drawing on the work of Esping-Anderson, these writers use the term 'recommodification' to describe the decline in workers' rights and security of employment that they observed characterised the employment situation of the home care workforce as it is increasingly privatised and commodified. While recourse to professional practices can help manage some of the consequences of contact with the abject – through inserting catheters, administering medications or organising toileting regimes – those without such professional resources are exposed more directly to the consequences of recommodification, as they have scant recourse to the intermediary structures of professionalisation. If nurses do dirty work, they can distance themselves not just at the end of a shift but also during their work time through a variety of 'professional practices' including of course maintaining a professional 'ethic' of care.

As levels of institutional provision for people aged above 65 have fallen (in relative terms at least), home care services have expanded (Bishop, 1999; Beringer et al., 2003; Boyd et al., 2012; Johnson, Rolph and Smith, 2010). In the process, a new work force has emerged – people in low pay work visiting older people in their homes to help keep them clean and tidy. This domestic work is undertaken, not as a result of the elite's reluctance to do their own dirty work, as in the past, but as a result of a pared down welfare state seeking to contain costs by sub-contracting labour to do society's dirty work without all the costs of upkeep and maintenance that are associated with public sector institutional care. As Aronson and Neysmith pointed out some time ago, 'the reductions in labor costs achieved by this work trans-fer...contribute to governments' attempts to cut public spending' (1996: 59). Across North America, Western Europe and Australasia, home care for frail old people has grown in size – though not in reputation. This whole sector has become a site for low-pay and often migrant labour where current cost pressures reduce any possibility of improving work conditions (Bonifacio, 2008; Fine and Mitchell, 2007; Hussein, Manthorpe and Stevens, 2011; Montgomery et al., 2005; van der Geist, Mul and Vermeulen, 2004; Weicht, 2011). A recent OECD (Organisation for Economic Co-operation and Development) report on the long-term care sector usefully summarises its main features and these are represented in Table 5.1.

Unlike the professional nursing and social work literature (which however circumspectly has begun to address professionals' dirty work – cf. Rudge and Holmes, 2010), care workers providing home care to old and frail people lack an academic or professional institu-tional base from which it might be possible to reflect upon, advocate for – and help re-frame their work and working conditions. Although a large volume of literature has grown up around informal or family care for frail older people, noting its many difficulties, stresses and points of breakdown, as well as its perceived value and rewards (cf. Dunkin and Anderson-Hanley, 1998; Han and Haley, 1999; Lim and

Table 5.1   Main features of the long-term home care workforce across the OECD

1	Ratio of clients to full time equivalent workers ranges from as low as 2 (Australia) to as high as 39 (Czech Republic)
2	Most workers are women, working part-time
3	Most have low qualifications, with the majority having no specific qualifications for the job
4	Benefits and wages are low; some home care workers are exempt from minimum wage and overtime protection laws (e.g., in US)
5	Home care workers often lack compensation for travel costs and team meetings and receive less support and supervision
6	There is high staff turnover; in US, more than two-thirds of home health aides leave in their first two years
7	Foreign-born workers play a growing role in the sector; they tend to work with shorter contracts, more irregular hours and for lower pay while serving the 'least favourable' care recipients

Source: Colombo et al., 2011. Reprinted with permission from OECD Publishing.

Zebrack, 2004; Torti et al., 2004; Walker, Pratt and Eddy, 1995), no such body of literature exists for paid home care workers.

In all of this it is important to note that significant differences exist between the formal and informal sectors of care. Spouses and children who care for their partner or parent, in the process often confront abject scenes. Their moral identity as 'family' however often serves to render invisible the abjection they face. Their practices in turn are less likely to 'other' their relative, even when they declare that s/he seems no longer to be the mother/father/husband/ wife s/he once was (Blieszner and Shifflet, 1990; Boylstein, 2012). While not immune from fears of 'contamination' of their own position within the field of the 'third age' by their partner's (or parent's) fourth age, or beliefs that the quality of the relationship had been profoundly transformed, theirs remains a historical relationship founded before the onset of impairment. As such, relatives can frame their care not as poorly rewarded dirty work but as an emotional and moral duty – even a labour of love. No such attributions are available to low paid care workers. Their poorly paid dirty work goes unrewarded by all but the cared for 'other' and/or his or her 'representative'. As stories emerge in the media about 'carer abuse' by home care workers, their position has begun to be the subject of moral anxiety – compounding the abjection of their clients with the potential disreputability of their jobs, as they risk being viewed as practitioners not of care but of abuse and exploitation.

Conclusions

Abjection defines the social imaginary of the fourth age just as much as frailty but unlike frailty it is not a 'topic' in gerontology or geriatric medicine. Abjection is neither a syndrome nor an index. It has little professional purchase and exists primarily within the context of social relationships, experienced and observed by the carer, and sometimes by the cared for, too. It flourishes in the disdain of the fit for the feeble, in the distance between those ageing successfully and those who are frailing; and in the division of labour that separates and keeps clean those who manage from those who give care and do not. That which is abject is not just that which disgusts, not just the expelled bodily fluids that people are taught to dispose of, objects to flush out of sight. It is attached to, and comes to reside in the person who cannot keep themselves clean, who cannot manage themselves and the mess they make of their lives. Abjection is pitiable at best, despicable at worst, a dirty kind of madness that most people prefer to steer clear of. But not everyone can, and not everyone chooses not to. Some choose to work with abjection – to tend those who seem unable or unaware of the need to keep himself or herself clean.

If the judgement of frailty implies the need – the moral imperative – to help and to care for the person judged frail, that judgement also contains whether or not we acknowledge it, the process of frailing the person so judged. Abjection itself is not a judgement; it is not the outcome of an assessment of need or the findings of a screening examination. It exists within, and cannot exist outside, a relationship. It is loaded with both meaning and feeling, the one incomprehensible without the other. Abject relations, first enunciated in Bataille's post-humously published essay, are not simply confined to, but rather still define the social relationships between the abject and the non-abject. In doing so, they also provide a distinct colour to caring, caring by doing things the carer would rather not have to or wish to do, care that is done not so much with love and reciprocity but through a sense of obligation.

The obligatory nature of the abject relationship is rendered most uncomfortable when it is experienced as the necessity of labour, an inescapable chore that can be avoided only by those whose caring labour is paid for by cash. Paid workers, however low paid, unqualified, unsupported and unsupervised can and do leave their jobs. Some stay, but stay without any moral obligation, and whose dislike for their job is expressed in their ambivalent relationship to those who appear to have made this their job, the care recipients. Whether or not they are the employers doesn't matter – they must be made to pay for this abjection – and they sometimes do, through the treatment of their person, whether this is done by their more utter frailing, by their being both frailed and fooled, or by the systematic annihilation of their identity and personhood.

Abjection and abuse are partners in the exchange of care, not only within the shadow of the fourth age, but especially there. Many carers of course do care, care for those frail people who seem most abject, with both a sense of moral obligation as well as a desire to protect them from their proximity to abjection. But even when the relationship is suffused with such obligatory moral care, the darkness of the abject is rarely absent, its dark imaginings ever present in the social mind. Because of such considerations we are led, in the next chapter, to address more fully the complex business of care and caring in later life.

Chapter 6

Care and the Moral Identity of the Fourth Age

Introduction

To speak of the fourth age as a social imaginary encompassing what is most feared, most distant and most impenetrable about old age might imply a lack of concern or respect for the circumstances of some of the most vulnerable citizens in modern societies. As we intimated in the last chapter, abjection and infirmity imply the need for care as well as an intrinsic difficulty with care. The frailty and perceived vulnerability of the fourth age furnish it with a moral identity that behoves society and its agents to assist those who seem most lost within its boundaries. But the moral identity that behoves care also preserves the fourth age's social imaginary just as it simultaneously strives to protect care recipients against its frailing consequences. In short, the moral imperative to care, and the narratives and practices of care form a third dimension from which the fourth age's social imaginary is constructed. These narratives and practices of care in turn embody and reflect the ambivalence that exists between the needs and the vulnerability associated with frailty and the distaste and the distancing that is associated with abjection. Our aim in this chapter is to consider, in some detail, what claims and what responses to those claims arise from this moral imperative to care for people whose attributed frailty and abjection places them within the reaches of the fourth age. In so doing, we hope to illuminate just how the responses of those who manage and/or provide care help fashion the very framework by which the fourth age acquires its particular imaginary.

As we have shown in previous chapters, many factors other than care contribute to shaping the social imaginary of the fourth age. These range from the historical representations of old age whose negative presence still permeates today's 'new' ageing to the inverted images of later life constructed by third age culture. Positing the fourth age as a social imaginary whose boundaries are formed by an objectifying frailty and a subjectively bounded abjection does not mean that it is a social space mapped solely by these corporeal coordinates. Through its abjection and frailty it embodies a moral identity, and through care it possesses a moral relationship with society as a whole. The various narratives and practices of care serve to 'realise' its imaginary form within morally calibrated social relationships. Despite the inconsistency and even incoherence in their articulation and enactment, the social imaginary of the fourth age lies as much within the practices and narratives of 'care' as it does in the communities of agedness and infirmity ascribed to the corporeal body. These practices, their narratives and their affective significance determine both a social and a moral identity framed by those who care, as much as by the bodies and behaviour of those who are cared for.

The boundary of care

A socially negotiated boundary demarcates the fourth age from the rest of society, where the usual attributions of agency, responsibility and social citizenship seem to no longer apply. Although this demarcation is determined by attributions of frailty and abjection, it is not simply a matter of society declaring that a certain degree of mental or physical infirmity must serve as a marker for those unable to make or maintain a distinct place for themselves within society in the way, for example, that age 70 or 65 has been designated as a marker for people to become pensioners. The boundaries of the fourth age are mapped out through the agency of others, others who contain and look after those deemed by themselves or more often by others incapable of managing themselves. In this sense 'institutionalisation' of those deemed unable to care for themselves has come to symbolise the social space within which the fourth age is most intensely imagined. It is a space delineated above all by agedness as Figure 6.1 illustrates. It shows the outcome of a national sample over a quarter of a million older people from Finland, by age group and gender, expressed as the proportions ending up institutionalised and dying during the course of a six-year follow up.

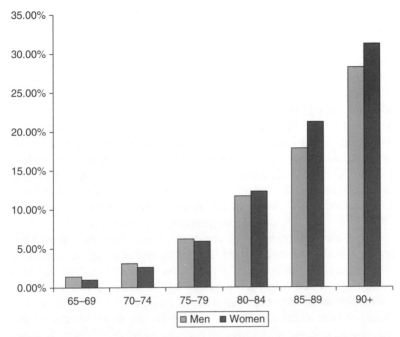

Figure 6.1   Percentage of Finnish men and women aged above 65 dying in an institution during a six-year follow up

Source: Authors' own figure based on tables 1 and 2, Martikainen, P. et al. (2009) *The Gerontologist,* 49 (1), 34–45.

The social outcome of institutionalisation represents a clear status transition – of going into care. It represents more than the social framing of 'power' relations, traditionally associated with sociological accounts from Goffman onwards with the internment of the poor and unruly. It also frames a moral identity for the individual older person that implies the necessity for action and an imperative to care – by others. This moral identity is not unique; it is one that has long been extended by society and its institutions to many of those whose 'corporeal citizenship' cannot or can no longer be supported by the agency of the person(s) concerned, irrespective of their age, ethnicity, gender or socio-economic status. It pre-dates modernity as institutions set up for the care of frail old people can be found in many urbanised, premodern societies from the period of late antiquity onwards. Although the family was (and remains) the first port of call in looking after infirm frail older people, institutions have long provided a place of last resort, established through religious orders and other charitable bodies most of which were eventually incorporated into the institutional machinery of the modern state. There has long been an expectation that families should care for their elderly frail relatives, but in the absence of family or in the absence of a family capable and willing to care, collective, civic institutions have always been expected to stand in. This longstanding imperative to care seems to apply to most urban societies, though the extent to which the institutions operate for the benefit of those admitted, compared with those setting up or employed within the institution has never been clear. By the nineteenth century, the institutions set up to care for frail elderly people were widely recognised to be inadequate to meet their needs – whether as people or as patients and the idea that 'something [more] must be done' was widely aired in the media of the time, as part of what Himmelfarb (2006 has called 'the moral imagination' of Victorian society.

But if the vulnerability of the frail elderly has long demanded action, it is also the case that, while eliciting our pity, they also provoke our distaste. In the previous chapter, we explored the disdain and disgust associated with the imaginary of the fourth age; here we are concerned more with the elicitation of pity, pity for those under the shadow of the fourth age. But in considering the moral identity of the fourth age, and the imperative to care, we need also to bear in mind the distaste and disdain for those whom we pity, as affects and attitudes into which we are also socialised, along with the expectations of care.

Care and moral identity

Within the discipline of psychology, moral identity has usually been interpreted as the integration of a sense of morality within the individual and his or her developing sense of self (Blasi, 1983: 201). The outcome of this proposed integration is the emergence of 'an explicit theory of one self as a moral agent' (Moshman, 2005: 121). In a sense, this reflects an amalgam of two developmental theories – Kohlberg's theory of moral development (1969 Kohlberg and Hersh, 1977) and Erikson's theory of the identity stage in psychosocial development (1963, 1968). Sometime in late adolescence or early adulthood, the recognition and acceptance of universal moral principles are thought to form a significant part of an individual's identity. While children will express ideas of right and wrong, good and bad, developmental psychology assumes that the internalisation of moral principles – rather than the simple knowledge of right and wrong – takes place in and after adolescence and settles down in adulthood to form a stable point of reference that enables adults to 'care for' others who are incapable of caring for themselves (expressed in Erikson's stages of intimacy and generativity).

In contrast to this life span developmental framework by which psychology understands the concept of 'moral identity', sociological uses of the term moral identity have usually considered it as a component of moral transactions, whereby actors impute similar or different qualities or competencies to themselves and to others (Katz, 1975). In this more interactional view, moral identities are not fixed qualities – not reflections of an acquired characteristic in one's self or in others – but assumptions made by ourselves and others about the determinants of a set of interactions or the narrative used to understand them. Finch (1989) has employed this interactional use of the term 'moral identity' when she described the nature of caregiving within families in terms of its moral character – a caring without reckoning. In taking this position, Finch was drawing on the earlier work of the anthropologist, Fortes, who argued that kinship relationships are uniquely binding, creating 'inescapable' moral claims and obligations (Finch, 1989: 231). At the same time, as Finch also acknowledges, in societies where kinship is more diffuse and where the distinction between kin and non-kin less totalising, the sense of such a distinction between caring with and without such a reckoning seems difficult to hold on to. Instead she suggests that the extent to which caring within families is characterised by instrumental versus obligatory relationships will vary based upon the social and historical nature of the relationship. Hence the moral identity of caring becomes itself a variable quantity co-determined on the one hand by society as a generalised 'other' and on the other, by the relationships of a particular family.

Adopting a somewhat similar relational perspective, but in the rather different context of a US community Muslim school and a local community action group, Suad-Nasir and Kirshner (2003) have outlined how moral identities are negotiated within these settings through a mixture of what they call 'social positioning', 'authoring' and 'framing'. Issues of relative and differential worth jostle with shared or contested assumptions about the affection, care and concern expressed by one individual toward another. Arguably the distinctiveness of family and non-family caregiving relationships is relative and the extent to which the social positioning and framing of moral identities varies between these different types of relationship may be one of degree rather than of a specific qualitative distinctiveness.

Moral identities, however framed, elicit accompanying moral senti-
ments. Caring – or not caring – about others implies not just an
evaluative framework – for whom should I care and why – but an
'affective' response mediated by that moral identity. This requires us
to examine what have been called the altruistic emotions, those feelings 'directed at the needs of others'. These typically include feelings
of pity, alongside those of sympathy and compassion (Carr, 1999: 411).
While sympathy might be considered as a more passive emotion,
requiring little in the way of response or action beyond the expression
of the emotion, feelings of pity and compassion imply much more.
Carr's writings drew attention to the similarities and differences
between these emotions. He writes that 'both pity and compassion…involve an appreciation of the suffering under which another
labours…[secondly] they involve a sympathetic reaction of distress
on the part of the agent – the one who feels pity or compassion; and
thirdly they involve the agent's being moved if possible to help to
alleviate that suffering' (1999: 411). What distinguishes them from
each other is according to Carr, that 'compassion rests upon an appreciation of the suffering as conceived by the one who suffers, whereas
pity involves a grasp of the misfortune of which the sufferer is
unaware' (428). In effect, he argues that compassion implies a con-
jointness of feeling, feeling 'with' the other, while pity exists without
that feeling with. Still, pity remains for Carr, primarily an altruistic
emotion and its elicitation a social virtue because it still involves
'feeling for' the other even if that does not extend to or require any
identification or feeling with the other. But, as with compassion, it
does imply a caring 'without reckoning'.

A further distinction is made between these two emotions by Callan.
He argues that compassion involves sorrow for another's plight, but
without thereby divesting the other of their autonomy, while pity is
evoked when there is an accompanying belief on the part of the agent
that the suffering other is incapable of alleviating their misfortune
(1988: 2). Callan states that 'in showing compassion for another I tacitly
affirm the common status we share as autonomous beings vulnerable
to misfortune; in showing pity I disavow that common status' (3). In
the case of caring with pity, obligation is not denied but what is
perhaps lacking is the reciprocity implicit in compassion. Hence, pity
is the more questionable feeling, its virtue more easily compromised
and its moral identity lacking a 'feeling with' core of human reciprocity. It implies, maybe introduces, an element of difference between the
self as pitying agent and the other as object of pity, a difference that
is easily framed as one of power, with the knowing and capable pitying

the unknowing and incapable, the person who pities is always superior to the pitied (Cartwright, 1988: 559).

Moral identity and care

A need for care is part of the 'moral imagination' of society, resulting in those deemed in need of care becoming part of the collective imaginary of the fourth age, just as caring and being cared for reflects and recreates the individual moral identities of both. Care is also a set of narratives and practices whose social templates are formed within the processes of social reproduction. Before and after the emergence of 'modernity', child care was practised by family members – typically the mother – and by non-family, either through 'domestic service' or as paid employment. This division – between nannies and mothers, between wives and wet nurses – is typically distinguished as informal and formal care. A similar division exists by extension to care for adults. Informal care for incapable adults is usually based upon a similar motif or template based upon the bonds of kinship and child-care (though the bonds of neighbourliness or friendship may also apply). Formal care is based upon different expectations – typically some contractual arrangement negotiated either by the household (private formal care) or by the state (public formal care). Whether individuals realise their 'moral identities' through their actions and interactions with others or through others' assumptions about their actions and interactions, care and the associated concern and consideration of others constitute the principal field in which attributions of moral identity are most often brought to bear.

The nature of those moral identities, the extent to which they confer an obligation to care 'without reckoning' and the affective responses that may or may not accompany those obligations are clearly different in the 'informal' and 'formal' sectors. Where prior affective bonds exist and where ties of friendship and/or kinship also feature, alongside some actual or perceived imbalance in power knowledge and agency, then a moral identity will be assigned to those who care as well as those who are cared for through the mutual negotiation that goes on in other family (or friendship) relations. In the case of children growing up with some form of mental or physical impairment or chronic ill health, various moral identities will develop within the family network, that may become more settled over time and more stable, but which may in due course be disrupted by unanticipated ruptures in the mutual balance of competencies and incapacities between children 'growing up' and parents 'growing older'. Similarly, in the case of a couple growing older together, settled and stable moral identities may be challenged by different experiences of health and illness, sturdiness and infirmity between the couple, leading to a degree of social re-positioning and a re-framing of their shared ties and moral identities. Such re-ordering of the relationship may shift as the health and fitness of each person changes without any fundamental break in mutual feeling for and with each other. Within this framework of stabilised moral identities, mutual care and compassion might be expected to overcome mutual irritation and frustration. The cared for partner feels with and for the carer – the responsibilities they shoulder, the constraints they labour under and the opportunities they forgo – just as the carer feels for the cared for, what they have done for them in the past, the sacrifices they have made, the constancy of the affection they have shown and the place they continue to occupy in their heart and their life.

Decades of research into caregiving relationships in later life attest to the importance of past commitments and present reciprocities in keeping going, keeping caring and maintaining compassion (Ablitt, Jones and Muers, 2009; Chen et al., 2013; Quinn, Clare and Woods, 2009). One of the most powerful determinants of continuing residence outside of an institution in later life is the nature of the household, which can be every bit as important as the nature and extent of the person's infirmities. Being widowed, divorced or unmarried, living on one's own, having few or no children and not owning one's own home all add to the risk of 'institutionalisation' in later life, irrespective of the older person's degree of rated physical or mental infirmity (Allen et al., 2012; Gaugler et al., 2009; Luppa et al., 2010b; Martikainen et al., 2009). Clearly having no-one to care for or about you enhances the risk of 'frailing'. But even within the framework of an informal care relationship (or network) once the ties of affection, the feeling with, as well as the feeling for, are severed, the moral identities of carer and cared for are hollowed out, and the previous capacity for mutual compassion dissipates.

Hence even in the context of an already existing caregiving relationship, the moral identity of the 'you' in that relationship can be replaced by that of a 'he' or a 'she' whom I care for, as feelings of reciprocity decline leaving little but the continuing feeling of obligation. When reciprocity declines, as it often does, obligation typically remains unchanged. The disappearance of the relational identity – the feeling of being 'as one' that makes helping one's partner akin to helping 'oneself' (Cialdini et al., 1997) – creates the space for 'othering' the person cared for, treating one's mentally frail partner or parent as a child, for example, or as no longer the husband/father/mother/wife whose former identity once shaped but which now distorts that of the non-frail partner (Quinn, Clare and Woods, 2009). In place of the unifying of identities that was conferred by affective reciprocity a different, less personal but no less moral identity emerges; the collective identity of dependency and otherness, of which the 'generic' child is perhaps the most acceptable form. This transformation creates a new moral and social domain for those for whom one is obliged to care, a person for whom one can feel pity but who has become irretrievably 'other' and who consequently no longer occupies the once distinct shared place in the life and heart of a particular, caring, compassionate other.

Unsurprisingly, such 'transitions to caregiving' have been found to lead to increased stress, depression and unhappiness of the caregiving family member (Marks, Lambert and Choi, 2002; Seltzer and Li, 2000). The effects on the cared for other, again not unsurprisingly have not been nearly so intensively studied. What does seem to be the case is that the extent of such effects seems to be mediated by the balance that carers feel between obligations and reciprocity. Feelings of reciprocity, unlike the feeling of obligation, reduce the burdensomeness of care and help maintain the caregiving relationship (del-Pino-Casado, Frias-Osuna and Palomino-Moral, 2011). Lack of reciprocity makes the cared for person seem more of another burden for the carer and seems also to affect the care recipient as well (Matire et al., 2002; McPherson et al., 2010). The mutual acceptance of dependency and need can sustain the well-being of the caregiving relationship (Feeney, 2007) but if obligation remains while reciprocity declines, mutual compassion is likely replaced by a different yet still altruistic affect, that of a pity. Pity – and being pitied – confers new moral identities. While factors other than age or frailty contribute to this transformation, there seems little doubt that mental frailty and accompanying problematic behaviours contribute heavily to such transitions, as love is changed, cruelly, to kindliness (Annerstedt et al., 2000; Nihtilä et al., 2008; Schneider et al., 1999; Torti et al., 2004).

One might expect reciprocity or compassion to play less of a part in the relationship between paid carers and the person they care, since these relationships are based primarily on contractual rather than affective obligations. In cases of formal care, there is rarely another shared identity and hence no loss to grieve over or still desire. The 'cared for's' identity is uncomplicatedly that of an 'other', from the moment the caregiving relationship begins. The care giver is expected to be the social agent 'in control' of that relationship and the moral identities it sustains. This raises concerns within the professional press, though not necessarily in the public media, since the ethic of care espoused by the 'caring professions' generally seeks to privilege compassion over pity and often denies or minimises the professional power that shapes the relationship (Gaut and Leineger, 1991; Leget and Olthuis, 2007; Von Dietze and Orb, 2000). Such evidence as exists suggests that introducing impaired older people to formal care generally weakens rather than sustains the informal bonds of care and consequently is associated with its subsequent breakdown (Allen et al., 2012; Gaugler et al., 2009). This is by not inevitably the case, but it has been observed sufficiently often to demand some explanation, especially as the professional narratives of 'good quality' care would claim otherwise, that empathic home care can enable infirm older people to age 'successfully' in place. To explore the processes whereby formal care might facilitate entry to, as often as it protects individuals from, the realms of the fourth age, we need to consider critically some of the assumptions underlying the professional ethics of compassionate care.

Care, compassion and professional ethics

Part of the wish to claim compassion as a professional virtue in medicine, nursing and social work practice has arisen within the evolving field of 'professional ethics'. Professional ethics emerged as a distinct academic domain during the 1970s – during the period of the 'bioethics revolution' (Baker and McCullough, 2007: 19). The first English language journal to be devoted to medical ethics was the _Journal of Medical Ethics_ published in 1975; the first journal on business ethics, the _Journal of Business Ethics_ was published in 1981; the first journal devoted to ethics and the legal profession was the _Notre Dame Journal of Law, Ethics & Public Policy_ which began in 1984; and the first nursing ethics journal _Nursing Ethics,_ was published in 1994. The emergence of these various academic journals on professional ethics and their accompanying narratives coincided with new public concerns over 'poor quality care' particularly in the institutions of the welfare state. Reports on abuses in the institutions of the late nineteenth and early twentieth century still housing large numbers of people with learning disability, psychiatric and geriatric patients began appearing in a number of countries during the 1960s, and a new call was made for these institutions to be replaced by 'community care'

(DHSS, 1981; Scull, 1985; Walker, 1981; Wing, 1981). The pressure to 'de-institutionalise' care and replace it with 'care in the community' created concerns over the efficiency and effectiveness of care. Following the 1980s 'crisis of the welfare state' and the rise of monetarist economics, a new managerialist direction was taken in the health and social care services, stimulating the ethic of 'consumerism' and 'client- or person-centred' care (Clarke, Gewirtz and McLaughlin, 2000). Each of these developments posed challenges to the identity of care, casting a new spotlight on its rhetoric and its practices.

Leaving to one side, for now, the determining influences for this shift in social policy, one consequence has been greater pressure on health and social care services to demonstrate that their 'clients' are at the centre of their concerns, much as the consumer (and not profit) is said to be the centre and focus of a conventional business's concerns. This pressure has been seemingly countered by a move toward an ethos of care within the services, which has in turn highlighted the importance of the altruistic emotions – of empathy, pity and compassion in their delivery. Particularly relevant has been what has been described as 'feminist ethics'. Drawing on insights from the women's movement feminist ethics privileges the relational aspects of care over the one sided principle of traditional (male- orientated) 'rights and duties' based principles.

Credit for articulating a feminist ethics of care is usually given to Gilligan (1982) in her critique of the gendered assumptions of Kohlberg's theory of moral development – published as *In a Different Voice*. Her position was elaborated further by Noddings in her book *Caring: A Feminist Approach to Ethics and Moral Education* (1984). Noddings describes the ethic of caring as representing a turning away from the principles of individualism espoused by Kant and his followers toward an ethic of 'natural caring' in which the right action is determined by fellow feeling and concern. Rather than follow abstract principles, irrespective of circumstances, Noddings argued for the privileging of empathy, of feeling with, being 'engrossed' by, and acting on behalf of the (cared for) other (1984: 33). A more general ethics of care was articulated by Tronto (1993). Concerned that what was being advocated was a partial, gender specific, contextual set of values limited to those areas of 'private life' concerned with distinct 'care practices', she sought to establish care as a generalised 'species' activity underlying all aspects of life and implicit in all the ways in which people maintain, develop and sustain their world (Tronto, 1993). Care, she argued, is commonly devalued, and our understanding of care 'fragmented' (2003: 112). While 'caring about' and 'taking care of' are the duties of the powerful, care-giving and care-receiving 'are left to the less powerful' (114). To integrate the valued with the de-valued aspects of care, Tronto argued, and in so doing restore the centrality of care to the general idea of morality, it is necessary to expand the definition of care. According to her account then, care consists of four elements or 'orientations': caring about or noticing the need to care; taking care of or assuming responsibility for care; caregiving or performing the care that needs to be done; and care-receiving or responding to care (1993: 127). Each of these elements of care embodies four related ethical values – of attentiveness, responsibility, competence and responsivity. People should be 'attentive' to the world around them and to others' needs; they should exercise 'responsibility' for dealing with people's dependency and vulnerabilities; they should exercise this responsibility competently so that the care outcome is good; and finally they should be responsive (1993: 127–137).

While others have extended, modified or elaborated Tronto's ethical framework, we shall focus here upon her original framework and its relevance to shaping the moral identity of the fourth age. First we should recognise that Tronto herself sees problems with her model. She writes that 'there are two primary dangers of care as a political ideal [which] arise inherently out of the nature of care itself' which she calls 'paternalism/maternalism' and 'parochialism' (1993: 170). The former reflects the imbalance of power that exists between those who manage the caring and those whose care is managed. This is typified through the parent/child template and making care a central ethic within society risks thereby institutionalising this inequality more broadly, in effect reinstating the 'single class' system of pre-modern society. The latter notion of parochialism risks reversing the universalism of enlightenment ethics, with the immediate demands of caring about those who are closest leading to the relative neglect of those to whom it is hardest to give attention – not just the needy in far off lands, but the needy who are least visible, who do not belong to anyone, the orphans of the community.

Other writers have been much more critical of the value (or virtue) of care, compassion and pity. What does pity do for the pitied, ask the activists of the disability movement. Disabled people it is claimed 'resent words that suggest they are sick, pitiful, childlike, dependent or objects of admiration' (Shapiro, 1994: 32). They should choose instead as one slogan puts it to 'piss on your pity', claiming an equality of access, an equality of respect and an equal voice – reciprocity, in other words, not the servility of being 'cared for'. The ambiguity that is contained in the feeling of pity has created a degree of resistance within the ranks of the disability movement toward the very idea of care and caring and books on disability written from the perspective of the disability movement rarely contain any reference to these terms (Watson et al., 2004: 336). Despite the difficulties of the disability movement's position (Thomas, 1999), it is still worth considering the objections to pity and care outlined by people within this movement, to get a sense of how moral identities may be compromised and eviscerated by such feelings and by the individual's embeddedness within the practices of one sided care.

Nietzsche is regarded by some as a touchstone when he 'teaches us that pity is demeaning both to the pitier and to the pitied' (Stocker, 2002: 137). Stocker argues that disabled people need to experience empathy not pity when they are 'helped' (not cared for). If disabled people fail to experience the former, then it is better they do without the latter. From this perspective, pity and care reflect a 'slave morality' (Paley, 2002). Pity is treated as an emotion through which people cultivate a sense of their own power – enhancing their moral identity as 'masters' at the expense of others who adopt the position of 'slaves'. Unlike the 'noble' lords of past eras, pity is a pale and weak expression of power exercised over sufferers who are 'easy prey' for the benefit of the carers. In denigrating those individuals who feel pity as much as those who are pitied, the philosopher Nietzsche argued that it 'is the most agreeable feeling among those who have little pride and no prospects of great conquests' (Nietzsche, *The Gay Science*, cited by Cartwright, 1988: 563). Though Carr (1999) sought to validate pity as an altruistic emotion, expressing the moral identity of the agent who pities, the 'new Nietzscheans' disdain its dubious altruism and the compromised moral identity of the caring/pitying agent. Such engagements with moral philosophy have their own consequences as Baker and McCullough have noted. Earlier 'moral revolutionaries' appropriated the writings of Nietzsche and Plato to argue in favour of the morality of 'mercy killing' disabled and chronically ill individuals (Baker and McCullough, 2007: 12–14). Despite the dubious history of medical ethics under National Socialism, several contemporary professional ethicists have allied themselves with those in the disability movement to devalue compassion, pity and care, arguing that 'those people who choose to work with a client group that is highly stigmatised are likely to have low self-esteem like their clients... [and hence]... remain connected with the disowned parts of themselves through contact with stigmatised people' (Marks, 1999: 109–110). Instead, reciprocity and alliance are advocated, through a shared political understanding of the exclusion and marginality of disabled people.

An alternative case has been made that care recipients should be placed in a position of control (power) over their care and hence over their carers (named assistants or helpers). The consequences, however, for allowing market forces to operate can just as easily lead to replacing one injustice with another, as the carer becomes the paid servant of the cared for – providing of course that he or she is minded to act as the master or mistress of his or her care. If one seeks to introduce alternative considerations into the contract that require not simply on demand service but on additional emotional labour, such that the carer must not only care on demand, but also care 'compassionately', the position of the long-term carer becomes ever more abject, reduplicating much of the master/slave position associated with the institutional scandals of the past.

Repositioning care as part of an alternative ethics to that of the autonomy and rights position espoused within the disability movement has thus been challenged by accusations that such an ethics of caring risks perpetuating the Nietzschean master/slave relationship, with the added expectation that the masters show compassion in return for – or as part of – their caring powers. Reversal of this position only duplicates this imbalance, without changing the basic configuration of care as control. In the end Tronto had to reach out to another ethics – of justice and fairness – in order to combat the limitations of her proposed ethic of caring and its inherent dangers (1993: 171). Returning in effect to a Kantian position of individual rights, one could argue that this diminishes the assumed centrality of a professional ethics of care, relying instead on the notion of people's rights, including the right to be cared for – with or without empathy, but perhaps not without pity, in effect claiming common citizenship rather than reciprocal 'personhood' (cf. Bartlett and O'Connor, 2007; Kelly and Innes, 2013).

Although we recognise that care, especially informal care, can serve to protect older people from the fourth age that very fact creates as its corollary the capacity of care to perform the very opposite function facilitating passage into the fourth age. Even with the 'right' type of care, even with care associated with some degree of 'reciprocal dependence' (Fine and Glendenning, 2005: 616) such 'journeys' may not always be preventable. There is no doubt an imperative to care beyond the boundaries of compassion, to act on behalf of the moral community and to manage care as best one can, including under conditions of an empathic veil of ignorance. But such duties do not extend to everyone and neither does everyone who is cared for want to be party to or even 'share' this particular journey toward the anticipated abyss that marks the fourth age.

The consequences of caring for the fourth age

Empirical research into informal or family 'dementia care' has clearly demonstrated how spouses are more likely to continue to care, to suffer less carer burden and to gain more satisfaction from looking after their partner, irrespective of the severity of his or her mental impairment compared with other caregiving arrangements (Pollitt, Anderson and O'Connor, 1991). Arguably this is because such relationship can be sustained for longer through the shared lives most couples live, making any re-framing of their identity almost undesirable as it risks 'unravelling' both of their lives. Although the transition from home care to institutional care can be difficult for informal carers, irrespective of their previous relationship, it seems particularly difficult when one spouse's dementia has acted as the trigger for nursing home admission. This is because of the difficulty of 'healing' the disruption in the relationship as feelings of commitment compete with feelings of alienation (Tilse, 1997: 32). While research suggests that most families maintain contact with their relative after admission into institutional care, the nature of that contact – the loss or continuity of 'compassion' and 'reciprocity' experienced – has not been so well studied (Gaugler, 2005). Intuitively it seems likely that, in the cases where carer and cared for live together, such a physical separation of two people's lives can lead only to a growing separation in their respective worlds, where the former carer is left alone to manage while the once cared for is more deeply enmeshed in care without commitment or the passive reciprocity of a once shared life.

  Does the experience of the estrangement of care facilitate the once cared for person's envelopment by a fourth age? Studies of the experience of relatives visiting their dependent in care suggest that along with feelings of guilt and pity is a reported sense of alienation – the feeling that their relative has become, emotionally, more of a stranger than before. Even when relatives recognise that their husband or wife, father or mother is 'no longer' the person they once were, such awareness of change does not necessarily consign the person to a state of 'otherness', of 'non-personhood' let alone 'social death'. As Pollitt and her colleagues noted 'the primary desire of the couples – both the dementing and non-dementing partners – was for life to continue as nearly as possible as it had always done or where it had radically changed, to maintain the status quo for as long as possible' (1991: 467).

For those older people who live alone and who have never experienced such care, the regime instituted by formal care represents a disjunction in their lives, one which evolves over time. Weekly visits from home care assistants become twice weekly, daily and eventually repeated visits each day. But home care services do not guarantee a constancy of personhood in either the carer or the cared for. The care provided by a caring agency is not typically responsive to the person cared for since it relies upon a system of timed and increasingly costed care practices. While a daughter may say to her mother that she can only pop in after work, or after the evening meal, and so on, such timing of care is pre-determined by the tasks of care but on the circumstances of the (informal) carer. It implies some kind of reciprocity – a negotiation of sorts – between the cared for mother and the caring daughter. Such reciprocity is neither presumed nor required in the case of formal care. Patterns and timings of care are determined by the carer, or more likely the carer's employing agency and their contractual arrangements with the paying authority and even when both carer and cared for can and do negotiate, such reciprocal negotiations must be conducted around the edges of the care contract (unless the cared for holds the contract himself or herself, of course, when a very different dynamic of power and moral identity holds sway).

Arguably the practices and consequences of formal care are even more attuned to the social imaginary of the fourth age than those enacted within networks of informal, family care. The aura of 'abjection' that surrounds the home care workforce shapes the social imaginary of the fourth age, devaluing both the carer and the cared for; added to the poor working conditions of long-term care has been the steady supply of reports in the media about the abuses of care as the new 'horrors' of community care replace the old 'horrors' of institutional care. People have been found less likely to report or perceive abuse from their relatives than they are from formal carers (Ziminski and Rempusheski, 2013) even though 'abuse' by family members is certainly not uncommon (Aciemo et al., 2010; Daley, Merchant and Jogerst, 2010). Epidemiological studies generally rely upon questioning older people who are able and willing to take part in such surveys, and their findings have limited power to illuminate either the extent or the determinants of abuse. Physical and mental frailty, social isolation and the degree of dependency upon the carer are widely considered risk factors for abuse, even in cultures with a persisting tradition of 'respect' for older people

(Kishimoto et al., 2013; Wang, 2006; Yan and Kwok, 2011). Such findings imply that a potential for some form of abuse or mistreatment resides in the nexus of care, irrespective of cultural traditions. The neediness of the care recipient, the capacity – or incapacity – of the carer to cope with that neediness and the degree of social isolation of the caregiving relationship are the more salient aspects to realising that potential for abuse while abuse itself arises most often during the more intimate personal care activities (Saveman et al., 1999; Sandvide et al., 2004). It seems that the more abject and intimate are the circumstances of carer and cared for, the more abusive can the relationship become. While institutional abuse is a matter of wider public concern, it may not be the most common site of abuse, precisely because of the institutional supports that are available – for the carers, at least (Habjanič and Lahe, 2012). Whether by caring less, or caring less intensely, formal carers may be less abusive toward those they care for, at the same time as being less compassionate and perhaps less mindful of their personal identity while recognising at the same time a fellow citizenship.

Unlike the less abject position associated with working in long-term nursing home care, with its better rates of pay, minimal travelling demands and more secure and more sociable working conditions, long-term home care poses problems that might well be thought to enhance the risk of abuse. In one sense long-term home care has taken over from nursing home care as the site of low-paid marginalised and precarious 'dirty work' (cf. Stannard, 1973; Jervis, 2001). Given the relatively recent expansion of this sector, it is not surprising that there is as yet relatively little research on the experiences of and the struggles over caregiving that takes place in the privacy of care recipients' homes (Genet et al., 2011). Even in the Nordic countries, where home care is a much less marginalised, precarious and unregulated occupation than elsewhere, approximately one-quarter of the home care workforce regularly report feeling inadequate to meeting the care recipient/client's needs (Trydegård, 2012: 124).

One of the few studies on abuse and neglect of home care 'clients' by their carers found that agency based carers more often neglected their clients' needs than did consumer-directed carers although there were few other differences in caregiving experiences (Matthias and Benjamin, 2003: 179). The authors also reported that *non-family* consumer-directed care workers more often neglected and physically and financially abused their clients compared with paid family carers, suggesting that, other circumstances being equal, the absence of a historically shared moral identity such as that which evolves within families renders care potentially more abject and more abusive.

The costs of being cared for

So far our attention has focused more upon the carer than the cared for, arguably because it is the agency of the carer that realises the fourth age not that of the person being cared for. The frail elderly person who is being cared for is not inherently or inextricably without agency; they are not in Haraway's terminology mere 'social actants' defined only by their corporeality (see Gilleard and Higgs 2013 for a fuller discussion of this distinction). But the attributions of, or the denial of the attributions of agency by the carer, toward the cared for, constitutes a site of contestation. That struggle is arguably one of contested imaginaries – whether of an imagined agency that the carer struggles to sustain, or of an imagined loss of agency, with which the carer struggles to accommodate. Care is realised within these struggles, care whose form and narratives affects the person being cared for, and not always in benign or helpful ways. Receiving care can lead an older infirm person to feel more aged, more useless and more depressed, and greater quantities of care can lead to a greater sense of agedness and, directly and indirectly, more abjection and misery (Cahill et al., 2009; Kwak, Ingersoll-Dayton and Burgard, 2014). This seems so whether or not the care comes from intimates or paid carers.

Reciprocity comes at a cost. To accept care is to accept dependency, returning as much as one can, but with some necessary sense of obligation toward the carer by the individual receiving care. In the absence of other exchangeable goods, these costs accrue to the person being cared for, creating a debt when there is often little means of paying it off. Homans (1958) in his paper 'Social behaviour as exchange' argued that much of human interactional behaviour can be understood through a system of mutual exchange whereby actors seek to minimise the costs of their exchange, while maximising their rewards. Its subsequent application to age and inter-generational relationships was first outlined by Dowd (1975, 1980), but its more specific application to the social relations of 'caregiving' and 'care receiving' in later life was developed in two papers exploring the relationship between reciprocity between adult caregiving children and their aged parents (Mutran and Reitzes, 1984; Stoller, 1985). Lowenstein and her colleagues (2007) provided cross-national evidence suggesting that older parents benefit more – in the sense of reporting greater well-being – when they see themselves giving more than they get from their children while the opposite – getting more than they give generally affected them negatively.

Such empirical studies are of course limited in their capacity to fully explore the complex meanings of social exchange. The simple addition of acts of giving and receiving do scant justice to the complexities of intimate relationships within and between generations. Nevertheless, what such studies illustrate is that giving is generally better than receiving, whether that is care or other types of gifts and services. The obvious unsurprising implication is that receiving care, however generously given, insidiously harms or devalues the recipient unless he or she can find some way to re-balance the exchange. Resistance to receiving care can be seen as an attempt to retain agency, to refuse to pay the price of pity. Sadly such resistance is often re-framed into the narratives of those with power and agency – the carers – as 'challenging' behaviour and met with medication or other 'psychosocial' interventions, or in the case of family, a sense of hurt that is only partly healed by attributions of otherness – she or he is no longer herself or himself. Without the power to articulate an alternative, commanding narrative, the fourth age can only darken its shadow.

Conclusions

We have argued in this chapter that it is through care that the fourth age is most intimately connected to society and that no social imaginary of the fourth age is complete without its realisation in some kind of caregiving relationship. While ideas of senility and ugly old age may form part of its narrative, the fourth age is embodied and realised within social relationships by the moral imperative of care. It is in this sense that care shapes the moral identity of the fourth age, through its neediness and abject helplessness which commands care. Care is neither disinterested nor pitiless, even at its most extreme, but the ethos of compassionate care that is proposed by many professional bodies is we believe just as imaginary, an imaginary ill fitted to reconstruct the contours of the fourth age.

Under the shadow of the fourth age, care operates through a dual regime, on the one hand positioning frail and abject older people within its imaginary while on the other striving to protect them from its harmful effects. The extent to which the former overrides the latter depends, we suggest, as much upon the moral identity of the care relationship as it does on the specific demands of care. Although compassion, empathic care and a sense of reciprocity between carer and cared for seem more protective, these narratives and their accompanying practices become less viable as the evidence to sustain reciprocity grows fainter and the caregiving relationship slowly becomes what has been described as 'a relationship of one'.

The more severe the cared for person's infirmities – particularly those that affect communication, memory and reflexivity – the greater the social isolation of the caregiving relationship. A lack of any historical connection between carer and cared for makes the demand for compassion even less realisable since there is no past credit of shared experience, of mutually exchanged gifts of kindness and love and care exchanged without compassion or reciprocity sooner becomes burdensome. At some point, reciprocity ceases to be a feature of even historically situated relationships and is replaced by a relationship whose compassion is largely constructed by the carer – or a felt obligation to sustain the caregiving relationship, where pity rather than compassion accompanies the caring. As the otherness of the person being cared for confronts the carer in each and every act of care, compassion is replaced with obligation. Then pity and responsibility must be aligned with power and though Nietzsche might not be pleased with this solution, we can only respond that neither Nietzsche (nor Noddings) are necessarily helpful adversaries in combatting the power of the fourth age imaginary and its one sided relationship with care. Otherwise, the pull of the gravitational field of the fourth age weakens further the boundaries of both self and other, carer and cared for, leading to the consequent dehumanisation – and abjection – of both parties. At some point, there is no other imaginary from which to draw on, other than that of the fourth age. That need not mean that the carer then stops or should stop caring, just that it may make it hard to insist upon accompanying that care with an obligatory sense of compassion.

Chapter 7

Bridges and Barriers between the Third and the Fourth Age

Introduction

As we have argued in previous chapters of this book, our way of understanding the fourth age is to regard it as a social imaginary of what is sometimes called 'real' or 'deep' old age. Though it is not unconnected to how we have theorised the third age, this conceptualisation of the fourth age is qualitatively distinct from it, and this separation is necessary if we are to fully appreciate the changes to old age that have occurred. Though it is possible to analyse both the third and fourth ages through the structuring influences of class (especially in the case of the third age) and gender (especially in the case of the fourth), much of their distinction lies outside these classical sociological structures. Hence our preference has been to formulate the fourth age as a social imaginary that cuts across the divisions of class and gender just as we have argued that the cultures of the third age cannot be easily read off from an infra-structure of class, cohort and community (Gilleard and Higgs, 2005: 165). This does not mean that participation in the cultures of the third age is not uninfluenced by older people's access to socio-economic resources or by their social and geographical settings. Our point is that the cultures of the third age are not constructed or determined by such structural differences. In the same way, we are aware that gender is clearly important in influencing how we imagine the fourth age and which persons we tend to most associate with this imaginary. But we would argue that neither class nor gender defines them. In the same way that we have chosen to treat the third age as an emergent cultural field (or fields) in which older people in general, (particularly but not exclusively, people in the more prosperous economies of the world) are engaged, so we think that it is more fruitful to interpret the fourth age as a distinct social (or cultural) imaginary, one that has a general purchase upon society's under-standing of later life, even as it is clearly associated with issues concerning especially gender.

Viewing the third age from what can be considered a Bourdieusian influenced perspective, we have identified choice, lifestyle and identity as key vectors through which the field emerges, changes and expands (Gilleard and Higgs, 2011a). Social agency plays a critical role in real-ising the third age, and individual lives possess iconic value in illustrat-ing and rehearsing what it means to participate within its cultural field. The fourth age is not like that. It functions primarily as a social imaginary, formed within the collective consciousness that society reflexively develops of itself, its institutions and its members and operating most powerfully within the social relations of care. While this imaginary and its links to the 'old' view of old age have been elaborated over long periods, it has been rendered darker and more diffuse in its contemporary form by the changing circumstances of our ageing societies. While many of the outlines of this imaginary can be discerned in the records of past societies, what is distinct is that this imaginary is now conveyed as forms of cultural knowledge through a combination of academic and professional writings and their appro-priation by the mass media, making the fourth age (understood vari-ously as 'deep', 'real' or 'extreme' old age) a social imaginary that is distinctly of our times.

The emergence of the third age and its active cultural separation from 'old age' has been an important contributor to that process of darkening and delineating the fourth age. In the first part of this chapter, we explore in some detail those processes whereby the social imaginary of the fourth age has been defined and elaborated by the very foregrounding of active successful later life and health styles. In the second part, we examine whether and how far the cultures of the third age – and its rhetoric of active 'successful' ageing might afford either some alleviation or amelioration of the otherwise intractable elements of the fourth age. These two processes by which the third age on the one hand delineates and on the other mollifies the fourth age imaginary are what we mean when we describe the boundaries and the bridges dividing or connecting the third age to the fourth age. We begin with its boundaries.

**Building the boundaries of the fourth age within the cultures
of the third age**

Old age is a necessary preoccupation of the third age. Though it is not
by any means its only preoccupation, it is a crucial one. Many of the
narratives supporting third age lifestyles centre upon not letting oneself
go, not looking or acting like an old man or an old woman, not exposing
too much, if at all, of one's material agedness. Although third age narratives and practices often sustain different identities and lifestyles and
draw upon points of reference unrelated to agedness – such as one's
sexuality, gender or ethnicity, or the uses of one's cultural and social
capital – many implicitly reference ageing and old age. This has given
cause for many writers and researchers on ageing and old age to criticise
the third age as a malignant cultural and social phenomenon, arguing
that the net result of promoting 'third ageism' is to increase the fear of
old age while diminishing its possibilities (George, 2011; Holstein, 2011).
This critique has been extended to or expressed as a critique of the
'successful ageing paradigm'. We shall take some space therefore to
outline the key features of what might be called the 'dividing practices'
of the third age as they have been articulated by its critics.

   Although we would argue for a conceptual distinction, links between
the concept of the third age and successful ageing have been made by
a number of authors (e.g., Holstein, 2011). 'Successful ageing' has been
deployed as a term in the gerontological literature for longer and
across a wider range of topics and disciplines than has that of the third
age. As a discursive frame, although successful aging has a long history
in academic writing on ageing, it has been very much 'anchored' as a
mainstream paradigm in gerontology by Rowe and Kahn in their
seminal article, *Human Aging: Usual and Successful* (1987). Dillaway
and Byrnes note that successful ageing is one among many terms
(productive aging, resourceful aging, independent aging, healthy aging,
active aging, aging well, positive aging and normal aging) that since
the 1970s have been used to express a positive view of later life (2009:
703). As a concept, it has proved more successful than other terminology, having more effect both on academic gerontology and on policy
(703). It has also received more critical analysis than these other terms,
hence our decision to focus upon these critiques to illustrate the 'costs'
associated with privileging 'positive' or 'successful' ageing and setting
this implicitly or explicitly against the subaltern position of 'unsuccessful' or 'negative ageing'.

   As Dillaway and Byrnes note, 'one of the most important and
growing critiques of the successful aging paradigm in recent years

revolves around the fact [sic] that successful aging terminology can only speak to privileged groups' experiences of aging...[and] thus successful aging can be an exclusionary and problematic term' (2009: 707). Others have argued that it 'fails to acknowledge the significance of later life thereby allowing society to avoid thinking about and creating a respected place for the oldest in society' (Davey and Glasgow, 2006). A third criticism has been made – the so-called 'political economy critique' – that the successful ageing paradigm emphasises individual responsibility for maintaining one's health, financial status and independence, thus minimising the role of the state in providing income support, health care and personal welfare with insufficient attention given 'to the needs of the frail old in policy and planning' (Davey and Glasgow, 2006: 25). A similar criticism has been mounted of the even more 'fiscally focused' concept of 'productive ageing' by Estes and Mahakian when they stated that 'to be aging successfully or productively, elders may be expected to take on more work (paid or unpaid) and to expect less from the state (government and the public sector)' (2001: 210). In consequence, whether intended or not, Estes argues that 'the concept of productive aging promotes the role of the market in addressing health-reinforcing, individual-based solutions and obfuscating the role of the state in addressing the structures that limit individuals' ability to actualize aging' (Estes and Associates, 2001: 199).

Clearly these arguments provide a thoughtful critique of the 'successful ageing' paradigm and while we believe they contain quite a few of their own contradictions, it is not our purpose here to descry them (but see Gilleard and Higgs, 2000 and Higgs and Jones, 2009 for discussions about these points). Rather we want to use them to illustrate the point that the third age, with its various narratives and performances realised in part through the discourses and practices that support 'successful ageing', foregrounds the virtues of autonomy, health and activity, thereby rendering the idea of 'unsuccessful' ageing as that marked by 'disability, dependency and ultimately death' (Holstein and Minkler, 2003: 793). Now while Holstein and Minkler argue that these narratives promote the 'cultural denial' of the downsides of life, it is perhaps more accurate to state that they promote the idea that (1) later life can be awful but (2) individuals can keep the awfulness of old age at bay. Such beliefs may have become quite common and many people in their 70s and 80s report maintaining their 'self respect through the ability to keep fear of frailty at a distance' (Hörder, Frändin and Larsson, 2013).

One powerful example of the growing effect of the social imaginary of the fourth age on the concerns of those living in later life is the fear of developing 'Alzheimer's'– that is, dementia. Williams, Higgs and Katz (2012) have described this process as an example of what they term 'neuroculture' which engages individuals in discussions about optimising or enhancing cognitive attributes through the use of brain training or pharmaceutical intervention where the aim is to slow down or prevent age-related memory problems. They point to the emergence of new medical conditions such as Mild Cognitive Impairment (MCI) which can be viewed either as a precursor to dementia or as a condition in its own right. Although there is debate on the utility of this diagnosis, the way in which it problematizes what was once 'normal' cognitive function in later life is probably more important in understanding its role as forming a component or theme within the cultures of the third age. Many older people have become wary of their potential cognitive problems and seek to prevent or at least slow down their occurrence by various methods including dieting, nutraceuticals and drugs. Not only has this created a potential market for the pharmaceutical industry and for various brain training programmes, but it also reflects and reinforces the distinction between those operating in the environment of the third age and those subject to the fourth age. MCI is a condition that creates ambiguity about the status of the individual in relation to the event horizon of the fourth age. In one way it normalises mental impairment as one of the vicissitudes of growing older at the same time as it establishes connections to the onset of dementia and all that '*sans everything*' that dementia is thought to entail. The shadow of the fourth age lies over this, and many other health promoting practices undertaken in later life and promoted at increasingly earlier ages to develop effective 'resistance' to old age and particularly that darker old age associated with 'senility'. These practices and their associated narratives are readily picked up by and elaborated in the mass media which then offer their own 'informed' solutions such as doing crossword puzzles daily, keeping your weight down by dieting, accessing 'innovative' drug therapies or by eating the necessary 'brain foods' such as berries or nuts, and so on.

The shadows of the fourth age cast in and by the third are not confined to those situations where particular diagnoses such as dementia, diabetes and hypertension threaten to destabilise the framework of post working life. In a study of financial decision making in older couples, Price et al. (2014) found that many of the people that they researched accepted that they would develop age-associated illnesses and disabilities as they grew older. Some made provision for this in their financial planning and anticipated making adaptations to their homes to optimise their future lives. But while their research subjects could envisage the onset of future disability, the issue of ending up needing long-stay care in a nursing home or other such institution was not so readily contemplated. Generally the respondents avoided the issue altogether or hoped to die before such eventuality occurred. The avoidance of the issue was not through lack of knowledge but rather because of the fearfulness attached to these outcomes. Money diverted to this end would both be costly and would constitute as they saw it 'wasted spending'. Consequently while there have been many calls in the UK for a full debate about the need to provide long-term care insurance or the construction of a better system of organising such care (Dilnot Commission, 2011), the failure of such debates to have public traction seem to us rooted much more in the imaginary of the fourth age than in any reluctance to take difficult political decisions. Contemplating ageing as not just an accumulation of deficits and disabilities but as 'ending up' in a nursing home with all that that is thought to entail further demonstrates the power of the fourth age as a social imaginary, that is already at work among those not yet even close to its gravitational pull.

Building bridges, building resistance

If many aspects of the cultures of the third age contribute to forcing old age deeper into the shadows of a fourth age through their 'anti-ageing' rhetoric and 'age-denying' practices, is it possible that some of these cultural strategies can also be used to mitigate some of the worst effects of the fourth age? We should say at the outset that we are sceptical of such possibilities. There are several reasons for such scepticism. First the fourth age in so far as it is created as a social imaginary by the discourses of the third age is based not upon the agency of individuals but as the assigned plight of an imagined collective, a collective othering of individuals as little more than figures of frailty. Such imagery is not dependent upon such visual signs as white hair, wrinkled skin, bent backs and sagging flesh, though such corporeal imagery may provide some of the context, but on the idea of 'unsuccess' itself, on a narrative of 'frailure'.

Those marked out by these third person narratives as frailed elders can be represented as sometimes sad, sometimes piteous and sometimes disgusting figures whose behaviour seems unstrategic, purposeless, helpless, exhibiting neither agency nor subjectivity.

Hence it makes little sense to argue that if the narratives and practices of the third age can be censored, changed or eliminated in order not to 'privilege' health, activity and agency, then this will lead to the disappearance of the fourth age from the collective imagination. Arguably, we could develop similar arguments about youth culture – that by privileging personal autonomy, physical attractiveness and reproductive fitness the non-young are rendered failures by comparison? If this is so, should we then deny them expressing such values – as if their cycling, skateboarding and dancing about was a strategy designed to disempower and render abject those less able to perform such 'youthful' activities? Health, activity, attractiveness, fitness, quickness of wit are all widely valued, not to 'oppress' those who lack these qualities but as goods that humanity – and society – have long sought to embody. Should we silence those who aspire to be so virtuous? And if it is argued that with age should also come changed values, might we not ask – at what age precisely should we stop desiring these things, and at what age precisely should we be chastised for valuing them? And even supposing these virtues were forbidden to those, say, aged more than 40 or 50 or 60; what exactly should they be replaced by – a love of sleep, of torpor, a 'transgressive' preference for abjection, inactivity and the faint odour of urine?

Within the social imaginary of the fourth age, there are no strategies to be deployed. The only challenges are to the imaginary itself. But shrinking the space it occupies in society – by redefining the chronology of what is 'really' old, by requiring ever greater degrees of mental and physical infirmity to meet the criteria of frailty and long-term care, by calling nursing homes 'assisted living facilities' or by demanding that formal and informal carers behave more kindly and compassionately – may paradoxically increase its gravitational pull, making the failure deeper, darker and more powerful than it already is. The densification of disability and dependency in long-term care that has characterised late modernity has taken away much of the potential agency that residents in old people's homes – and before them the inmates of the workhouse infirmaries – once possessed. Shrinking the boundaries of what constitutes 'old age' *in extremis* may paradoxically make matters worse. And if shrinking is not the solution, should we consider its opposite, expanding and thus diluting its power, in much the same fashion as the early modern parish did under the old poor law, lowering the threshold for outdoor and indoor relief and including both workers and the unemployed as deserving of relief?

Reversing trends that began in the mid-nineteenth century – classical modernity – seems an implausible political shift in strategy, one that was not even considered in the enthusiastic heyday for welfare during those glorious decades from 1945 to 1975 – once known by the French as *les trentes glorieuses* (Fourastié, 1979; Pierson, 1998). Even if size matters, there seems little prospect of increasing the range and variety of care support and personal sustenance available to people in later life in the developed, let alone in developing societies, as politicians and policy makers struggle with the 'increasing pressure...to control and monitor long-term care spending' (Doyle and Timonen, 2007: 127). Already there is concern that in Europe, the numbers of people 'needing' residential and home based long-term care will rise by between 100 per cent and 200 per cent over the next 50 years and as a result 'the supply of [long-term] care is unlikely to keep pace with demand' (Geerts and Willemé, 2012: 9). We have explored issues of long-term care in Chapter 2 and the associated 'apocalyptic demography' of later life in Chapter 3, and it is safe to conclude that the reports coming out of international bodies such as the EU, OECD and World Bank make it improbable that there will be any expansion or 'loosening' of the criteria entitling older people to receive generously funded long-term home and residential care.

Are all collective solutions to the challenges of the fourth age improbable then? Can the emphasis upon individualisation that characterises third age cultures be applied instead as a strategy of resistance against the fourth age? The promotion of individual strategies of resistance to the fourth age is as we noted at the beginning of this chapter, an important element in third age cultures. Ever since Galen patented his six 'non-naturals', the combination of taking the air, exercising, being regular in one's bowel and bladder habits, avoiding stress and eating sensibly has been promoted as the way to age well (Gilleard, 2013). Might such strategies be extended to offer a reasonable and inexpensive option for minimising the risks of becoming a frail elder, of delaying, deferring or avoiding altogether the crossing of the boundary into the fourth age? Arguments that ageing societies are experiencing a 'compression' of morbidity in later life – or if not its compression, then its deferment – have been rehearsed earlier and it seems reasonable to believe that despite the decline of collective welfare observed since the 1980s, an increasingly consumerist individualistic self-reflexive 'late modern' society has seen a steady, if uneven expansion in absolute and relative terms of active healthy later life (Cai and Lubitz, 2007; Costa, 2005; Doblhammer and Kytir, 2001; Fries et al., 2011; Hessler et al., 2003; Stewart, Cutler and Rosen, 2013). Evidence that planned 'lifestyle' interventions can predict or prevent such proxies for the fourth age as dementia, disability, frailty and multi-morbidity is not strong (Keysor, 2003; Plassman et al., 2010;

van Haastregt et al., 2000) although Fries (2005) is certainly optimistic about the potential of such interventions. Arguably, even if there were effective, evidence based interventions that delay or prevent these problems, as Moody (1995) has pointed out describing the potential risk of 'double jeopardy', what of those fated to fail to achieve such positive outcomes – would there not be a further shrinking, a further 'densification' and an even greater sense of 'unsuccessful' ageing attached to those not obtaining any benefits – would they not fall even deeper into the community of the frailed and the failed?

Is it possible to develop alternative structural approaches to build greater universal resistance to the fourth age – to reduce its gravitational pull on us all? In some sense the answer has to be yes and no. Since the fourth age is, according to our argument, a social imaginary – a collective representation of all that is feared and found most distasteful about old age – it might seem possible that such a collective imagining can be changed or undermined as a result, for example, of changes in the quality of long-term care, developments in preventive medicine or the application of new assistive technologies to better address the situation of those whose circumstances place them close to the shadows of the fourth age. Just as palliative care has claimed to take the pain and suffering out of dying with cancer, so might one envisage a form of palliative care that attempts to reduce the abjection and indignity associated with illness and impairment in old age. Illustrative of such approaches is the ambitious national strategy adopted by Sweden of targeting resources upon the most sick or fragile of the population aged above 65. The state has established a series of targets including measurable gains in access to comprehensive palliative care, less harmful uses of anti-psychotic medication, regular surveillance of mental and physical disabilities, improved management of ulcers and so forth.

Even so, because it is an imaginary, an imaginary whose historical representations have long roots reaching well beyond modernity, it might be that the fourth age resists such modernist agendas because it serves a necessary function, promoting a sense of comparative well-being among the increasing number of people in later life who do not consider themselves either 'frail' or 'abject'. By not thinking of themselves as frailed, by maintaining an idea of frailty that distances them from its abject position, many older people may feel either blessed or pleased with themselves for managing to 'protect' themselves from such a fate. The next section addresses this problem by considering the potential for a future 'un-imagining' of the fourth age.

Can we imagine later life without a fourth age?

In this final section, we consider the question of whether later life can be experienced outside the framework of a fourth age. To some extent it is easier to imagine not participating in the third age than it is escaping the pull of the fourth. Those older people who continue working full-time doing the same job or staying in the same business that they had before they entered later life may die without ever retiring or developing a post-work 'later lifestyle'. Others may seem to transition abruptly from being a productive adult to becoming an infirm elder, as a result, for example, of a severe acute illness or trauma that brings their active lives to an end. In either case, it is possible to imagine lives lived largely outside of the third age just as it is possible to imagine someone dying abruptly before experiencing a prolonged period of enfeeblement or incapacity. But while in the case of the third age, it is possible to argue that the person never, or perhaps only very marginally, engaged with the cultures of the third age it is not clear that by avoiding living with infirmity one necessarily avoids any engagement with the fourth age. If the fourth age is a social imaginary and not a stage of life, and if it is not a set of cultural practices either, it is capable of touching everyone without that element of agency and subjectivity that the third age requires.

So is it possible to imagine later life without recourse to the social imaginary of the fourth age? Those who have argued for a moral economy of the life course offer a vision that embraces vulnerability as part of our common humanity (Baars, 2012; Vincent, 2003). Such writers seek thereby to 'humanise' the fourth age, investing it with its own meaning and purpose – in effect 're-imagining' the fourth age as a 'real' old age whose reality is constituted from moral purpose – exercising what Himmelfarb (2006) has called 'the moral imagination'. It can be argued that the 'moral economy' approach toward later life is primarily concerned with inter-personal relations. It is said by some to reflect 'the place of consensual assumptions about reciprocal obligations' within and between various groups, including of course between 'age groups' (Minkler and Cole, 1999: 40). As these authors note, there is something of a disconnection between those consensual views that concern old age and economic justice – where the majority of young and old agree that the non-working elderly deserve material and social support – and the value given to old age itself – which is low (43). Arguably if the creation and sustainability of third age culture is a product of the former, the fourth age is a victim of the latter.

The moral economy approach calls not just for 'norms of reciprocity' within society, and between the generations, but for an equal valuing of each stage in life from infancy to old age. An example of one such moral 'reordering' of the life course is that of Baars' 'aging as finitization' (2012: 236–238). Baars suggests that the perspective of finitude and 'the inevitability of change can inspire us to appreciate the uniqueness of persons' (236). Inevitably however such notions of individual development (including, e.g., Erikson's model of the development of 'integrity' in old age) privilege a view of the self-reflexivity of persons that is conspicuous by its absence within the fourth age's imaginary. Moreover, any moral re-ordering of the life course is no longer quite as easy to outline as it was in pre-modern societies where all forms of life were given meaning by divine law and religious practice (Sears, 1986). Trying to answer the question of what old age is 'for' in a society less caught up with such beliefs and practices only yields a multiplicity of answers that arguably reflect little more than the fragmentation and destandardisation of the modern 'institutional' life course.

Even if one accepts the futility of any moral re-ordering of the life course, it is still possible to articulate a different moral economy approach based upon the expectations of and toward people as citizens, citizens from the cradle to the grave, with rights throughout life that reflect the ethos of the modern post-war welfare state. This might include decent standards of child care, prevention of abuse of children and of people in care, provision of educational and employment opportunities for all, civic and material support of close personal relationships throughout adulthood and opportunities for a secure retirement in later life with reliable, secure access to health and social care at all times, and especially during periods of vulnerability. Arguably, that was the culminating vision of Beck's Modernity One; whether it can be re-vitalised in Modernity Two is less clear (Beck and Lau, 2005).

Still, such re-imaginings can help undermine some of the negative imagery of those 'in the shadow of' the fourth age, although it may be doubted if such policy initiatives would ever eliminate the kind of negative talk about 'bones' and 'vegetables' that is often observed among the residents of nursing homes (Gubrium and Holstein, 2002: 202) or the informal 'hidden' curriculum that pervades medical training which sees 'eldercare' as either boring, frustrating or unrewarding (Higashi et al., 2012, 2013). Perhaps the point is not to demand professionalised, manualised 'compassionate person-centeredness' or indeed any compulsory affective valuing of older people who are felt to be

'abject' or deemed to be 'frail'. Arguably, the moral economy of ensuring 'fairness' and 'support' throughout the lifespan should not be
renegotiated either through the lens of an apocalyptic demography or
through the practices of frailing but by avoiding moralising altogether
focusing instead upon funding fair care for all, for the long-term and
as needed to people who are conceptualised first and foremost as
citizens rather than as needy or vulnerable 'persons' (Bartlett and
O'Connor, 2007). Perhaps the nearest that we have so far got in this
attempt to encapsulate the fourth age within the totality of citizenship
is the so-called 'Nordic model' of care, a model suffused if not with
morality then at least with a certain optimism that societies can do
better, fail better, by their oldest and most frailed citizens (Albaek
et al., 2014; Rostgaard, 2014). The fact that such societies also seem to
offer the most satisfying later life for all is at least one reason for
remaining hopeful (cf. Global AgeWatch Index, 2014).

Conclusions

We have argued in this chapter that the contemporary social imaginary of the fourth age is in part the product of third age culture and
its aversion toward and rejection of old age as 'agedness'. This antag-
onism plays its part in making of the fourth age something to be feared
and avoided. At the same time other policy related factors within the
prosperous nations play an equal, almost complementary part. These
include the promotion of policies favouring 'active' and/or 'productive'
ageing and the pervasive use of an apocalyptic demography that is
employed in international models of the rising costs of health care
and the growing burden of long-term care that are linked to the rising
numbers of dependent, frail elderly people in our ageing societies.

In considering these factors, we have explored the possibilities of
'resistance' to the fourth age imaginary through three different means –
the use of individualised 'third age strategies' to thwart the ascriptions
of the fourth age from settling upon people in later life; second, the
development of policies reversing the densification of disability within
long-term care, by lowering the threshold for eligibility and/or expanding the range of more inclusive long-term care service options; and
third, the re-imagining of old age free from the darker and more
distant imagining of the fourth age by a moral re-ordering of the life
course that seeks to give a more positive meaning to vulnerability and
dependency at all stages in the life-course. None of these strategies
we believe are likely to prove successful. The fourth age cannot be

re-imagined otherwise; its imaginary must be faced without flinching or wishing that it was otherwise. In real life, constant attempts to keep as many people as possible from traversing its 'event horizon' will and need to be made – by older people themselves when resisting the attributions of frailty, by partners in care who cling together through thick and thin in the face of their mutual abjection, as well as by enabling more comprehensive long-term care services and, finally, a matter that deserves much greater discussion than we can provide in this book, namely giving people the option of not having to approach so close to the metaphorical black hole of the fourth age at all.

Chapter 8

Fashioning a Future for Fourth Age Studies

Our aim in this book has been to contribute to the understanding of later life in late modernity. Once secured by the institutions of the modern welfare state, later life has already begun to lose its coherence as a chronologically bound social category. This 'loss of identity' is, we suggest, a phenomenon of late modernity, part of the broader destandardisation of the life course that is taking place in these 'liquid times' (Bauman, 2007). Not only has old age lost its distinct status, its categorical boundaries; ageing itself has ceased to be seen as a process of pre-determined biological decline, ticking away to its own, inimitable timetable. Ageing and old age now appear contingent, rendering later life more uncertain, more unsettling and, at the same time, more pregnant with opportunity. Out of this fluidity and contingency, the fourth age has emerged as a revived and revised 'social imaginary' of 'old' old age, still replete with the distaste, fear and pity that old age has long inspired.

As we have noted earlier, there is much more later life in society and much more to later life than ever before. There are greater numbers of older people – people aged above 60 – and more people of all ages who are confronting ageing and old age. This 'multitude' of age makes generalisations about old age harder to establish and even harder to sustain. The heterogeneity of experience, lifestyle and status in later life has become too difficult to assimilate into the collective consciousness of society. As morbidity and mortality during the first decades of life has declined, the patterning of development has become clearer and more predictable. The opposite has become true for ageing. As paid employment becomes less common for children and adolescents the world over and as education provides an imperative for 'normal development', the moral panics and collective anxieties over childhood and youth now centre on the readiness of today's youth to become the active, healthy and productive older adults of tomorrow. In contrast, for today's older adults there is no unanimity over the timing or the tasks of later life. People's experience of navigating through this period of life has become more diverse and more contradictory. The distinction between participating in post-working life and participating in life outside work has become blurred. Expectations of life are no longer tightly tied to life expectancy. Yet despite the fact that markets, media and the state continually reiterate the mantra that 'older people' are now 'younger', such statements fail to reassure. The new ageing can no doubt put pressure on some and make others feel a failure for feeling so old even as it opens out opportunities of ageing differently for many. The older ways of understanding later life – as old age – still remain hidden in the shadows. They have not left the social imagination; they are just harder to reconcile with the everyday experience and expectations of contemporary later life.

Such residual imaginings of old age frame the fourth age as a negatively charged social imaginary. That is the gist of the argument presented in this book. In introducing the concept of old age as a social imaginary, we have drawn upon the work of two social theorists, Castoriadis (1987) and Taylor (2004). These writers, albeit from different perspectives, have made the social imaginary an important, if contested term in the social sciences as well as in cultural studies (Elliott, 2002; Gaonkar, 2002; Strauss, 2006). The value of the term, which as one writer has pointed out can at times be simply read as 'cultural knowledge in new clothes' (Strauss, 2006: 322) is that it encapsulates how the meaning of so many contemporary social institutions and practices cannot be reduced to or read off by existing structures of power or tradition. It is as if the more liquid the society the more diversely its institutions are understood and the greater scope for imagined communities and commonalities to emerge in a contested space.

Within this context, it becomes culturally and sociologically fruitful to think of the fourth age as a prime example of such a social imaginary, an attempt to re-imagine old age as a new 'institution' whose fluid boundaries are framed by the idea of frailty, whose power lies in its prediction of pervasive decline and whose images of incivility and abjection point to an ever deeper ageing of individuals and society. In exploring this idea, we have argued that while the fourth age has

emerged as a social imaginary fuelled by the fears stoked by the contemporary culture[s] of the third age and the apocalyptic demography
of ageing societies, its meaning reaches back to a historical bedrock
of fear and distaste for the indignities of agedness that have endured
across the centuries.

Frailty – pathway to the fourth age

Contemporary conceptualisations of frailty and its biomedical operationalization has made it a new centre of gravity arising as geriatric
medicine began to lose its place within the health care system and
'care of the elderly infirm' became commoditised and privatised by
increasingly non-medical corporate players. This centralisation of
frailty is not just the consequence of changes within geriatric medicine.
It also echoes the reason societies first provided charity to, and secured
support for old people – help to widows and orphans because they
lacked an adult male to support them and help to those infirm elderly
people whose families were unable to help them. In a similar way to
being orphaned or being widowed, frailty seems to serve as a straight-
forward enough criterion for help and for care. However, if geriatric
medicine is to avoid being relegated to the rules of the old 'poor law'
infirmaries, the search for a new 'biomedical legitimacy' is required.
Hence the investment in establishing frailty's scientific credentials, the
inevitable failure to fully realise them and the consequent expansion
of the imaginary as frailty reverts to being the reason for caring.

Of course, 'old' old age meant more than simple frailty; it contained
the contradictions of its own abjection. While widows and orphans
were seen as weak, vulnerable individuals, there was nothing disgusting about their state; to have lost one's parents or one's husband was
a misfortune, after all, a reason for charity and for pity, even compassion. But infirm old age was less a misfortune, less a reason for pure
pity, let alone compassion. It was instead the mark of man's mortality – man's mortality, for women frailty was otherwise positioned.
Frailty was long gendered its female form indicative of women's
greater inherent fragility and the ephemeral nature of their value as
youth, beauty and fecundity. Implicitly (and often explicitly) old age
was as an undesirable, unpleasant and unattractive state only rendered
sensible by its proximity to death or the experience assumed to accrue
with longer life. Wisdom or spirituality may not have required a fit or
well-formed body, but both qualities nevertheless implied a fit and
well-formed mind.

Loss of capacity – the foolishness of age – marked the boundary between a burdensome and a pathetic old age, between an elder citizen and a senile dotard, between a matron and a crone. Such distinctions and the weight given to them no doubt varied over place and time, but until the modern chronological categorisation of old age, these characterisations served as the blueprint for all subsequent distinctions between the fit and the frail, being the master of one's agedness or being its slave. If senescence was the marker of civilised ageing, senility was that of its sad and ugly failure. It had no redeeming features. It was – is – the pre-cursor of the fourth age. Senility was not measured, the way modern mental status tests assign individuals to categories of incapacity, and it was used loosely until in the mid-twentieth century assessment procedures were gradually introduced into long-term care settings to distinguish formally the unsuccessfully aged from the rest, those who were defined by their need for care from those who were judged capable of representing themselves as other than the 'aged infirm'. Behind these judgements, these distinctions and the imaginaries that they convey lay another factor, the essentially 'social' component of the fourth age – the need for others to care.

The fourth age and the moral imperative to care

In writing of the link between the social imaginary of the fourth age and the moral imperative to care we have argued that care provides the major context for the social realising of the fourth age's imaginary. Care, we argued, gives the fourth age real traction because it both seeks to protect older people from, and at the same time creates the conditions for their entry, to the fourth age. It is commonly believed that until the twentieth century, frail, infirm and incapacitated people were generally treated badly – even within their own families. Institutional care was seen as altogether harsh, unfeeling and based upon a minimum of giving. Yet however harshly provided, people were still taken into care. There was no collective refusal to support, and almshouses, asylums, hospitals and infirmaries and the like were established and maintained for such hapless sick and infirm people. This indicates both the persistence of a moral imperative to care and the contradictions contained within those institutions of care.

In discussing such problems as immobility, incontinence and confusion, we have tried to identify the frequent difficulties faced by those who care – alongside the problems of those who are cared for. Abuse, we have suggested, becomes an inherently potential dimension arising from the contradictory position that such care engenders. While once it was deemed sufficient to provide care, out of charity and pity, the new 'ethic of care' that has emerged during the period of post-1960s 'de-institutionalisation' demands more – a compassionate caring, given equally by the hands, the heart and the head. As this new ethics has been extended to the care given 'under the shadow of the fourth age', more attention is paid to the antithesis of compassionate care – care given without pity, in other words, the cruelties of care.

This concern for the ethics of care has led to a belief that the 'real' problem lies in a failure to recognise personhood among those subject to the fourth age. As a consequence person-centred approaches have been promoted for use in settings where people with dementia are being cared for, and attention has been focused on the 'malignant social psychology' of the social care setting. Researchers such as Kitwood have argued that people with dementia are denied the positionality of personhood, and it was this denial that lay behind many of the difficulties experienced by people with dementia (Kitwood and Bredin, 1992; Kitwood, 1997). However, once again such notions of personhood are attributed to the people concerned rather than asserted by them. Agency still seems out of reach. How this can lead to more compassionate care remains a moot point and one which brings us back to the social imaginary of the fourth age.

How does an imaginary become socially realised? The question of 'who whom'?

Expectations have material consequences. The existence and form of the fourth age's social imaginary affects the lives of all those who come under its shadow, whether as elderly patients in hospital, residents in nursing homes, relatives, partners and friends of infirm older people at home or in care, as well as community nurses, home care workers, social workers, physicians and surgeons – the list is long and getting longer as the care sector evolves in line with society's expectations. But do we need to go beyond examining the material consequences of this particular cultural imaginary to explore its social construction – its role in the structures of power and influence within society – hence our use of Lenin's famous question – 'who whom?' (Lenin quoted in Žižek, 2001:113–114) at the beginning of this section. Is the fourth age a social imaginary fashioned by more than a universal fear of 'ageing out of control' and the corporeality of ageing – is it also a social imaginary constructed through systems of power and organised by political institutions to the benefit of some and the cost of others?

In our second chapter on the institutions of long-term care, we pointed out how the transition from the alms-house to the workhouse affected the standing of age and frailty within society, in part because of the status of those admitted into these very different institutions. Granted that the residents of the alms-houses were not only the 'genteel poor', but also in many cases less frail, less dependent on help in the activities of daily living and perhaps also less aged, is it possible to view the association between lack of status, want and need and 'ending up' in the workhouse infirmary as establishing a class and power differential such that those abject inmates in the black hole of the infirmary were tainted by the scandal of pauperism? Using Bataille's terms, the inmates of the infirmaries were representatives of Victorian society's abject classes, looked after by others rendered similarly abject by their close association with the aged sick of the workhouse.

The demise of the workhouse and its disappearance from the collective imagination during the 'golden decades' of the post-war welfare state suggests that any such links rest more upon the cultural lag of history than on the contemporary ordering of class. Means and Smith have noted how the period between 1942 and 1948 witnessed a major reform in long-term residential care for elderly people in England (1998: 70–80) from public assistance institution to small- and medium-sized 'hotel-like' institutions as required by the 1948 National Assistance Act, open to all those deemed aged and in need, irrespective of rank and income. In Scandinavia, a similar attempt was made to break the association between long-term institutional care for older people and poor relief so that old people's homes should 'cease to be homes for the poor and instead be open to all old people in need of care, regardless of their private economy' (Edebalk, 2009: 9).

Even after these reforms, social factors continued to influence which category of elderly person ended up in institutional settings. Townsend's (1981) classic paper on the social creation of dependency in later life argued that lack of resources – familial as well as financial – played a large part in determining admission into Britain's old age homes in the 1960s and 1970s as did physical incapacity. Similar findings were reported in the US. Reviewing research conducted in the 1960s and early 1970s in America, Dunlop (1976), like Townsend, concluded that two groups of social factors influenced admission to institutions – lack of social resources and lack of financial resources. He summarised his findings thus: 'The possession of familial or financial resources keeps many elderly persons from ever entering an institution and postpones the day of admission for many others' (82). Other studies of the time reached similar conclusions. Examining US nursing home admissions data from the mid-1960s, Vicente and her colleagues concluded that 'The association between factors such as old age and poverty, on the one hand, and increased risk of institutionalization on the other, indicate that medical need may not be the sole or even major determinant of entry or length of stay in nursing homes' (1979: 367).

Clearly the disruption of the link between financial and physical neediness sought by the post-war welfare state failed to achieve its goal, and admission to nursing homes or residential homes continued to be marked by distinctions in social rank as much as in physical dependency. But as the golden decades of welfare faded, new research emerged suggesting that social inequalities influenced physical functioning itself, in later life, implying that those who grew old in relative poverty were also rendered less resilient and physically frailer than those whose life had not been limited by lack (Cambois, Robine and Hayward, 2001; Chandola et al., 2007; Lynch, Kaplan and Shema, 1997). Such research tended however to emphasise differences in disability in 'early old age'. When extended to the later years (e.g., after age 75), there seemed less consistent evidence of the effects of socio-economic inequality (Beckett, 2000; Herd, 2006). Relative inequalities in mortality do seem to decrease with age, while absolute inequalities increase; the debate still rages (Huisman et al., 2004; 2005).

But if one compares research into the predictors of long-term institutional care in the last couple of decades (1990–2010) with that from the 1960s and 1970s, it is clear that the effect of poverty – low income – on nursing home admission has declined markedly, while the influence of family support – living alone or with family – remains. Most important of all in predicting entry into institutional care in the twenty-first century are age and dementia. Does this then mean that the infirmity and neediness associated with institutional care has ceased to be socially structured? Has the influence of class, poverty and social disadvantage faded, under the more all encompassing shadows of infirmity and sheer agedness? We have argued that this is indeed so, even though the idea of 'ending up in care' has itself lost none of the dread that was once attached to the workhouse and its infirmary (Gilleard and Higgs, 2011b).

Indeed it could be argued that the dread of ending up in care has grown as it becomes less socially structured and more widely shared by the misfortune of rich and poor alike, in the dubious democracy of Alzheimer's. Though there is no doubt that there are inequalities in nursing home care and in the quality of the long-term care environment, for the majority of older people even the most luxuriously appointed nursing home scarcely seems preferable to a place that one can nevertheless still call 'home'. Of course, there are limits to such comparisons. It would be egregious to deny that the indignities of a lonely life lived with extreme physical dependency in an inaccessible top floor flat in a deprived urban neighbourhood might well render a person worse off – both as a citizen and as a human being – compared with living in a comfortable assisted living apartment outside Copenhagen, Oslo or Stockholm.

But do not social circumstances play a 'hidden' role in the onset and progress of infirmity in old age? Have we too easily skipped over the social determinants of mental and physical frailty – ignoring, for example, the effects of education, occupation and gender on the incidence of cancer and heart disease, on dementia and diabetes, on liver and kidney disease, and on Parkinson's disease and stroke? Given that dementia offers the greatest likelihood of admission into long-term institutional care – that is,nursing homes or their equivalent – should we have been more mindful of the role that social factors play in this particular infirmity – that is the onset and progression of Alzheimer's and related neurological diseases?

The fourth age and the social structure of dementia

Some time ago, a book was published with the provocative title '*The Social Construction of Dementia*' (Harding and Palfrey, 1997). In their book, the authors argued that the apocalyptic demography of dementia leads to a view of the 'demented' as needing to be controlled either 'within the walls of institutions' or through the less expensive option of 'community care' (143). The 'demented' are represented as the poor ones were, but with a reverse direction of travel observe – from indoor to outdoor 'relief'. But while there is plenty of evidence of the social structuring of the workhouse population as well as the inmates of the public assistance institutions and local authority homes that followed (Townsend, 1962), there is very little evidence in the twenty-first century of class inequalities among those admitted with a diagnosis of dementia into the nursing and residential care sector. Even the incidence of dementia, let alone admission into care, seems unrelated to one's socio-economic position in early mid or even later working life, although educational level might be influential (Karp et al., 2004).

Nevertheless there has been a growing interest in the idea of 'preventing' Alzheimer's disease, fuelled by the steady deflation over the last decade in the anti-dementia drug enthusiasm that was so prevalent during the last decade of the twentieth century (cf. Kachaturian et al., 2008; Imtiaz et al., 2014; Solomon et al., 2014). However few writers have implied that a reduction in socio-economic inequality, the amelioration of lifelong economic disadvantage or improved welfare might form a basis for such strategies, which rely instead upon the usual '*res non natura*' – diet, exercise, fresh air (not smoking) and the cultivation of contentment. Strategies to reduce the risk of institutionalisation have also ignored such radical possibilities, focusing instead upon the protection and nurturance of 'social bonds' through caregiver 'education', 'support' and 'family therapy' (Spijker et al., 2008).

Another more radical alternative has now been promoted in Sweden. This is simply to eliminate the concept of a nursing home altogether, reclassifying 'institutional care' as 'assisted living'. Whether the bad press that followed Sweden's earlier privatisation and retrenchment of institutional care for infirm elderly citizens (Kemeny, 2005) has played any part in this re-framing of care is difficult to know, but one can only admire the boldness of this 'linguistic' turn: social construction deconstructed, Scandinavian style. However, it is our contention that because both social constructionist accounts of dementia and structural deterministic accounts of dementia do not provide a convincing account of the issues involved in understanding the condition that we need to see it as better understood through the idea of the fourth age.

Fourth age studies: the value of pursuing the fourth age

Where does focussing on the fourth age take us? The backdrop to this book is the extensively commented upon phenomenon of population ageing and the idea that a deeper and darker old age is beginning to overshadow the enthusiasm over the third age that first emerged toward the end of the twentieth century. Consequently, we have concentrated on old age's representation in the social imaginary of the fourth age. We have done so knowing that any adequate understanding of later life has nevertheless to consider this in the context of the third age. The considerable social and cultural changes that mark postworking life in the twenty-first century have rendered many of the traditional approaches to old age obsolete. It is no longer possible to see the older population primarily in terms of their 'roleless roles'; their 'disengagement'; or indeed their 'structured dependency' (Higgs and Jones, 2009). The diversity of the 'cultures of ageing', as we put it in an earlier book, have meant that later life can no longer be represented by old age or as a residual category of social and health policy. It has become a much more complex phenomenon and even social and health policies are adapting to the changing context of later life. Twenty years ago it was still possible for international bodies and national governments to believe that they could stay in control of pension regimes and health care policies; in the contemporary environment, such hopes seem overly ambitious. The virtue of what could be described as 'third age studies 'is that it accepts this reflexively charged contingency about age and seeks to understand it rather than trying to categorise it and return it to the 'safer' processes of social administration. Following this approach has meant that many new areas of study have opened up in order to deal with the 'accepted truths' of older people's lives. These have included areas such as consumption and expenditure; leisure and sport; tourism and travel; interpersonal relationships and sexuality.

The creation of a parallel 'fourth age studies' can similarly take the study of ageing and later life forward, looking at some of gerontology's and geriatric medicine's traditional themes in a different light. The changing nature of old age affects equally on those who might be understood as experiencing 'real' old age as it does on those who are busy 'successfully' ageing. This does not mean, however, that present circumstances are the same as those who were in similar situations in previous decades. As we have tried to show, the power of the social imaginary of the fourth age has considerable consequences for positioning the vulnerability of highly dependent older people – through the assessment of frailty, the targeting of the most sick and the resulting densification of disability and the elaboration of narratives of care that are daily dissonant with the logics of practice. The purpose of fourth age studies is not simply to describe and delineate the parameters of this social and cultural imaginary; it is also about identifying the pervasive power of the fourth age and finding ways to challenge or subvert it. By being more aware of its operations, and the traps that it offers to 'solve' what are often insoluble problems, policy makers and practitioners as well as older people and their families can have some chance of mitigating – even undermining – its more baleful and negative effects. Only by confronting the abject and tragic aspects of age and its infirmities, and recognising the capacity for those who care as well as those who are the object of care to be pulled into the otherness of the fourth age, can there be any chance of rendering the fourth age more tractable and more contingent.

The moral imperative to care is part of this social imaginary. Just as caring derives from the imaginary of the fourth age, so it also shapes it. Between the abstractions of policy and the abjections of practice lie the everyday un-successes of age and the ignominies that accompany the struggle to care. Even if these problems cannot be 'solved', we can still seek to understand how those deemed frail are frequently further failed and how, in Beckett's (2009) words, we can learn to 'fail better'. This struggle to confront, optimistically, what Trilling called 'the essential immitability of the human condition' represents a crucial part in any programme of fourth age studies (Trilling, 1972). What such studies should not be about however is descrying the existence of the fourth age seeking an alternative by re-naming or re-labelling it with kinder words or seeking to eliminate its power by denying opportunities for third age cultures to flourish. The route of those advocating a 'moral economy' approach often only seems to diminish human potential at all ages. Instead, we would argue that we must persist in contesting abjection while acknowledging the humanity behind frailty. Fourth age studies, we would contend, is a way of realising that agenda.

References

Aarons, H. J., Bosworth, B. & Burtless, G. (1989). *Can America Afford to Grow Old? Paying for Social Security.* Washington, DC: Brookings Institution.

Ablitt, A., Jones, G. V. & Muers, J. (2009). Living with Dementia: A Systematic Review of the Influence of Relationship Factors. *Aging & Mental Health,* 13(4), 497–511.

Achenbaum, W. A. (1986). *Social Security: Visions and Revisions.* New York: Cambridge University Press.

Aciemo, R., Hernandez, M. A., Amstadter, A. B., Resnick, H. S., Steve, K., Muzzy, W. & Kilpatrick, D. G. (2010). Prevalence and Correlates of Emotional, Physical, Sexual, and Financial Abuse and Potential Neglect in the United States: The National Elder Mistreatment Study. *American Journal of Public Health,* 100(2), 292–297.

Adams, T. M. (1990). *Bureaucrats and Beggars: French Social Policy in the Age of the Enlightenment.* New York: Oxford University Press.

Adelman, R. C. (1995). The Alzheimerization of aging. *The Gerontologist,* 35(4), 526–532.

Agüero-Torres, H., Fratiglioni, L., Guo, Z., Viitanen, M., von Strauss, E. & Winblad, B. (1998). Dementia Is the Major Cause of Functional Dependence in the Elderly: 3-Year Follow-Up Data from a Population-Based Study. *American Journal of Public Health,* 88(10), 1452–1456.

Agüero-Torres, H., von Strauss, E., Viitanen, M., Winblad, B. & Fratiglioni, L. (2001). Institutionalization in the Elderly: The Role of Chronic Diseases and Dementia. Cross-Sectional and Longitudinal Data from a Population-Based Study. *Journal of Clinical Epidemiology,* 54(8), 795–801.

Aiken, L. H., Sloane, D. M., Cimiotti, J. P., Clarke, S. P., Flynn, L., Seago, J. A., Spetz, J. & Smith H. L. (2010). Implications of the California Nurse Staffing Mandate for Other States. *Health Services Research,* 45(4), 904–921.

Aitola, P., Lehto, K., Fonsell, R. & Huhtala, H. (2010). Prevalence of Faecal Incontinence in Adults Aged 30 Years or More in General Population. *Colorectal Disease,* 12(7), 687–691.

Akpan, A., Gosney, M. A. & Barrett, J. (2006). Privacy for Defecation and Fecal Incontinence in Older Adults. *Journal of Wound Ostomy & Continence Nursing,* 33(5), 536–540.

Al-Ameel, T., Andrew, M. K. & MacKnight, C. (2010). The Association of Fecal Incontinence with Institutionalization and Mortality in Older Adults. *The American Journal of Gastroenterology,* 105(8), 1830–1834.

Albæk, K., Andersen, T. M., Asplund, R., Erling, B., Bratsberg, B., Calmfors, L., Kauhanen A., et al. (2014). *The Nordic Model–Challenged but Capable of Reform.* Copenhagen: Nordisk Ministerråd.

Allen, S. M., Lima, J. C., Goldscheider, F. K. & Roy, J. (2012). Primary Caregiver Characteristics and Transitions in Community-Based Care. *The Journals of Gerontology Series B: Psychological Sciences and Social Sciences*, 67(3), 362–371.

Alvarado, B. E., Zunzunegui, M. V., Béland, F. & Bamvita, J. M. (2008). Life Course Social and Health Conditions Linked to Frailty in Latin American Older Men and Women. *The Journals of Gerontology Series A: Biological Sciences and Medical Sciences*, 63(12), 1399–1406.

Andersen, S. L., Sebastiani, P., Dworkis, D. A., Feldman, L. & Perls, T. T. (2012). Health Span Approximates Life Span Among Many Supercentenarians: Compression of Morbidity at the Approximate Limit of Life Span. *The Journals of Gerontology Series A: Biological Sciences and Medical Sciences*, 67(4), 395–405.

Anderson, B. (1983). *Imagined Communities*. London: Verso.

Annerstedt, L., ElmstÅhl, S., Ingvad, B. & Samuelsson, S. M. (2000). An Analysis of the Caregiver's Burden and the "Breaking-Point" when Home Care becomes Inadequate. *Scandinavian Journal of Public Health*, 28(1), 23–31.

Arie, T. & Jolley, D. (1983). 'The Rising Tide'. *British Medical Journal*, 286(6362), 325–326.

Aronson, J. & Neysmith, S. M. (1996). 'YOU'RE NOT JUST IN THERE TO DO THE WORK': Depersonalizing Policies and the Exploitation of Home Care Workers' Labor. *Gender & Society*, 10(1), 59–77.

Ata, T., Terada, S., Yokota, O., Ishihara, T., Fujisawa, Y., Sasaki, K. & Kuroda, S. (2010). Wandering and Fecal Smearing in People with Dementia. *International Psychogeriatrics*, 22(03), 493–500.

Baars, J. (2012). *Aging and the Art of Living*. Baltimore, MD: Johns Hopkins University Press.

Baker, R. & McCullough, L. B. (2007). Medical Ethics' Appropriation of Moral Philosophy: The Case of the Sympathetic and the Unsympathetic Physician. *Kennedy Institute of Ethics Journal*, 17(1), 3–22.

Baltes, M. M. (1998). The Psychology of the Oldest-Old: The Fourth Age. *Current Opinion in Psychiatry*, 11(4), 411–415.

Baltes, P. B. & Smith, J. (2003). New Frontiers in the Future of Aging: From Successful Aging of the Young Old to the Dilemmas of the Fourth Age. *Gerontology*, 49(2), 123–135.

Barer, M. L., Evans, R. G., Hertzman, C. & Lomas, J. (1987). Aging and Health Care Utilization: New Evidence on Old Fallacies. *Social Science & Medicine*, 24(10), 851–862.

Barlow, J. H., Turner, A. P. & Wright, C. C. (2000). A Randomized Controlled Study of the Arthritis Self-Management Programme in the UK. *Health Education Research*, 15(6), 665–680.

Bartlett, R. & O'Connor, D. (2007). From Personhood to Citizenship: Broadening the Lens for Dementia Practice and Research. *Journal of Aging Studies*, 21(2), 107–118.

Bataille, G. (1999). Abjection and Miserable Forms. In S. Lotringer (ed.), *More & Less*. Cambridge, MA: MIT Press, 8–13.

Bauer, J. M. & Sieber, C. C. (2008). Sarcopenia and Frailty: A Clinician's Controversial Point of View. *Experimental Gerontology*, 43(7), 674–678.

Bauman, Z. (2007). *Liquid Times*. Cambridge: Polity Press.

Baylis, D., Bartlett, D. B., Syddall, H. E., Ntani, G., Gale, C. R., Cooper, C., Lord, J.M. & Sayer, A. A. (2013). Immune-endocrine biomarkers as predictors of frailty and mortality: a 10-year longitudinal study in community-dwelling older people. *Age*, 35(3), 963–971.

Beck, U. & Lau, C. (2005). Second Modernity as a Research Agenda: Theoretical and Empirical Explorations in the 'Meta-Change' of Modern Society. *The British Journal of Sociology*, 56(4) 525–557.

Beckett, M. (2000). Converging Health Inequalities in Later Life – an Artifact of Mortality Selection? *Journal of Health and Social Behavior*, 41(1), 106–119.

Beckett, S. (2009). Worstward Ho!, in *Company, Ill Seen Ill Said, Worstward Ho, Stirrings Still*. London: Faber and Faber.

Beier, A. L. (1985). *Masterless Men: The Vagrancy Problem in England 1560–1640*. London: Methuen.

Beringer T. R. O., Crawford V. L. S., Montgomery A. & Gilmore D. H. (2003). Institutional Care for Elderly People in North and West Belfast: A Decade of Change from 1989–1999. *Ageing Clinical and Experimental Research*, 15(1), 38–42.

Bharucha, A. E., Zinsmeister, A. R., Locke, G. R., Seide, B. M., McKeon, K., Schleck, C. D. & Melton III, L. J. (2005). Prevalence and Burden of Fecal Incontinence: A Population-Based Study in Women. *Gastroenterology*, 129(1), 42–49.

Bharucha, A. J., Pandav, R., Shen, C., Dodge, H. H. & Ganguli, M. (2004). Predictors of Nursing Facility Admission: A 12-Year Epidemiological Study in the United States. *Journal of the American Geriatrics Society*, 52(3), 434–439.

Bishop, C. E. (1999). Where Are the Missing Elders? The Decline in Nursing Home Use, 1985 and 1995. *Health Affairs*, 18(4), 146–155.

Black B., Muralee S. & Tampi R. R. (2005). Inappropriate Sexual Behaviors in Dementia. *Journal of Geriatric Psychiatry and Neurology*, 18(2), 155–162.

Blasi, A. (1983). Moral Cognition and Moral Action: A Theoretical Perspective. *Developmental Review*, 3(2), 178–210.

Blieszner, R. & Shifflet, P. A. (1990). The Effects of Alzheimer's Disease on Close Relationships between Patients and Caregivers. *Family Relations*, 39(1), 57–62.

Blomqvist, P. (2004). The Choice Revolution: Privatization of Swedish Welfare Services in the 1990s. *Social Policy & Administration*, 38(2), 139–155.

Boas, F. & Michelson, N. (1932). The Graying of Hair. *American Journal of Physical Anthropology*, 17(2), 213–228.

Bonifacio, G. L. A. T. (2008). I Care for You, Who Cares for Me? Transitional Services of Filipino Live-in Caregivers in Canada. *Asian Women*, 24(1), 25–50.

Bortz, W. (2010). Understanding Frailty. *Journals of Gerontology: Medical Science*, 65A, 255–256.

Boyd, M., Bowman, C., Broad, J. B. & Connolly, M. J. (2012). International Comparison of Long-Term Care Resident Dependency across Four Countries (1998–2009): A Descriptive Study. *Australasian Journal on Ageing*, 31(4), 233–240.

Boyd, M., Broad, J. B., Kerse, N., Foster, S., von Randow, M., Lay-Yee, R., Chelimo, C., Whitehead, N. & Connolly, M. J. (2011). Twenty-Year Trends in Dependency in Residential Aged Care in Auckland, New Zealand: A Descriptive Study. *Journal of the American Medical Directors Association*, 12(7), 535–540.

Boylstein, C. (2012). Reconstructing Marital Closeness while Caring for a Spouse with Alzheimer's. *Journal of Family Issues*, 33(5), 584–612.

Bowman, C. E. Whistler J. E. & Ellerby, M. (2004). A National Census of Care Home Residents. *Age and Ageing*, 33(6), 561–566.

Breyer, F., Costa-Font, J. & Felder, S. (2010). Ageing, Health, and Health Care. *Oxford Review of Economic Policy*, 26(4), 674–690.

Broad, J. B., Boyd, M., Kerse, N., Whitehead, N., Chelimo, C., Lay-Yee, R., von Randow, M., Foster, S. & Connolly, M. J. (2011). Residential Aged Care in Auckland, New Zealand 1988–2008: Do Real Trends Over Time Match Predictions? *Age and Ageing*, 40(4), 487–494.

Brocklehurst, J. C. (1967). The Management of Incontinence. *Postgraduate Medical Journal*, 43(502), 527–533.

Brookmeyer, R., Johnson, E., Ziegler-Graham, K. & Arrighi, H. M. (2007). Forecasting the Global Burden of Alzheimer's Disease. *Alzheimer's & Dementia*, 3(3), 186–191.

Brundage, A. (2002). *The English Poor Laws, 1700–1930*. Basingstoke: Palgrave Macmillan.

Brunk, J. M. (2007). *Frailty: Meaningful Concept Or Conceptual Muddle?* (Doctoral dissertation, Miami University, Ohio).

Burgess, E. W. (1960). Aging in Western Culture. In E. W. Burgess (ed.), *Aging in Western Societies*. Chicago: University of Chicago Press, 4–28.

Cahen, L. (1904). *Le Grand Bureau des Pauvres de Paris au milieu du XVIIIe siecle*. Paris : Bibliotheque d'Histoire Moderne, I(iii), 436–512.

Cai, L. & Lubitz, J. (2007). Was There Compression of Disability for Older Americans from 1992 to 2003? *Demography*, 44(3), 479–495.

Calasanti, T. & King, N. (2011). A Feminist Lens of the Third Age: Refining the Framework. In D. Carr & K. Komp (eds), *Gerontology in the Era of the Third Age*. New York: Springer, 67–85.

Callan, E. (1988). The Moral Status of Pity. *Canadian Journal of Philosophy*, 18(1), 1–12.

Cambois, E., Robine, J. M. & Hayward, M. D. (2001). Social Inequalities in Disability-Free Life Expectancy in the French Male Population, 1980–1991. *Demography*, 38(4), 513–524.

Carandang, R., Seshadri, S., Beiser, A., Kelly-Hayes, M., Kase, C. S., Kannel, W. B. & Wolf, P. A. (2006). Trends in incidence, lifetime risk, severity, and 30-day mortality of stroke over the past 50 years. *JAMA*, 296(24), 2939–2946.

Carr, B. (1999). Pity and Compassion as Social Virtues. *Philosophy*, 74(3), 411–429.

Cartwright, D. E. (1988). Schopenhauer's Compassion and Nietzsche's Pity. *Schopenhauer Jahrbuch*, 69, 557–567.

Casale-Martínez, R. I., Navarrete-Reyes, A. P. and Ávila-Funes, J. A. (2012), Social Determinants of Frailty in Elderly Mexican Community-Dwelling Adults. *Journal of the American Geriatrics Society*, 60, 800–802.

Castle, N. G. (1998). Physical Restraints in Nursing Homes: A Review of the Literature Since the Nursing Home Reform Act of 1987. *Medical Care Research and Review*, 55(2), 139–170.

Castoriadis, C. (1987). *The Imaginary Institution of Society*. Cambridge: Polity Press.

Cavallo, S. (1990). Patterns of poor-relief and patterns of poverty in eighteenth-century Italy: the evidence of the Turin Ospedale di Carità. *Continuity and Change*, 5(1), 65–98.

Chandola, T., Ferrie, J., Sacker, A. & Marmot, M. (2007). Social Inequalities in Self-Reported Health in Early Old Age: Follow-Up of Prospective Cohort Study. *British Medical Journal*, 334(7601), 990.

Chen, C. K., Uzdawinis, D., Schölmerich, A. & Juckel, G. (2014). Effects of Attachment Quality on Caregiving of a Parent with Dementia. *The American Journal of Geriatric Psychiatry*, 22(6), 623–631.

Chief Medical Officer. (1928). *Annual Report of the Chief Medical Officer, 1928*. London: Ministry of Health, HMSO.

Cialdini, R. B., Brown, S. L., Lewis, B. P., Luce, C. & Neuberg, S. L. (1997). Reinterpreting the Empathy–Altruism Relationship: When One into One Equals Oneness. *Journal of Personality and Social Psychology*, 73(3), 481–494.

Clark, R. L. & Spengler, J. J. (1980). *The Economics of Individual and Population Aging*. Cambridge: Cambridge University Press.

Clarke, J., Gewirtz, S., McLaughlin, E. (2000). *New Managerialism, New Welfare?* London: Sage.

Cohen-Mansfield J., Marx M. S. & Rosenthal, A. S. (1989). A Description of Agitation in a Nursing Home. *Journals of Gerontology: Medical Sciences*, 44, M77–M84.

Collard, R. M., Boter, H., Schoevers, R. A. & Oude Voshaar, R. C. (2012). Prevalence of Frailty in Community-Dwelling Older Persons: A Systematic Review. *Journal of the American Geriatrics Society*, 60(8), 1487–1492.

Collerton, J., Martin-Ruiz, C., Davies, K., Hilkens, C. M., Isaacs, J., Kolenda, C. & Kirkwood, T. B. (2012). Frailty and the Role of Inflammation, Immunosenescence and Cellular Ageing in the Very Old: Cross-Sectional Findings from the Newcastle 85+ Study. *Mechanisms of Ageing and Development*, 133(6), 456–466.

Colombo, F., Llena-Nozel, A., Mercier, J. & Tjadens, F. (2011). Long-Term Care Workers: Needed but Often Undervalued. In (eds) C. Francesca, L.N. Ana, M.

Jérôme & T. Frits. *Help Wanted? Providing and Paying for Long-Term Care*. Paris: OECD Publishing (http://dx.doi.org/10.1787/9789264097759-10-en, accessed 31 March 2014).

Costa, D. L. (2000). Understanding the Twentieth-Century Decline in Chronic Conditions Among Older Men. *Demography*, 37(1), 53–72.

——. (2002). Changing Chronic Disease Rates and Long Term Declines in Functional Limitation Among Older Men. *Demography*, 39(1), 119–138.

——. (2005). Causes of Improving Health and Longevity at Older Ages: A Review of the Explanations. *Genus*, 51(1), 21–38.

Covino, D. C. (2000). Abject Criticism. *Genders*, 32(2), 3.

Cowgill, D. O. & Holmes, L. D. (1972). *Aging and Modernization*. New York: Appleton-Century-Crofts.

Cruz-Jentoft, A. J., Baeyens, J. P., Bauer, J. M., Boirie, Y., Cederholm, T., Landi, F. & Zamboni, M. (2010). Sarcopenia: European Consensus on Definition and Diagnosis Report of the European Working Group on Sarcopenia in Older People. *Age and Ageing*, 39(4), 412–423.

Cruz-Jentoft, A. J. & Michel, J. P. (2013). Sarcopenia: A Useful Paradigm for Physical Frailty. *European Geriatric Medicine*, 4(2), 102–105.

Cullum, P. H. (1991). *Cremetts and Corrodies: Care of the Poor and Sick at St. Leonard's Hospital, York, in the Middle Ages*. Borthwick Publications, no. 79, York: Borthwick Institute.

Daatland, S. O. (1985). Managing Everyday Life: The Trivial Round Made Significant. In A. Butler (ed.), *Aging: Recent Advances and Creative Responses*. London: Croom Helm, 67–77.

Daniels, Ramon, van Rossum, Erik, de Witte, Luc, Kempen, Gertrudis, I. J. M. & den Heuvel, Wim van. (2008). Interventions to Prevent Disability in Frail Community-Dwelling Elderly: A Systematic Review. *BMC Health Services Research*, 8, 278. doi: 10.1186/1472-6963-8-278.

Davey, J. & Glasgow, K. (2006). Positive Ageing: A Critical Analysis. *Policy Quarterly*, 2(4), 21–27.

De Beauvoir, S. (1977). *Old Age*. (Trans. P. O'Brien), Harmondsworth: Penguin Books.

Decker, F. H. (2005). *Nursing Homes, 1977–1999: What Has Changed, What Has Not?* Washington: National Center for Health Statistics. (http://www.cdc.gov/nchs/data/nnhsd/NursingHomes1977_99.pdf, accessed 3/2/2013).

de Grey, A. D. (2008). Rejuvenation Research in 2007. *Rejuvenation Research*, 11(4), 837–839.

de la Maisonneuve, C. & Martins J. O. (2013). A Projection Method for Public Health and Long-Term Care Expenditures, *OECD Economics Department Working Papers, No. 1048*, OECD Publishing, Paris. (http://dx.doi.org/10.1787/5k44v53w5w47-en)

Del-Pino-Casado, R., Frias-Osuna, A. & Palomino-Moral, P. A. (2011). Subjective Burden and Cultural Motives for Caregiving in Informal Caregivers of Older People. *Journal of Nursing Scholarship*, 43(3), 282–291.

de Meijera, C., Koopmanschapa, M. Bago d' Uvac, T. & van Doorslaera, E. (2011). Determinants of Long-Term Care Spending: Age, Time to Death or Disability? *Journal of Health Economics*, 30(2011), 425–438.

de Rijke, J. M., Schouten, L. J., Hillen, H. F., Kiemeney, L. A., Coebergh, J. W. W. & van den Brandt, P. A. (2000). Cancer in the Very Elderly Dutch Population. *Cancer*, 89(5), 1121–1133.

Dillaway, H. E. & Byrnes, M. (2009). Reconsidering Successful Aging a Call for Renewed and Expanded Academic Critiques and Conceptualizations. *Journal of Applied Gerontology*, 28(6), 702–722.

Dilnot Commission. (2011). *Commission on Funding of Care and Support*. London: Department of Health.

Diokno, A. C., Brock, B. M., Brown, M. B. & Herzog, A. R. (1986). Prevalence of Urinary Incontinence and Other Urological Symptoms in the Noninstitutionalized Elderly. *The Journal of Urology*, 136(5), 1022–1025.

Doblhammer, G. & Kytir, J. (2001). Compression or Expansion of Morbidity? Trends in Healthy-Life Expectancy in the Elderly Austrian Population between 1978 and 1998. *Social Science & Medicine*, 52(3), 385–391.

Dormont, B., Grignon, M. & Huber, H. (2006). Health Expenditure Growth: Reassessing the Threat of Ageing. *Health Economics*, 15(9), 947–963.

Douglas, M. (1988). *Purity and Danger*. London: Routledge Kegan & Paul.

Dowd, J. J. (1975). Aging as Exchange: A Preface to Theory. *Journal of Gerontology*, 30(5), 584–594.

——. (1980). Exchange Rates and Old People. *Journal of Gerontology*, 35(4), 596–602.

Doyle, M. & Timonen, V. (2007). *Home Care for Ageing Populations: A Comparative Analysis of Domiciliary Care in Denmark, the United States and Germany*. Cheltenham: Edward Elgar Publishing.

Dunkin, J. J. & Anderson-Hanley, C. (1998). Dementia Caregiver Burden: A Review of the Literature and Guidelines for Assessment and Intervention. *Neurology*, 51(1), S53–S60.

Dunlop, B. (1976). Need for and Utilization of Long-Term Care Among Elderly Americans. *Journal of Chronic Diseases*, 29(2), 79–87.

Dupre, M. E., Liu, G. & Gu, D. (2008). Predictors of longevity: Evidence from the oldest old in China. *American Journal of Public Health*, 98(7), 1203–1208.

Edebalk, P. G. (2009). From Poor Relief to Universal Rights: On the Development of Swedish Old-Age Care, 1900–1950. *Lunds Universitet Socialhogskolan Working Paper Series 2009: 3*, Lund University, Lund.

Edwards, B. K., Howe, H. L., Ries, L. A. G., Thun, M. J., Rosenberg, H. M., Yancik, R., Wingo, P. A., Jemal, A. & Feigal E. G. (2002). Annual Report to the Nation on the Status of Cancer, 1973–1999, Featuring Implications of Age and Aging on US Cancer Burden. *Cancer*, 94(10), 2766–2792.

Edwards, C. (1999). Age-Based Rationing of Medical Care in Nineteenth Century England. *Continuity and Change*, 14(2), 227–265.

Elliott, A. (2002). The Social Imaginary: A Critical Assessment of Castoriadis's Psychoanalytic Social Theory. *American Imago*, 59(2), 141–170.

El Safoury, O. S. & Ibrahim, M. (2011). A Clinical Evaluation of Skin Tags in Relation to Obesity, Type 2 Diabetes Mellitus, Age, and Sex. *Indian Journal of Dermatology*, 56(4), 393.

Englander, D. (1998). *Poverty and Poor Law Reform in 19th Century Britain, 1834–1914: From Chadwick to Booth*. London: Routledge.

Erikson, E. H. (1963). *Childhood and Society* (Revised edition). New York: W. W. Norton.

—. (1968). *Identity: Youth and Crisis*. New York: W. W. Norton.

Esser, D. E. & Ward, P. S. (2013). Ageing as a Global Public Health Challenge: From Complexity Reduction to Aid Effectiveness. *Global Public Health: An international journal of research, policy and practice*, 8(7), 745–768.

Estes, C. L. & Associates. (2001). *Social Policy and Aging: A Critical Perspective*. Thousand Oaks, CA: Sage.

Estes, C. L. & Mahakian, J. L. (2001). The political economy of productive aging. In (eds) N. Morrow-Howell, J. Hinterlong & M. Sherraden, *Productive Aging: Concepts and Challenges*, (197–213), Baltimore: John Hopkins University Press..

Etman, A., Burdorf, A., Van der Cammen, T. J., Mackenbach, J. P. & Van Lenthe, F. J. (2012). Socio-Demographic Determinants of Worsening in Frailty Among Community-Dwelling Older People in 11 European Countries. *Journal of Epidemiology and Community Health*, 66(12), 1116–1121.

Ewart, C. T. (1910). Eugenics and Degeneracy. *Journal of Mental Science*, 56(235), 678–679.

Falkner, T. M. & De Luce, J. (eds). (1989). *Old age in Greek and Latin literature*. New York: SUNY Press.

Feeney, B. C. (2007). The Dependency Paradox in Close Relationships: Accepting Dependence Promotes Independence. *Journal of Personality and Social Psychology*, 92(2), 268–285.

Felder, S., Werblow, A. & Zweifel, P. (2010). Do Red Herrings Swim in Circles? Controlling for the Endogeneity of Time to Death. *Journal of Health Economics*, 29(2), 205–212.

Feller, E. (2000). L'Assistance républicaine aux vieillards : de l'assistance obligatoire (1905) au fonds national de solidarité (1956). *Bulletin d'Histoire de la Sécurité Sociale*, vol. 38, (July 1998), 4–39.

Felson, D. T., Naimark, A., Anderson, J., Kazis, L., Castelli, W. & Meenan, R. F. (1987). The Prevalence of Knee Osteoarthritis in the Elderly: The Framingham Osteoarthritis Study. *Arthritis & Rheumatism*, 30(8), 914–918.

Finch, J. (1989). *Family Obligations and Social Change*. Cambridge: Polity Press.

Fine, M. & Glendinning, C. (2005). Dependence, Independence or Inter-Dependence? Revisiting the Concepts of 'Care' and 'Dependency'. *Ageing and Society*, 25(04), 601–621.

Fine, M. D. & Mitchell, A. (2007). Immigration and the Aged Care Workforce in Australia: Meeting the Deficit. *Australasian Journal on Ageing*, 26(4), 157–161.

Fischer, D. H. (1978). *Growing Old In America*. New York: Oxford University Press.

Fisher, A. L. (2005). Just What Defines Frailty? *Journal of the American Geriatrics Society*, 53, 2229–2230.

Fisk, E. L. (1926). Old Age Must Come...(Correspondence). *The Lancet*, 17 April, p. 844.

Floyd, K. C., Yarzebski, J., Spencer, F. A., Lessard, D., Dalen, J. E., Alpert, J. S.,Gore, J.M. & Goldberg, R. J. (2009). A 30-Year Perspective (1975–2005) into the Changing Landscape of Patients Hospitalized with Initial Acute Myocardial Infarction Worcester Heart Attack Study. *Circulation: Cardiovascular Quality and Outcomes*, 2(2), 88–95.

Formiga, F., Ferrer, A., Sanz, H., Marengoni, A., Alburquerque, J., and Pujol, R. (2013). Patterns of Comorbidity and Multimorbidity in the Oldest Old: The Octabaix Study. *European Journal of Internal Medicine*, 24(1), 40–44.

Foucault, M. (1975). *Surveiller et punir* (Discipline and Punish) Editions Gallimard (Vol. 225): Paris.

——. (1977). *Discipline and Punish: The Birth of the Prison*. Harmondsworth: Penguin.

Fourastié, J. (1979). *Les trente glorieuses: ou la Révolution invisible de 1946 à 1975*. Paris: Fayard.

Fried, L. P., Ferrucci, L., Darer, J., Williamson, J. D. & Anderson, G. (2004). Untangling the Concepts of Disability, Frailty and Co-Morbidity: Implications for Improved Targeting and Care. *Journals of Gerontology: Medical Science*, 59A(3), 255–263.

Fried, L. P., Tangen, C. M. & Walston, J. (2001). Frailty in Older Adults: Evidence for a Phenotype. *Journals of Gerontology: Medical Science*, 56A, M146–M156.

Fried, L. P., Xue, Q. L., Cappola, A. R., Ferrucci, L., Chaves, P., Varadhan, R., Guralnick, A. M. & Bandeen-Roche, K. (2009). Nonlinear Multisystem Physiological Dysregulation Associated with Frailty in Older Women: Implications for Etiology and Treatment. *The Journals of Gerontology Series A: Biological Sciences and Medical Sciences*, 64(10), 1049–1057.

Fries, J. F. (1980). Aging, Natural Death and the Compression of Morbidity. *New England Journal of Medicine*, 303(3), 130–135.

——. (2005). Frailty, Heart Disease, and Stroke: The Compression of Morbidity Paradigm. *American Journal of Preventive Medicine*, 29(5), Supplement 1, 164–168.

Fries, J. F., Bruce, B. & Chakravarty, E. (2011). Compression of Morbidity 1980–2011: A Focused Review of Paradigms and Progress. *Journal of Aging Research*, Article ID 261702.

Frohman, L. (2008). *Poor Relief and Welfare in Germany from the Reformation to World War I*. Cambridge: Cambridge University Press.

Fukuyama, F. (1995). *Trust: The Social Virtues and the Creation of Prosperity*. New York: Free Press.

Fultz, N. H. & Herzog, A. (2001). Self-Reported Social and Emotional Impact of Urinary Incontinence. *Journal of the American Geriatrics Society*, 49(7), 892–899.

Frost, H., Haw, S. & Frank, J. (2012). Interventions in Community Settings That Prevent or Delay Disablement in Later Life: An Overview of the Evidence. *Quality in Ageing and Older Adults*, 13(3), 212–230.

Gaonkar, D. P. (2002). Toward New Imaginaries: An Introduction. *Public Culture*, 14(1), 1–19.

Gaugler, J. E. (2005). Family Involvement in Residential Long-Term Care: A Synthesis and Critical Review. *Aging & Mental Health*, 9(2), 105–118.

Gaugler, J. E., Yu, F., Krichbaum, K. & Wyman, J. F. (2009). Predictors of Nursing Home Admission for Persons with Dementia. *Medical Care*, 47(2), 191–198.

Gaut, D. & Leininger, M. M. (1991). *Care: The Compassionate Healer*. New York: National League for Nursing.

Gee, E. & Gutman, G. (eds). (2000). *The Overselling of Population Ageing: Apocalyptic Demography, Intergenerational Challenges, and Social Policy*. Oxford: Oxford University Press.

Gee, E. M. (2002). Misconceptions and Misapprehensions about Population Ageing. *International Journal of Epidemiology*, 31(4), 750–753.

Geerts, J. & Willemé, P. (2012). Projections of Use and Supply of Long-Term Care in Europe: Policy Implications. *Enepri Policy Brief No. 12*, ENEPRI, European Network of Economic Policy Research Institutes.

Genet, N., Boerma, W.G.W., Kringos, D.S., Bouman, A., Francke, A.L., Fagerström, C., Melchiorre, M.G., Greco, C. and Devillé, W. (2011). Home Care in Europe: A Systematic Literature Review. *BMC Health Services Research*, 11(1), 207.

George, L. K. (2011). The Third Age: Fact or Fiction – Or Does It Matter? In D. C. Carr & K. Komp (eds), *Gerontology in the Era of the Third Age: Implications and Next Steps*. New York: Springer, 245–260.

Gerber, Y., Jacobsen S. J., Frye R. L., Weston S. A., Killian J. M. & Roger V. L. (2006). Secular Trends in Deaths from Cardiovascular Diseases. *Circulation*, 113, 2285–2292.

Geremek, B. (1997). *Poverty: A History*. Oxford: Blackwell.

Gilleard, C. (2013). Renaissance Treatises on 'Successful Ageing'. *Ageing and Society*, 33(2), 189–215.

Gilleard C. & Higgs P. (2000). *Cultures of Ageing: Self, Citizen and the Body*. Prentice Hall: Harlow.

——. (2005). *Contexts of Ageing: Class, Cohort and Community*. Cambridge: Polity Press.

——. (2009). The Third Age: Field, Habitus or Identity. In I. R. Jones, P. Higgs, & D. Ekerdt (eds), *Consumption and Generational Change: The Rise of Consumer Lifestyles and the Transformation of Later Life*. New Jersey: Transactions Press, 23–36.

——. (2010).Theorizing the Fourth Age: Aging without Agency. *Aging and Mental Health*, 14(1), 121–128.

——. (2011a). The Third Age as a Cultural Field. In D. C. Carr & K. Komp (eds), *Gerontology in the Era of the Third Age: Implications and Next Steps*. New York: Springer, 33–49.

—— (2011b). Frailty, Disability and Old Age: A Re-Appraisal. *Health*, 15(5), 475–490.

——. (2013). *Ageing, Corporeality and Embodiment*. London: Anthem Press.

——. (2014). Revisionist or Simply Wrong? a Response to Armstrong's Article on Chronic Illness. *Sociology of Health & Illness*, 36(7), 1111–1115.

Gilligan, C. (1982). *In a Different Voice*. Cambridge, MA: Harvard University Press.

Goode, P. S., Burgio, K. L., Richter, H. E. & Markland, A. D. (2010). Incontinence in Older Women. *JAMA*, 303(21), 2172–2181.

Goose, N. (2014). Accommodating the elderly poor: almshouses and the mixed economy of welfare in England in the second millennium. *Scandinavian Economic History Review*, 62(1), 35–57.

Goose, N. & Looijesteijn, H. (2012). Alms Houses in England and the Dutch Republic Circa 1350–1800: A Comparative Perspective. *Journal of Social History*, 45(4), 1049–1073.

Grenier, A. (2007). Constructions of Frailty in the English Language, Care Practice and the Lived Experience. *Ageing and Society*, 27(3), 425–446.

——. (2012). *Transitions and the Life Course: Challenging the Constructions of 'Growing Old'*. Bristol: Policy Press.

Grenier, A. & Hanley, J. (2007). Older Women and 'Frailty': Aged, Gendered and Embodied Resistance. *Current Sociology*, 55(2), 211–228.

Gruenberg, E. M. (1977). The Failures of Success. *Milbank Memorial Fund Quarterly*, 55(1), 3–24.

Gubrium, J. F. & Holstein, J. A. (1995). Qualitative Inquiry and the Deprivatization of Experience. *Qualitative Inquiry*, 1(2), 204–222.

Gubrium, J. & Holstein, J. A. (1999). The Nursing Home as a Discursive Anchor for the Ageing Body. *Ageing & Society*, 19(4), 519–538.

Gubrium, J. L. & Holstein, J. A. (2002). Going Concerns and Their Bodies. In L. Andersson (ed.), *Cultural Gerontology*. Westport, CT: Greenwood Publishing Group, 191–205.

Gutton, J. P. (1988). *Naissance du vieillard: essai sur l'histoire des rapports entre les vieillards et la société en France*. Paris: Aubier.

Habjanič, A. & Lahe, D. (2012). Are Frail Older People Less Exposed to Abuse in Nursing Homes as Compared to Community-Based Settings? Statistical Analysis of Slovenian Data. *Archives of Gerontology and Geriatrics*, 54(3), e261–e270.

Hägglund, D., Walker-Engström, M. L., Larsson, G. & Leppert, J. (2003). Reasons Why Women with Long-Term Urinary Incontinence do not Seek Professional Help: A Cross-Sectional Population-Based Cohort Study. *International Urogynaecology Journal*, 14(5), 296–304.

Han, B. & Haley, W. E. (1999). Family Caregiving for Patients with Stroke Review and Analysis. *Stroke*, 30(7), 1478–1485.

Harper, R. I. (1983). A Note on Corrodies in the Fourteenth Century. *Albion: A Quarterly Journal Concerned with British Studies*, 15(2), 95–101.

Harding, N. & Palfrey, C. (1997). *The Social Construction of Dementia: Confused Professionals?* London: Jessica Kingsley.

Health Advisory Service. (1982). Care in the Community: A Consultative Document on Moving Resources for Care in England. London: HMSO.

Heath, J. & Potter, A. (2005). *The Rebel Sell: How the Counterculture became Consumer Culture* Chichester: Capstone.

Herd, P. (2006). Do Functional Health Inequalities Decrease in Old Age? Educational Status and Functional Decline Among the 1931–1941 Birth Cohort. *Research on Aging*, 28(3), 375–392.

Hessler, R. M., Eriksson, B. G., Dey, D., Gunilla, S., Valter & Steen, B. (2003). The Compression of Morbidity Debate in Aging: An Empirical Test Using the Gerontological and Geriatric Population Studies in Göteborg, Sweden (H70). *Archives of Gerontology and Geriatrics*, 37(3), 213–222.

Higashi, R. T., Tillack, A. A., Steinman, M., Harper, M. & Johnston, C. B. (2012). Elder Care as 'Frustrating' and 'Boring': Understanding the Persistence of Negative Attitudes toward Older Patients Among Physicians-in-Training. *Journal of Aging Studies*, 26(4), 476–483.

Higashi, R. T., Tillack, A., Steinman, M. A., Johnston, C. B. & Harper, G. M. (2013). The 'Worthy' Patient: Rethinking the 'Hidden Curriculum' in Medical Education. *Anthropology & Medicine*, 20(1), 13–23.

Higgs, P. & Gilleard, C. (2006). Departing the Margins: Social Class and Later Life in a Second Modernity. *Journal of Sociology*, 42(3), 219–226.

Higgs P. & Jones I. R (2009). *Medical Sociology and Old Age: Towards a Sociology of Health in Later Life*. London: Routledge.

Higgs, P., Leontowitsch, M., Stevenson, F. & Jones, I. R. (2009). Not Just Old and Sick-the 'Will to Health' in Later Life. *Ageing and Society*, 29(5), 687–707.

Himmelfarb, G. (2006). *The Moral Imagination: From Edmund Burke to Lionel Trilling*. Chicago: Ivan R. Dee.

Hirsch, C., Anderson, M. L., Newman, A., Kop, W., Jackson, S., Gottdiener, J., Tracy, R. & Fried, L. P. (2006). The Association of Race with Frailty: The Cardiovascular Health Study. *Annals of Epidemiology*, 16(7), 545–553.

Hoeymans, N., Wong, A., van Gool, C. H., Deeg, D. J., et al. (2012). The Disabling Effect of Diseases: A Study on Trends in Diseases, Activity Limitations, and Their Interrelationships. *American Journal of Public Health*, 102(1), 163–70.

Hogan, D. B., Freiheit, E. A., Strain, L. A., Patten, S. B., Schmaltz, H. N., Rolfson, D. & Maxwell, C. J. (2012). Comparing Frailty Measures in Their Ability to Predict Adverse Outcome Among Older Residents of Assisted Living. *BMC Geriatrics*, 12(56), 1–11.

Holmes, D., Perron, A. & O'Byrne, P. (2006). Understanding Disgust in Nursing: Abjection, Self, and the Other. *Research and Theory for Nursing Practice*, 20(4), 305–316.

Holstein, M. (2011). Cultural Ideals, Ethics and Agelessness: A Critical Perspective on the Third Age. In D. Carr & K. Komp (eds), *Gerontology in the Era of the Third Age*, New York: Springer, 225–243.

Holstein, M. B. & Minkler, M. (2003). Self, Society, and the 'New Gerontology'. *The Gerontologist*, 43(6), 787–796.

Homans, G. C. (1958). Social Behavior as Exchange. *American Journal of Sociology*, 63(6), 597–606.

Hörder, H. M., Frändin, K. & Larsson, M. E. (2013). Self-Respect through Ability to Keep Fear of Frailty at a Distance: Successful Ageing from the Perspective of Community-Dwelling Older People. *International Journal of Qualitative Studies on Health and Well-being* 2013, 8: 20194 – http://dx.doi.org/10.3402/qhw.v8i0.20194.

Houles, M., van Kan, G. A., Rolland, Y., Andrieu, S., Anthony, P., Bauer, J., M., Beauchet, O., M. Bonnefoy, M., Cesari, M., Donini, L. -M., Gillette-Guyonnet, S., Inzitari, M., Jurk, I. Nourhashemi, F., Offord-Cavin, E., Onder G., Ritz, P., Salva, A., Visser, M. & Vellas, B. (2010). La vitesse de marche comme critère de fragilité chez la personne âgée vivant au domicile. *Les Cahiers de L'année Gérontologique*, 2(1), 13–23.

Huber, E. & Stephens, J. D. (2001). *Development and Crisis of the Welfare State: Parties and Policies in Global Markets*. Chicago: University of Chicago Press.

Huisman, M., Kunst, A. E., Andersen, O., Bopp, M., Borgan, J. K., Borrell, C., Costa, G., Deboosere, P., Desplanques, G., Donkin, A., Gadeyne, S., Minder C., Regidor E., Spadea, T., Valkonen T. & Mackenbach, J. P. (2004). Socioeconomic Inequalities in Mortality Among Elderly People in 11 European Populations. *Journal of Epidemiology and Community Health*, 58(6), 468–475.

Huisman, M., Kunst, A. E., Bopp, M., Borgan, J. K., Borrell, C., Costa, G., Deboosere, P., Gadeyne, S., Glickman, M., Marinacci, C., Minder, C., Regidor E., Valkonen T. & Mackenbach, J. P. (2005). Educational Inequalities in Cause-Specific Mortality in Middle-Aged and Older Men and Women in Eight Western European Populations. *The Lancet*, 365(9458), 493–500.

Hummert, M. L., Garstka, T. A. & Shaner, J. L. (1997). Stereotyping of Older Adults: The Role of Target Facial Cues and Perceiver Characteristics. *Psychology and Aging*, 12(1), 107.

Hussein, S., Manthorpe, J. & Stevens, M. (2011). Social Care as First Work Experience in England: A Secondary Analysis of the Profile of a National Sample of Migrant Workers. *Health & Social Care in the Community*, 19(1), 89–97.

Imtiaz, B., Tolppanen, A. M., Kivipelto, M. & Soininen, H. (2014). Future Directions in Alzheimer's Disease from Risk Factors to Prevention. *Biochemical Pharmacology*, 88, 661–670.

Ineichen, B. (1987). Measuring the Rising Tide: How Many Dementia Cases Will There Be by 2001? *The British Journal of Psychiatry*, 150(2), 193–200.

Isaacs, B. (1972). Toward a Definition of Geriatrics. *Journal of Chronic Diseases*, 25(8), 425–432.

Isaacs, B. & Walkey, F. A. (1964). A Survey of Incontinence in Elderly Hospital Patients. *Gerontologia Clinica*, 6(6), 367–376.

Italian Longitudinal Study on Aging Working Group. (1997). Prevalence of Chronic Diseases in Older Italians: Comparing Self-Reported and Clinical Diagnoses. *International Journal of Epidemiology*, 26(5), 995–1002.

Jafferany, M., Huynh, T. V., Silverman, M. A., Zaidi, Z. (2012). Geriatric Dermatoses: A Clinical Review of Skin Diseases in an Aging Population. *International Journal of Dermatology*, 51(5), 509–522.

Jemal, A., Siegel, R., Xu, J. & Ward, E. (2010). Cancer Statistics, 2010. *CA: A Cancer Journal for Clinicians*, 60(5), 277–300.

Jervis, L. L. (2001). The Pollution of Incontinence and the Dirty Work of Caregiving in a US Nursing Home. *Medical Anthropology Quarterly*, 15(1), 84–99.

Johnson, P., Conrad, C. & Thomson, D. (eds) (1989). *Workers versus Pensioners: Intergenerational Justice in an Ageing World*. Manchester: Manchester University Press.

Jones, I. R., Hyde, M., Victor, C., Wiggins, D., Gilleard, C. & Higgs, P. (2008). *Ageing in a Consumer Society: From Passive to Active Consumption in Britain*. Bristol: Policy Press.

Jones I. R. & Higgs, P. (2010). The Natural, the Normal and the Normative: Contested Terrains in Ageing and Old Age *Social Science and Medicine*, 71(8), 1513–1519.

Jütte, R. (1994). *Poverty and Deviance in Early Modern Europe*. Cambridge: Cambridge University Press.

Kachaturian, Z.S., Petersen, R.C., Gauthier, S., Buckholtz, N., Corey-Bloom, J.P., Evans, B. et al., (2008). A Roadmap for the Prevention of Dementia: The Inaugural Leon Thal Symposium. *Alzheimer's & Dementia*, 4(3), 156–163.

Kanapuru, B. & Ershler, W. B. (2009). Inflammation, coagulation, and the pathway to frailty. The *American Journal of Medicine*, 122(7), 605–613.

Karlsson, M. & Klohn, F. (2011). Some Notes on How to Catch a Red Herring: Ageing, Time-to-Death & Care Costs for Older People in Sweden. *Darmstadt Discussion Papers in Economics, Nr. 207*, Technische Universität Darmstadt.

Karp, A., Kåreholt, I., Qiu, C., Bellander, T., Winblad, B. & Fratiglioni, L. (2004). Relation of Education and Occupation-Based Socioeconomic Status to Incident Alzheimer's Disease. *American Journal of Epidemiology*, 159(2), 175–183.

Katz, J. (1975). Essences as Moral Identities: Verifiability and Responsibility in Imputations of Deviance and Charisma. *American Journal of Sociology*, 80(6), 1369–1390.

Katz, M. B. (1986). *In the Shadow of the Poorhouse: A Social History of Welfare in America*. New York: Basic Books.

Kaufman, S. R. (1994). The Social Construction of Frailty: An Anthropological Perspective. *Journal of Aging Studies*, 8(1), 45–58.

Kelly, F. & Innes, A. (2013). Human Rights, Citizenship and Dementia Care Nursing. *International Journal of Older People Nursing*, 8(1), 61–70.

Kemeny, J. (2005). 'The Really Big Trade-Off' between Home Ownership and Welfare: Castles' Evaluation of the 1980 Thesis and a Reformulation 25 Years on. *Housing, Theory & Society*, 22(2), 59–75.

Keysor, J. J. (2003). Does Late-Life Physical Activity or Exercise Prevent or Minimize Disablement? a Critical Review of the Scientific Evidence. *American Journal of Preventive Medicine*, 25(3), 129–136.

Kirkwood, T. B. (1999). *Time of Our Lives: The Science of Human Aging.* Oxford University Press: Oxford.

Kishimoto, Y., Terada, S., Takeda, N., Oshima, E., Honda, H., Yoshida, H., Yokota, O. & Uchitomi, Y. (2013). Abuse of People with Cognitive Impairment by Family Caregivers in Japan (a cross-sectional study). *Psychiatry Research*, 209(3), 699–704.

Kitwood, T. (1997). *Dementia Reconsidered.* Buckingham: Open University Press.

Kitwood, T. & Bredin, K. (1992). Towards a theory of dementia care: personhood and well-being. Ageing and Society, 12(3), 269–287.

Kohlberg, L. (1969). *Stages in the Development of Moral Thought and Action.* New York: Holt Rinehart & Wilson.

Kohlberg, L. & Hersh R. H. (1977). Moral Development: A Review of the Theory. *Theory into Practice*, 16(2), 53–59.

Kotlikoff, L.J. (1992). *Generational Accounts.* New York: Free Press.

Kotlikoff, L. J. & Burns, S. (2005). *The Coming Generational Storm: What You Need to Know about America's Economic Future.* Cambridge, MA: MIT Press.

Kramer, M. (1980). The Rising Pandemic of Mental Disorders and Associated Chronic Diseases and Disabilities. *Acta Psychiatrica Scandinavica*, 62(S285), 382–397.

Kraus, M., Czypionka, T., Riedel, M., Mot, E. & Willemé, P. (2011). *How European Nations Care For Their Elderly: A New Typology of Long-Term Care Systems.* ENEPRI Policy Brief no. 7. European Network of Economic Policy Research Institutes.

Kristeva, J. (1982). *Powers of Horror, An Essay on Abjection.* New York: Columbia University Press.

Kuklo, C. (2000). Elderly Women in the Cities of Central Europe in the Eighteenth Century. *The History of the Family*, 5(4), 451–471.

Kukull, W. A. (2006). The Growing Global Burden of Dementia. *The Lancet Neurology*, 5(3), 199–200.

Laing & Buisson. (2013). *Care of Elderly People UK Market Survey 2012/13.* Laing & Buisson.

——. (2013). *Domiciliary Care UK Market Report 2012, 12th edition.* Laing & Buisson.

Lancet, The. (1865). Report of the Sanitary Commission for Investigating the State of the Infirmaries of Workhouses. *The Lancet*, v. 86(2183) 1 July, p.16.

——. (1894). Old Age as a Law of Nature. *The Lancet*, v. 143(3671) 6 January, p.41.

——. (1946). The Old in an Overcrowded World. *The Lancet*, v. 247(6390) 16 February, p.244.

——. (1951). Old People. *The Lancet*, v. 258(6889) 10 November, p.880.

Larson, E. B. (2010). Prospects for Delaying the Rising Tide of Worldwide, Late-Life Dementias. *International Psychogeriatrics*, 22(8), 1196–1202.

Larsson, K., Kåreholt, I. & Thorslund, M. (2008). Care Utilisation in the Last Years of Life in Relation to Age and Time to Death: Results from a Swedish Urban Population of the Oldest Old. *European Journal of Ageing*, 5(4), 349–357.

Laslett, P. (1989). *A Fresh Map of Life: The Emergence of the Third Age*. London: Weidenfeld & Nicolson.

Laslett, P. (1996). *A Fresh Map of Life: The Emergence of the Third Age*. 2nd edition. London: Palgrave Macmillan.

Leget, C. & Olthuis, G. (2007). Compassion as a Basis for Ethics in Medical Education. *Journal of Medical Ethics*, 33(10), 617–620.

Lehnert, T., Heider, D., Leicht, H., Heinrich, S., Corrieri, S., Luppa, M. & König, HH. (2011). Review: Health Care Utilization and Costs of Elderly Persons with Multiple Chronic Conditions. *Medical Care Research and Review*, 68(4), 387–420.

Lewin, C. G. (2003). *Pensions and Insurance before 1800: A Social History*. East Linton: Tuckwell Press.

Liang, J., Liu, X., Tu, E. & Whitelaw, N. (1996). Probabilities and Lifetime Durations of Short-Stay Hospital and Nursing Home Use in the United States, 1985. *Medical Care*, 34(10), 1018–1036.

Lievesley, N., Crosby, G. & Bowman, C. (2011). *The Changing Role of Care Homes*. London: BUPA/CPA.

Lim, J. W. & Zebrack, B. (2004). Caring for Family Members with Chronic Physical Illness: A Critical Review of Caregiver Literature. *Health and Quality of Life Outcomes*, 2(50), 1–9.

Liu, C. K. & Fielding, R. A. (2011). Exercise as an Intervention for Frailty. *Clinics in Geriatric Medicine*, 27(1), 101–110.

Liu, Z. (2000). The Probability of Nursing Home Use Over a Lifetime in Australia. *International Journal of Social Welfare*, 9(3), 169–180.

Ljunggren, G., Phillips, C. D. & Sgadari, A. (1997). Comparisons of Restraint Use in Nursing Homes in Eight Countries. *Age and Ageing*, 26(2), 43–47.

Looijesteijn, H. (2012). Funding and Founding Private Charities: Leiden almshouses and their founders, 1450–1800. *Continuity and Change*, 27, 199–239.

Lorig, K. R. & Holman, H. R. (2003). Self-Management Education: History, Definition, Outcomes, and Mechanisms. *Annals of Behavioral Medicine*, 26(1), 1–7.

Lövheim, H., Sandman, P. O., Kallin, K., Karlsson, S. & Gustafson, Y. (2008). Symptoms of Mental Health and Psychotropic Drug Use Among Old People in Geriatric Care, Changes between 1982 and 2000. *International Journal of Geriatric Psychiatry*, 23(3), 289–294.

Lowe, C. R. & McKeown, T. (1949). The Care of the Chronic Sick I. Medical and Nursing Requirements. *British Journal of Social Medicine*, 3(3), 110–126.

Lowenstein, A., Katz, R. & Gur-Yaish, N. (2007). Reciprocity in Parent–Child Exchange and Life Satisfaction Among the Elderly: A Cross-National Perspective. *Journal of Social Issues*, 63(4), 865–883.

Lubitz, J., Beebe, J. & Baker, C. (1995). Longevity and Medicare expenditures. *New England Journal of Medicine*, 332(15), 999–1003.

Lunde, O. (1984) A study of body hair density and distribution in normal women. *American Journal of Physical Anthropology*, 64(2), 179–184

Lundgren, A. S. & Ljuslinder, K. (2011a). Problematic Demography: Representations of Population Ageing in the Swedish Daily Press. *Journal of Population Ageing*, 4(3), 165–183.

——. (2011b). 'The Baby-Boom Is Over and the Ageing Shock Awaits': Populist Media Imagery in News-Press Representations of Population Ageing. *International Journal of Ageing & Later Life*, 6(2), 39–71.

Luppa, M., Luck, T., Matschinger, H., König, H. H. & Riedel-Heller, S. G. (2010a). Predictors of Nursing Home Admission of Individuals without a Dementia Diagnosis before Admission-Results from the Leipzig Longitudinal Study of the Aged (LEILA 75+). *BMC Health Services Research*, 10(1), 186.

Luppa, M., Weyerer, T., Konig, S., Hans-Helmut, Brahler, E. & Riedel-Heller, S. (2010b). Prediction of Institutionalization in the Elderly: A Systematic Review. *Age and Ageing*, 39(1), 31–38.

Luppa, M., Riedel-Heller, SG., Luck, T., Wiese, B., van den Bussche, H., Haller, F., Sauder, M., Mösch, E., Pentzek, M., Wollny, A., Eisele, M., Zimmermann, T., König HH., Maier, W., Bickel, H., Werle, J. & Weyerer, S. (2012). Age-Related Predictors of Institutionalization: Results of the German Study on Ageing, Cognition and Dementia in Primary Care Patients (AgeCoDe). *Social Psychiatry and Psychiatric Epidemiology*, 47(2), 263–270.

Lynch, J. W., Kaplan, G. A. & Shema, S. J. (1997). Cumulative Impact of Sustained Economic Hardship on Physical, Cognitive, Psychological, and Social Functioning. *New England Journal of Medicine*, 337(26), 1889–1895.

Manton, K. G., Gu, X. & Lamb, V. L. (2006). Change in chronic disability from 1982 to 2004/2005 as measured by long-term changes in function and health in the US elderly population. *Proceedings of the National Academy of Sciences*, 103(48), 18374–18379.

Marengoni, A., Winblad, B., Karp, A. & Fratiglioni, L. (2008). Prevalence of Chronic Diseases and Multimorbidity Among the Elderly Population in Sweden. *American Journal of Public Health*, 98(7), 1198.

Marengoni, A., Angleman, S., Melis, R., Mangialasche, F., Karp, A., Garmen, A., Meinow, B. & Fratiglioni,L. (2011). Aging with Multi-Morbidity: A Systematic Review of the Literature. *Aging Research Reviews*, 10(4), 430–439.

Marks, N. F., Lambert, J. D. & Choi, H. (2002). Transitions to Caregiving, Gender, and Psychological Well-Being: A Prospective US National Study. *Journal of Marriage and Family*, 64(3), 657–667.

Martikainen, P., Moustgaard, H., Murphy, M., Einiö, E. K., Koskinen, S., Martelin, T. & Noro, A. (2009). Gender, Living Arrangements, and Social Circumstances as Determinants of Entry into and Exit from Long-Term Institutional Care at Older Ages: A 6-Year Follow-Up Study of Older Finns. *The Gerontologist*, 49(1), 34–45.

Martin, R. Williams, C. & O'Neill, D. (2009). Retrospective Analysis of Attitudes to Ageing in *the Economist*: Apocalyptic Demography for Opinion Formers? *British Medical Journal*, 339, b4914, 1435–1437.

Matire, L. M., Stephens, M. A. P., Druley, J. A. & Wojno, W. C. (2002). Negative Reactions to Received Spousal Care: Predictors and Consequences of Miscarried Support. *Health Psychology*, 21(2), 167–176.

Matthias, R. E. & Benjamin, A. E. (2003). Abuse and Neglect of Clients in Agency-Based and Consumer-Directed Home Care. *Health & Social Work*, 28(3), 174–184.

McEwan, P. & Laverty, S. G. (1949). Chronic Sick and Elderly in Hospital: Conclusions from a Bradford Survey. *The Lancet*, 254(6589), 1098–1099.

McHugh, T. (2007). *Hospital Politics in Seventeenth Century France*. Aldershot: Ashgate Publishing.

McIntosh, M. K. (2012). *Poor Relief in England, 1350–1600*. Cambridge: Cambridge University Press.

McKenzie, S., St John, W., Wallis, M. & Griffiths, S. (2013). Men's Management of Urinary Incontinence in Daily Living: Implications for Practice. *International Journal of Urological Nursing*, 7(1), 43–52.

McKeowan, T. (1976). *The Role of Medicine: Dream, Mirage or Nemesis?* London: Nuffield Provincial Hospitals Trust.

McPherson, C. J., Wilson, K. G., Chyurlia, L. & Leclerc, C. (2010). The Balance of Give and Take in Caregiver–Partner Relationships: An Examination of Self-Perceived Burden, Relationship Equity, and Quality of Life from the Perspective of Care Recipients Following Stroke. *Rehabilitation Psychology*, 55(2), 194.

Meacher, M. (1972). *Taken for a Ride: Special Residential Homes for Confused Old People: A Study of Separatism in Social Policy*. London: Longman.

Means, R. & Smith, R. (1998). *From Poor Law to Community Care: The Development of Welfare Services for Elderly People, 1939–1971*. London: The Policy Press.

Menninghaus, W. (2003). *Disgust: Theory and History of a Strong Sensation*, (transl. H. Eiland & J. Golb). Albany, NY: State University of New York Press.

Michielse, H. C. M. (1990). Policing the Poor: J L Vives and the Sixteenth Century Origins of Modern Social Administration. *Social Service Review*, 64(1), 1–21.

Miller, W. I. (1997). *The Anatomy of Disgust*. Cambridge, MA: Harvard University Press.

Milne, J.S., Williamson, J., Maule,M.M. & Wallace, E.T. (1972). Urinary Symptoms in Older People. *Modern Geriatrics*, 3:198–212.

Minassian, V. A., Drutz, H. P. & Al-Badr, A. (2003). Urinary Incontinence as a Worldwide Problem. *International Journal of Gynecology & Obstetrics*, 82(3), 327–338.

Minkler, M. & Cole, T. R. (1999). Political and Moral Economy: Getting to Know One Another. In M. Minkler & C. L. Estes (eds), *Critical Gerontology*: Perspectives from Political and Moral Economy. Amityville, NY: Baywood Publishing, 37–49.

Misztal, B. A. (1996). *Trust in Modem Societies*. Cambridge, MA: Polity Press.

Mitchison, R. (2000). *The Old Poor Law in Scotland: The Experience of Poverty, 1574–1845*. Edinburgh: Edinburgh University Press.

Mitniski, Arnold B., Mogilner, Alexander J., MacKnight, C. & Rockwood, K. (2002). The Mortality Rate as a Function of Accumulated Deficits in a Frailty Index. *Mechanisms of Ageing and Development*, 123, 1457–1460.

Montgomery, R. J., Holley, P. L., Deichert, J. & Kosloski, K. (2005). A Profile of Home Care Workers from the 2000 Census: How It Changes What We Know. *The Gerontologist*, 45(5), 593–600.

Moody, H. R. (1995). Ageing, Meaning and the Allocation of Resources. *Ageing and Society*, 15(02), 163–184.

Morton, D. J., Kritz-Silverstein, D., Riley, D. J., Barrett-Connor, E. L. & Wingard, D. L. (2007). Premature Graying, Balding, and Low Bone Mineral Density in Older Women and Men The Rancho Bernardo Study. *Journal of Aging and Health*, 19(2), 275–285.

Moshman, D. (2005). *Adolescent Psychological Development: Rationality, Morality, and Identity*. 2nd Edition. Hove, Sussex: Psychology Press.

Mot, E. & Willemé, P. (eds). (2012). *Assessing Needs of Care in European Nations*. ENEPRI Policy Brief no. 14, European Network of Economic Policy Research Institutes.

Mot, E. Faber, R., Geerts, J. & Willemé, P. (eds). (2012). *Performance of Long-Term Care Systems in Europe*. ENEPRI Research Report no. 117, European Network of Economic Policy Research Institutes.

Mullan, P. (2000). *The Imaginary Time Bomb: Why an Ageing Population Is Not a Social Problem*. London: I. B. Tauris.

Munson, H. W. (1930). The Care of the Sick in Alms-Houses. *The American Journal of Nursing*, 30(10), 1226–1230.

Murtaugh, C. M., Kemper, P. & Spillman, B. C. (1990). The Risk of Nursing Home Use in Later Life. *Medical Care*, 28(10), 952–962.

Mutran, E. & Reitzes, D. C. (1984). Intergenerational Support Activities and Well-Being Among the Elderly: A Convergence of Exchange and Symbolic Interaction Perspectives. *American Sociological Review*, 49(2), 117–130.

Nagaratnam, N., Patel, I. & Whelan, C. (2003). Screaming, Shrieking and Muttering: The Noise-Makers amongst Dementia Patients. *Archives of Gerontology and Geriatrics*, 36(3), 247–258.

Neuberger, J. (2009). *Not Dead Yet: A Manifesto for Old Age*. London: HarperCollins.

Neugarten, B. L. (1974). Age groups in American society and the rise of the young-old. The *Annals of the American Academy of Political and Social Science*, 415(1), 187–198.

Newman, J. L. (1962). Old Folk in Wet Beds. *British Medical Journal*, 1(5295), 1824.

Nicholls, A. (2012). 'A Comfortable Lodging and One Shilling and Fourpence a Day': The Material Benefits of an Alms-House Place. *Family & Community History*, 15(2), 81–94.

Nihtilä, E. K., Martikainen, P. T., Koskinen, S. V., Reunanen, A. R., Noro, A. M. & Häkkinen, U. T. (2008). Chronic Conditions and the Risk of Long-Term Institutionalization Among Older People. *The European Journal of Public Health*, 18(1), 77–84.

Noddings, N. (1984). *Caring: A Feminine Approach to Ethics and Moral Education*. Berkeley, CA: University of California Press.

Nowak, A. & Hubbard, R. E. (2009). Falls and Frailty: Lessons from Complex Systems. *Journal of the Royal Society of Medicine*, 102, 98–102.

'Nunquam' (1892). A Socialist View of the Poor Law. *The Clarion*, 17 September.

O'Brien, G. (1982). The Establishment of Poor-Law Unions in Ireland, 1838–1843. *Irish Historical Studies*, 23(90), 97–120.

O'Connor, J. (1987). *The Meaning of Crisis*. Oxford: Blackwell.

O'Flaherty, M., Buchan, I. & Capewell, S. (2013). Contributions of Treatment and Lifestyle to Declining CVD Mortality: Why Have CVD Mortality Rates Declined So Much Since the 1960s? *Heart*, 99(3), 159–162.

OECD. (1988a). *Reforming Public Pensions*. Paris: OECD.

——. (1988b). *Ageing Populations: The Social Policy Implications*. Paris: OECD.

——. (2006). Projecting OECD Health and Long-Term Care Expenditures: What Are the Main Drivers? *Economics Department Working Papers no. 477*, ECO/WKP(2006)5, OECD, Paris.

——. (2013a). 'What Future for Health Spending?' *OECD Economics Department Policy Notes, No. 19* OECD, Paris.

——. (2013b). Public Spending on Health and Long-Term Care: A New Set of Projections. *Main Paper, Economic Policy Paper no. 6* (accessed 10/02/2014: http://www.oecd.org/eco/growth/Health%20FINAL.pdf).

——. (2013c) *Health at a Glance, 2013*. OECD, Paris.

Ogden, L. L. & Adams, K. (2009). Poorhouse to Warehouse: Institutional Long-Term Care in the United States. *Publius: The Journal of Federalism*, 39(1), 138–163.

O'Hare, A. M., Choi, A. I., Bertenthal, D., Bacchetti, P., Garg, A. X., Kaufman, J. S., Walter, L. C., Mehta, K. M., Steinman, M. A., Allon, M., McClellan, W. M. & Landefeld, C. S. (2007). Age Affects Outcomes in Chronic Kidney Disease. *Journal of the American Society of Nephrology*, 18(10), 2758–2765.

Olshansky, S. J. & Ault, A. B. (1986). The Fourth Stage of the Epidemiologic Transition: The Age of Delayed Degenerative Diseases. *The Milbank Quarterly*, 64(3), 355–391.

Olshansky, S. J., Passaro, D. J., Hershow, R. C., Layden, J. Carnes, B. A., Brody, J., Hayflick, L., Butler, R. N., Allison, D. B. & Ludwig, D. S. (2005). A Potential Decline in Life Expectancy in the United States in the 21st Century. *New England Journal of Medicine*, 352(11), 1138–1145.

Olshansky, S. J., Rudberg, M. A., Carnes, B. A., Cassel, C. K. & Brody, J. A. (1991). Trading Off Longer Life for Worsening Health: The Expansion of Morbidity Hypothesis. *Journal of Aging and Health*, 3(2), 194–216.

Omran, A. R. (1971). The Epidemiologic Transition: A Theory of the Epidemiology of Population Change. *The Milbank Memorial Fund Quarterly*, 49(4), 509–538.

Orgel, L. E. (1963). The Maintenance of the Accuracy of Protein Synthesis and Its Relevance to Ageing. *Proceedings of the National Academy of Sciences of the United States of America*, 49(4), 517–523.

Paley, J. (2002). Caring as a Slave Morality: Nietzschean Themes in Nursing Ethics. *Journal of Advanced Nursing*, 40(1), 25–35.

Pekkarinen, L., Elovainio, M., Sinervo, T., Finne-Soveri, H. & Noro, A. (2006). Nursing Working Conditions in Relation to Restraint Practices in Long-Term Care Units. *Medical Care*, 44(12), 1114–1120.

Pel-Littel, R. E., Schuurmans, M. J., Emmelot-Vonk, M. H. & Verhaar, H. J. J. (2009). Frailty: Defining and Measuring of a Concept. *JNHA-The Journal of Nutrition, Health and Aging*, 13(4), 390–394.

Perry, S., Shaw, C., McGrother, C., Matthews, R. J., Assassa, R. P., Dallosso, H., Williams, K., Brittain, K. R., Azam, U., Clarke, M., Jagger, C., Mayne, C., Castleden, C. M. & the Leicestershire MRC Incontinence Study Team. (2002). Prevalence of Faecal Incontinence in Adults Aged 40 Years or More Living in the Community. *Gut*, 50, 480–484.

Peterson, P. G. (1999). Gray Dawn: The Global Aging Crisis. *Foreign Affairs*, 78(1), 42–55.

Phillips, C. D., Hawes, C., Mor, V., Fries, B. E., Morris, J. N. & Nennstiel, M. E. (1996). Facility and Area Variation Affecting the Use of Physical Restraints in Nursing Homes. *Medical Care*, 34(11), 1149–1162.

Piantanelli, L. (1988). Cancer and Aging: From the Kinetics of Biological Parameters to the Kinetics of Cancer Incidence and Mortality. *Annals of the New York Academy of Sciences*, 521, 99–109.

Pickard, S. (2010). Role of Governmentality in the Establishment, Maintenance and Demise of Professional Jurisdictions: The Case of Geriatric Medicine. *Sociology of Health and Illness*, 32(7), 1072–1086.

—— (2011). Health, Illness and Normality: The Case of Old Age. *BioSocieties*, 6, 323–341.

Pierson, C. (1998). *Beyond the Welfare State: The New Political Economy of Welfare*. Cambridge: Polity Press.

Plassman, B. L., Williams, J. W., Burke, J. R., Holsinger, T. & Benjamin, S. (2010). Systematic Review: Factors Associated with Risk for and Possible Prevention of Cognitive Decline in Later Life. *Annals of Internal Medicine*, 153(3), 182–193.

Polder, J. J., Barendregt, J. J. & van Oers, H. (2006). Health Care Costs in the Last Year of Life — the Dutch Experience. *Social Science & Medicine*, 63(7), 1720–1731.

Pretlove, S. J., Radley, S., Toozs-Hobson, P. M., Thompson, P. J., Coomarasamy, A. & Khan, K. S. (2006). Prevalence of Anal Incontinence According to Age and Gender: A Systematic Review and Meta-Regression Analysis. *International Urogynecology Journal*, 17(4), 407–417.

Price D., Bisdee D., Daly T., Livsey L. & Higgs P. (2014). Financial Planning for Social Care in Later Life: The 'Shadow' of Fourth Age Dependency. *Ageing and Society*, 34(3), 388–410.

Prince, M., Acosta, D., Albanese, E., Arizaga, R., Ferri, C. P., Guerra, M., Huang, Y., Ks Jacob, Jimenez-Velazquez, I. Z., Rodriguez, J. L., Salas, A., Sosa, A. L., Sousa, R., Uwakwe, R., Van Der Poel, R., Williams, J. & Wortmann, M. (2008). Ageing and Dementia in Low and Middle Income Countries: Using Research to Engage with Public and Policy Makers. *International Review of Psychiatry*, 20(4), 332–343.

Pullan, B. (1999). The Counter-Reformation, Medical Care and Poor Relief. In (eds) Ole Peter Grell, Andrew Cunningham & John Arrizabalaga, *Health Care and Poor Relief in Counter-Reformation Europe*, London: Routledge, 18–39.

Puts, M. T. E., Deeg, D. J. H., Hoeymans, N., Nusselder, W. J. & Schellevis, F. G. (2008). Changes in the Prevalence of Chronic Disease and the Association with Disability in the Older Dutch Population between 1987 and 2001. *Age and Ageing*, 37(2), 187–193.

Quinn, C., Clare, L. & Woods, B. (2009). The Impact of the Quality of Relationship on the Experiences and Wellbeing of Caregivers of People with Dementia: A Systematic Review. *Aging and Mental Health*, 13(2), 143–154.

Rapoport, J., Jacobs, P., Bell, N. R. & Klarenbach, S. (2004). Refining the Measurement of the Economic Burden of Chronic Diseases in Canada. *Chronic Diseases in Canada*, 25(1), 1–14.

Rau, R., Soroko, E., Jasilionis, D., & Vaupel, J. W. (2008). Continued reductions in mortality at advanced ages. *Population and Development Review*, 34(4), 747–768.

Reistetter, T. A., Graham, J. E., Deutsch, A., Markello, S. J., Granger, C. V. & Ottenbacher, K. J. (2011). Diabetes Comorbidity and Age Influence Rehabilitation Outcomes after Hip Fracture. *Diabetes Care*, 34(6), 1375–1377.

Rentoul, R. (1906). *Race Culture or Race Suicide?* Liverpool: Cornish Brothers. (accessed on 7 April 2014, via http://archive.org/stream/racecultureorrac00rent/racecultureorrac00rent_djvu.txt.)

Resnick, N. M., Yalla, S. V. & Laurino, E. (1989). The Pathophysiology of Urinary Incontinence among Institutionalized Elderly Persons. *New England Journal of Medicine*, 320(1), 1–7.

Robb, B. (1967). *Sans Everything: A Case to Answer*. London: Nelson. Robertson, A. (1990). The Policies of Alzheimer's Disease: A Case Study in Apocalyptic Demography. *International Journal of Health Services*, 20(3), 429–442.

——. (1997). Beyond Apocalyptic Demography: Towards a Moral Economy of Interdependence. *Ageing and Society*, 17(4), 425–446.

Robine, J. M. & Paccaud, F. (2005). Nonagenarians and Centenarians in Switzerland, 1860–2001: A Demographic Analysis. *Journal of Epidemiology and Community Health*, 59(1), 31–37.

Rockwood, K., Stadnyk, B., MacKnight, C., McDowell, I., Hebert, R. & Hogan, D. B. (1999). A Brief Clinical Measure of Frailty. *The Lancet*, 353, 205–206.

Rodrigues, R., Huber, M. & Lamura, G. (2012). *Facts and Figures on Healthy Ageing and Long-Term Care.* Itävalta, Vienna: European Centre for Social and Welfare Policy and Research.

Rodríguez-Mañas, L., Féart, C., Mann, G., Viña, J., Chatterji, S., Chodzko-Zajko, W., Gonzalez-Colaço, M. Bergman, H., Carcaillon, L., Nicholson, C., Scuteri, A., Sinclair,A., Pelaez, M., Van der Cammen, T., Beland, F., Bickenbach, J., Delamarche, P., Ferrucci, L., Fried, L.P., Gutiérrez-Robledo, L.M., Rockwood, K., Artalejo, F.R., Serviddio, G. & Vega, E. (2013). Searching for an operational definition of frailty: a delphi method based consensus statement. The frailty operative definition-consensus conference project. *The Journals of Gerontology Series A: Biological Sciences and Medical Sciences*, 68(1), 62–67.

Roebuck, J. (1979). When Does 'Old Age' Begin? the Evolution of the English Definition. *Journal of Social History*, 12(3), 416–428.

Rømmen, K., Schei, B., Rydning, A., Sultan, A. H. & Mørkved, S. (2012). Prevalence of Anal Incontinence Among Norwegian Women: A Cross-Sectional Study. *British Medical Journal Open*, 2(4).

Ronald, I., Fought, R. L. & Ray, W. A. (1994). Changes in Antipsychotic Drug Use in Nursing Homes during Implementation of the OBRA-87 Regulations. *JAMA*, 271(5), 358–362.

Rostgaard, T. (2014). *The Nordic Welfare Model Caring for Old.* Paper presented at the 22nd Nordic Congress of Gerontology, Goteborg, 26 May.

Rothgang, H. (2010). Social Insurance for Long-term Care: An Evaluation of the German Model. *Social Policy & Administration*, 44(4), 436–460.

Rothman, M. D., Leo-Summers, L. & Gill, T. M. (2008). Prognostic Significance of Potential Frailty Criteria. *Journal of the American Geriatrics Society*, 56(12), 2211–2216.

Rothwell, P. M., Coull, A. J., Giles, M. F., Howard, S. C., Silver, L. E., Bull, L. M., Gutnikov, S., Edwards, P., Mant, D., Sackley, C., Farmer, A., Sandercock, P., Dennis, M., Warlow, C., Bamford, J., & Anslow, P. (2004). Change in Stroke Incidence, Mortality, Case-Fatality, Severity, and Risk Factors in Oxfordshire, UK from 1981 to 2004 (Oxford Vascular Study). *The Lancet*, 363(9425), 1925–1933.

Roubenoff, R. & Hughes, V. A. (2000). Sarcopenia Current Concepts. *The Journals of Gerontology Series A: Biological Sciences and Medical Sciences*, 55(12), M716–M724.

Rowe, J. W. & Kahn, R. L. (1987). Human Aging: Usual and Successful. *Science*, 237(4811), 143–149.

Rozanova, Julia, Northcott, Herbert C. & McDaniel, Susan A. 2006. Seniors and Portrayals of Intra-Generational and Inter-Generational Inequality in the Globe and Mail. *Canadian Journal on Aging / La Revue canadienne du vieillissement*, 25(4), 373–386.

Rudge, T. & Holmes, D. (eds). (2010). *Abjectly Boundless: Boundaries, Bodies, and Health Work*. Farnham: Ashgate Publishing.

Salive, M. (2013). Multimorbidity in Older Adults. *Epidemiologic Reviews*, 35(1), 75–83.

Samuelsson, E., Månsson, L. & Milsom, I. (2001). Incontinence Aids in Sweden: Users and Costs. *BJU International*, 88(9), 893–898.

Sandvide, Å., Åström, S., Norberg, A. & Saveman, B. I. (2004). Violence in Institutional Care for Elderly People from the Perspective of Involved Care Providers. *Scandinavian Journal of Caring Sciences*, 18(4), 351–357.

Saveman, B. I., Åström, S., Bucht, G. & Norberg, A. (1999). Elder Abuse in Residential Settings in Sweden. *Journal of Elder Abuse & Neglect*, 10(1–2), 43–60.

Scharf, T. (2009). Too Tight to Mention: Unequal Income in Older Age. In P. Cann & M. Dean (eds), *Unequal Ageing: The Untold Story of Exclusion in Old Age*. Bristol: Policy Press, 25–52.

Schmidt M, Jacobsen JB, Lash TL, Bøtker HE, Sørensen HT. (2012). 25 Year Trends in First Time Hospitalisation for Acute Myocardial Infarction, Subsequent Short and Long Term Mortality, and the Prognostic Impact of Sex and Comorbidity: A Danish Nationwide Cohort Study. *British Medical Journal*, 344:e356.

Schneider, E. L. & Brody, J. A. (1983). Aging, Natural Death and the Compression of Morbidity: Another View. *New England Journal of Medicine*, 309(14), 854–856.

Schneider, J., Murray, J., Banerjee, S. & Mann, A. (1999). EUROCARE: A Cross-National Study of Co-Resident Spouse Carers for People with Alzheimer's Disease: I—Factors Associated with Carer Burden. *International Journal of Geriatric Psychiatry*, 14(8), 651–661.

Schnohr, P., Lange, P., Nyboe, J., Appleyard, M. & Jensen, G. (1995). Gray Hair, Baldness, and Wrinkles in Relation to Myocardial Infarction: The Copenhagen City Heart Study. *American Heart Journal*, 130(5), 1003–1010.

Schoeni, R. F., Freedman, V. A. & Martin, L. G. (2008). Why is late-life disability declining? *Milbank Quarterly*, 86(1), 47–89.

Scull, A. (1985). Deinstitutionalization and Public Policy. *Social Science & Medicine*, 20(5), 545–552.

Sears, E. (1986). *The Ages of Man: Medieval Interpretations of the Life Cycle*. Princeton, NJ: Princeton University Press.

Selbæk, G., Kirkevold, Ø. & Engedal, K. (2007). The Prevalence of Psychiatric Symptoms and Behavioural Disturbances and the Use of Psychotropic Drugs in Norwegian Nursing Homes. *International Journal of Geriatric Psychiatry*, 22(9), 843–849.

Seltzer, M. M. & Li, L. W. (2000). The Dynamics of Caregiving Transitions during a Three-Year Prospective Study. *The Gerontologist*, 40(2), 165–178.

Seshamani, M. & Gray, A. (2004). Ageing and Health-Care Expenditure: The Red Herring Argument Revisited. *Health Economics*, 13(4), 303–314.

Shang, B. & Goldman, D. (2008). Does Age or Life Expectancy Better Predict Health Care Expenditures? *Health Economics*, 17(4), 487–501.

Shapiro, J. P. (1994). *No Pity: People with Disabilities Forging a New Civil Rights Movement*. New York: Random House.

Siddiqui, N. Y., Levin, P. J., Phadtare, A., Pietrobon, R. & Ammarell, N. (2013). Perceptions about Female Urinary Incontinence: A Systematic Review. *International Urogynecology Journal*, 1–9.

Sirven, N. (2012). On the Socio-Economic Determinants of Frailty: Findings from Panel and Retrospective Data from SHARE. *Working Paper No.52*, Institut de Recherche et Documentation en Économie de la Santé (IRDES), Paris.

Sloane, P. D., Hoeffer, B., Mitchell, C. M., McKenzie, D. A., Barrick, A. L., Rader, J. & Koch, G. G. (2004). Effect of Person-Centered Showering and the Towel Bath on Bathing-Associated Aggression, Agitation, and Discomfort in Nursing Home Residents with Dementia: A Randomized, Controlled Trial. *Journal of the American Geriatrics Society*, 52(11), 1795–1804.

Smith, F. B. (1990). *The People's Health, 1830–1910*. London: Weidenfeld & Nicolson.

Solomon, A., Mangialasche, F., Richard, E., Andrieu, S., Bennett, D. A., Breteler, M., Fratiglioni, L., Hooshmand, B., Khachaturian, A.S., Schneider, L.S., et al. (2014). Advances in the Prevention of Alzheimer's Disease and Dementia. *Journal of Internal Medicine*, 275(3), 229–250.

Soloway, R. A. (1990). *Demography and Degeneration: Eugenics and the Declining Birthrate in Twentieth-Century Britain*. Chapel Hill, NC: University of North Carolina Press.

Sousa, R. M., Ferri, C. P., Acosta, D., Albanese, E., Guerra, M., Huang, Y., Jacob, K.S., Jotheeswaran, A.T., Rodriguez, J.J., Pichardo, G.R., Rodriguez, M.C., Salas, A., Sosa, A.L., Williams, J., Zuniga, T. & Prince, M. Lancet. (2009). Contribution of Chronic Diseases to Disability in Elderly People in Countries with Low and Middle Incomes: A 10/66 Dementia Research Group Population-Based Survey. *The Lancet*, 374(9704), 1821–1830.

Spijker, A., Vernooij-Dassen, M., Vasse, E., Adang, E., Wollersheim, H., Grol, R. & Verhey, F. (2008). Effectiveness of Nonpharmacological Interventions in Delaying the Institutionalization of Patients with Dementia: A Meta-Analysis. *Journal of the American Geriatrics Society*, 56(6), 1116–1128.

Spijker, J. & MacInnes, J. (2013). Population Ageing: The Timebomb That Isn't? *British Medical Journal*, 347, f6598

Splaine, Mike. (2008). Campaign Advocacy in Brief: Dementia Care Policy Strategies and Recommendations. *Alzheimer's Care Today*, 9(2),145–146.

Stannard, C. I. (1973). Old folks and Dirty Work: The Social Conditions for Patient Abuse in a Nursing Home. *Social Problems*, 20(3), 329–342.

Stewart, S. T., Cutler, D. M. & Rosen A. B. (2013). US Trends in Quality-Adjusted Life Expectancy from 1987 to 2008: Combining National Surveys to More Broadly Track the Health of the Nation. *American Journal of Public Health*, 103(11), e78–e87.

Stocker, S. S. (2002). Facing Disability with Resources from Aristotle and Nietzsche. *Medicine, Health Care and Philosophy*, 5(2), 137–146.

Stoller, E. P. (1985). Exchange Patterns in the Informal Support Networks of the Elderly: The Impact of Reciprocity on Morale. *Journal of Marriage and the Family*, 47(2), 335–342.

Strauss, C. (2006). The Imaginary. *Anthropological Theory*, 6(3), 322–344.

Strehler B. L. (1962). *Time, Cells and Aging*. New York: Academic Press.

Suad Nasir, N. I. & Kirshner, B. (2003). The Cultural Construction of Moral and Civic Identities. *Applied Developmental Science*, 7(3), 138–147.

Szanton, S. L., Seplaki, C. L., Thorpe, R. J., Allen, J. K. & Fried, L. P. (2010). Socioeconomic Status Is Associated with Frailty: The Women's Health and Aging Studies. *Journal of Epidemiology and Community Health*, 64(1), 63–67.

Taylor, C. (2004). *Modern Social Imaginaries*. Durham, NC: Duke University Press.

Thane, P. M. (2000). *Old Age in English History: Past Experiences, Present Issues*. Oxford: Oxford University Press.

Theou, O., Brothers, T. D., Mitnitski, A. & Rockwood, K. (2013). Operationalization of Frailty Using Eight Commonly Used Scales and Comparison of Their Ability to Predict All-Cause Mortality. *Journal of the American Geriatrics Society*, 61(9), 1537–1551.

Theou, O., Brothers, T. D., Rockwood, M. R., Haardt, D., Mitnitski, A. & Rockwood, K. (2013). Exploring the Relationship between National Economic Indicators and Relative Fitness and Frailty in Middle-Aged and Older Europeans. *Age and Ageing*, 42(5), 614–619.

Thomas, C. (1999). *Female Forms: Experiencing and Understanding Disability*. Buckingham: Open University Press.

Thomas, P. K. & Ferriman, D. G. (1957). Variation in facial and pubic hair growth in white women. *American Journal of Physical Anthropology*, 15(2), 171–180.

Thomas, T. M., Plymat, K. R., Blannin, J. & Meade, T. W. (1980). Prevalence of Urinary Incontinence. *British Medical Journal*, 281(6250), 1243–1245.

Thompson, A. P. (1949). Problems of Ageing and Chronic Sickness. – I. *British Medical Journal*, 2(4621), 243.

Thomson, D. (1983). Workhouse to Nursing Home: Residential Care of Elderly People in England Since 1840. *Ageing and Society*, 3(1), 43–69.

Tilse, C. (1997). She Wouldn't Dump Me: The Purpose and Meaning of Visiting a Spouse in Residential Care. *Journal of Family Studies*, 3(2), 196–208.

Tobin, S. S. & Lieberman, M. A. (1976). *Last Home for the Aged*. San Francisco: Jossey-Bass. Torti Jr, F. M., Gwyther, L. P., Reed, S. D., Friedman, J. Y. & Schulman, K. A. (2004). A Multinational Review of Recent Trends and Reports in Dementia Caregiver Burden. *Alzheimer Disease & Associated Disorders*, 18(2), 99–109.

Townsend, P. (1962). *Last Refuge*. London: Routledge and Kegan Paul.

Townsend, P. (1963). *The Family Life of Old People: An Inquiry in East London*. Harmondsworth: Penguin Books.

Townsend, P. (1981). The Structured Dependency of the Elderly: A Creation of Social Policy in the Twentieth Century. *Ageing and Society*, 1(1), 5–28.

Tredgold, A. F. (1909). The Feeble-Minded – Social Danger. *The Eugenics Review*, 1(2), 97–104.

Trilling, L. (1972). *Sincerity and Authenticity*. Cambridge, MA: Harvard University Press..

Tronto, J. C. (1993). *Moral Boundaries: A Political Argument for an Ethic of Care*. New York: Routledge.

Trydegård, G. B. (2012). Care Work in Changing Welfare States: Nordic Care Workers' Experiences. *European Journal of Ageing*, 9(2), 119–129.

Tunstall-Pedoe, H. (2012). Decline in Coronary Heart Disease: Did It Fall or Was It Pushed? *British Medical Journal*, 344:d7809

Turner, B. S. (2009). *Can We Live Forever? A Sociological and Moral Inquiry*. London: Anthem Press.

Tyler, I. (2009). Against Abjection. *Feminist Theory*, 10(2), 77–98.

van Gorp, B. & Vercruysse, T. (2012). Frames and Counter-Frames Giving Meaning to Dementia: A Framing Analysis of Media Content. *Social Science & Medicine*, 74, 1274–1281.

van Haastregt, J., Diederiks, J. P., van Rossum, E., de Witte, L. P. & Crebolder, H. F. (2000). Effects of Preventive Home Visits to Elderly People Living in the Community: Systematic Review. *British Medical Journal*, 320(7237), 754–758.

van Hooren, F. & Becker, U. (2012). One Welfare State, Two Care Regimes: Understanding Developments in Child and Elderly Care Policies in the Netherlands. *Social Policy & Administration*, 46(1), 83–107.

van Iersel, M. B. & Rikkert, M. G. (2006). Frailty Criteria Give Heterogeneous Results when Applied in Clinical Practice. *Journal of the American Geriatric Society*, 54(4), 728–729.

van Kan, G. A., Rolland, Y., Houles, M., Gillette-Guyonnet, S., Soto, M. & Vellas, B. (2010). The Assessment of Frailty in Older Adults. *Clinics in Geriatric Medicine*, 26(2), 275–286.

van Leeuwen, Marco H. D., Meerkerk, Elise van Nederveen and van Voss, Lex Heerma. (2014). Provisions for the Elderly in North-Western Europe: An International Comparison of Alms-Houses, Sixteenth–Twentieth Centuries. *Scandinavian Economic History Review*, 62(1), 1–16.

Verbrugge, L. M. (1984). Longer Life but Worsening Health? Trends in Health and Mortality of Middle-Aged and Older Persons. *The Milbank Memorial Fund Quarterly*, 62(3), 475–519.

——. (1992). Disability Transitions for Older Persons with Arthritis. *Journal of Aging and Health*, 4(2), 212–243.

Vermeulen, J., Neyens, J. C., van Rossum, E., Spreeuwenberg, M. D. & de Witte, L. P. (2011). Predicting ADL Disability in Community-Dwelling Elderly People Using Physical Frailty Indicators: A Systematic Review. *BMC Geriatrics*, 11(1), 33.

Vetter, N., Jones, D. & Victor, C. (1981). Urinary Incontinence in the Elderly at Home. *The Lancet,* 318(8258), 1275–1277.

Vicente, L., Wiley, J. A. & Carrington, R. A. (1979). The Risk of Institutionalization before Death. *The Gerontologist,* 19(4), 361–367.

Vickers, K. (2007). Aging and the Media: Yesterday, Today, and Tomorrow. *Californian Journal of Health Promotion,* 5(3), 100–105.

Victoroff, J., Mack, W. J. & Nielson, K. A. (1997). Psychiatric Complications of Dementia: Impact on Caregivers. *Dementia and Geriatric Cognitive Disorders,* 9(1), 50–55.

Vincent, J. (2003). *Old Age.* London: Routledge.

Vladeck, B. C. (1980). *Unloving Care: The Nursing Home Tragedy.* New York: Basic Books.

Von Dietze, E. & Orb, A. (2000). Compassionate Care: A Moral Dimension of Nursing. *Nursing Inquiry,* 7(3), 166–174.

Walker, A. (1981). Community Care and the Elderly in Great Britain: Theory and Practice. *International Journal of Health Services,* 11(4), 541–557.

Walker, A. J., Pratt, C. C. & Eddy, L. (1995). Informal Caregiving to Aging Family Members: A Critical Review. *Family Relations,* 44(4), 402–411.

Walston, J., Hadley, E. C., Ferrucci, L., Guralnik, J. M., Newman, A. B., Studenski, S. A., Ershler, W. B., Harris, T. &. Fried, L. P. (2006). Research Agenda for Frailty in Older Adults: Toward a Better Understanding of Physiology and Etiology: Summary from the American Geriatrics Society/National Institute on Aging Research Conference on Frailty in Older Adults. *Journal of the American Geriatrics Society,* 54(6), 991–1001.

Warren, M. (1946). Care of the Chronic Aged Sick. *The Lancet,* 247(6406), 841–843.

Watson, N., McKie, L., Hughes, B., Hopkins, D. & Gregory, S. (2004). (Inter) Dependence, Needs and Care the Potential for Disability and Feminist Theorists to Develop an Emancipatory Model. *Sociology,* 38(2), 331–350.

Weaver, C. L. (1987). Support of the Elderly before the Depression: Individual and Collective Arrangements. *Cato Journal,* 7(2), 503–525.

Webster, C. (1994). The Elderly and the Early National Health Service. In M Pelling & R. M. Smith (eds), *Life Death and the Elderly: Historical Perspectives.* London: Routledge, 165–193.

Weicht, B. (2011). Embodying the Ideal Carer: The Austrian Discourse on Migrant Carers. *International Journal of Ageing and Later Life,* 5(2), 17–52.

Werblow, A., Felder, S. & Zweifel, P. (2007). Population Aging and Health Care Expenditure: 'a School of Red Herrings'? *Health Economics,* 16(10), 1109–1126.

Wilińska, M. & Cedersund, E. (2010). 'Classic Ageism' or 'Brutal Economy'? Old Age and Older People in the Polish Media. *Journal of Aging Studies,* 24(4), 335–343.

Williams S., Higgs P. & Katz S. (2012). Neuroculture, Active Ageing and the 'Older Brain': Problems, Promises and Prospects. *Sociology of Health and Illness,* 34, 64–78.

Williamson, J. B. (1984). Old Age Relief Policy Prior to 1900: The Trend toward Restrictiveness. *American Journal of Economics and Sociology*, 43(4), 369–384.

Wimo, A., Rönnbäck, E., Nyberg, A., Granholm, O. & Thorslund, M. (1999). Nursing Load in Different Care Alternatives in Sweden during 18 Years. *Archives of Gerontology and Geriatrics*, 28(3), 205–216.

Wing, J. K. (1981). From Institutional to Community Care. *Psychiatric Quarterly*, 53(2), 139–152.

Wingo, P. A., Ries, L. A., Rosenberg, H. M., Miller, D. S. & Edwards, B. K. (1998). Cancer Incidence and Mortality, 1973–1995. *Cancer*, 82(6), 1197–1207.

Wolff, J. L., Boult, C., Boyd, C & Anderson, G. (2005). Newly Reported Chronic Conditions and Onset of Functional Dependency. *Journal of the American Geriatrics Society*, 53(5), 851–855.

Woo, J., Goggins, W., Sham, A. & Ho, S. C. (2005). Social Determinants of Frailty. *Gerontology*, 51(6), 402–408.

Woo, J., Leung, J. & Morley, J. E. (2012). Comparison of Frailty Indicators Based on Clinical Phenotype and the Multiple Deficit Approach in Predicting Mortality and Physical Limitation. *Journal of the American Geriatrics Society*, 60(8), 1478–1486.

World Bank (1994). Averting the Old Age Crisis: Policies to Protect the Old and Promote Growth. New York: Oxford University Press.

Yan, E. & Kwok, T. (2011). Abuse of Older Chinese with Dementia by Family Caregivers: An Inquiry into the Role of Caregiver Burden. *International Journal of Geriatric Psychiatry*, 26(5), 527–535.

Yarnell, J. W. G. & St Leger, A. S. (1979). The Prevalence, Severity and Factors Associated with Urinary Incontinence in a Random Sample of the Elderly. *Age and Ageing*, 8(2), 81–85.

Yoshida, D., Suzuki, T., Shimada, H., Park, H., Makizako, H., Anan, Y., Tsutsumimoto, K., Uemura, K., Ito, T. & Lee, S. (2014). Using Two Different Algorithms to Determine the Prevalence of Sarcopenia. *Geriatrics & Gerontology International*, 14(S1), 46–51.

Yuan, H. B., Williams, B. A. & Liu, M. (2011). Attitudes toward Urinary Incontinence among Community Nurses and Community-Dwelling Older People. *Journal of Wound Ostomy & Continence Nursing*, 38(2), 184–189.

Zeilig, H. (2014). Dementia as a Cultural Metaphor. *The Gerontologist*, 54(2), 258–267.

Zhang, Y. & Jordan, J. M. (2010). Epidemiology of Osteoarthritis. *Clinics in Geriatric Medicine*, 26(3), 355–369.

Ziminski, P. C. & Rempusheski, V. F. (2013). Examining barriers to self-reporting of elder physical abuse in community-dwelling older adults. *Geriatric Nursing* (New York, NY), 35(2), 120–125.

Žižek, S. (2001). *On Belief*. London: Routledge.

——. (2002). *Welcome to the Desert of the Real: Five Essays on September 11 and Related Dates*. London: Verso.

Zuidema, S. U., de Jonghe, J. F., Verhey, F. R. & Koopmans, R. T. (2010). Environmental correlates of neuropsychiatric symptoms in nursing home patients with dementia. *International Journal of Geriatric Psychiatry*, 25(1), 14–22.

Zweifel, P., Felder, S. & Meiers, M. (1999). Ageing of population and health care expenditure: A red herring? *Health Economics*, 8(6), 485–496.

Website

1 Help Age International, 2014. Global Rankings Table
http://www.helpage.org/global-agewatch/population-ageing-data/global-rankings-table/

2 Life expectancy in England & Wales, 1951–2010
https://www.gov.uk/government/uploads/system/uploads/attachment_data/file/223190/life_Expectancy.pdf

3 McIntosh, 2012, Online Appendix 6 and 7
http://www.cambridge.org/us/academic/subjects/history/british-history-after-1450/poor-relief-england-13501600?format=HB

Index